GRANT
ME
A
HIGHER LOVE

How to Go from the
Relationship from Hell
to One that's Heaven Sent
by Scaling The Ladder of Love

Cindi Sansone-Braff

ISBN: 1-4196-6262-7
ISBN-13: 9781419662621
Library of Congress Control Number: 2007901567

Visit www.booksurge.com to order additional copies.

DEDICATION

To God, Who has been so patient with me, lifetime after lifetime – I finally heard Your Divine Message loud and clear: *Only love matters.* This labor of love is humbly offered in celebration of You, My Lord.

To the many blessed *Soul Mates,* both platonic and romantic ones, including those who have come and gone and those who, mercifully, still remain a vital part of my life.

To the many *Karmic Mates, Cellmates,* and *Razor's Edge Mates* who've helped me in my soulful journey, and to my *Group Soul Mates* whose love, friendship, and support contributed greatly to this work.

Most of all, to my beloved daughter, Shana, whose brilliant light broke through my darkness and showed me the way.

This book is further dedicated to anyone in search of love.

Peace be with you now and always.

Ever yours,
Cindi

ACKNOWLEDGEMENTS

I most humbly acknowledge and give thanks to the entire cosmos for illuminating the way. Special thanks must be given to the many angels, spirit guides, and Ascended Masters who surrounded me with support, guidance, and comfort throughout this long process.

I send abundant gratitude to the thousands of people who allowed me to read their Tarot cards, giving me complete access into their hearts, minds, and souls, and for granting me permission to open their Akashic records. The information that was channeled through me and revealed to me during these sessions has been an invaluable source of insight and knowledge, making this book of love possible in the first place.

I respectfully give thanks to those souls who have crossed over and who came through me so lovingly and honestly to give counsel and advice to the loved ones they had left behind. Sometimes these discarnate beings came to share their regrets and remorse. Many times they came through to confess sadly to their loved ones, "I never told you how much I loved you when I had the chance, and for this, I am eternally sorry." Often they came to apologize for the many *Errors in Thinking* they were guilty of perpetuating. All in all, these telepathic communications have proven invaluable in my study of love, and for this I am most grateful.

Additional thanks go out to the authors of the books I've read and now highly recommend throughout *Grant Me a Higher Love*. Quite honestly, I couldn't have written this book without the insight and wisdom these books provided.

Last, but not least, I would like to acknowledge my fantastic editor, Susan A. O'Doherty, Ph.D., Licensed Clinical Psychologist.

CONTENTS

CONTENTS

CONTENTS

- Similarities and Differences Between *Mirror Soul* Reunions and *Twin Soul* Reunions 224
- The Many Faces of *Mirror Souls* 225
- The *Magic Mirror Effect* 226
- The *Blessed Platonic Duad* 227
- The *Serene Sacred Duad* 227
- How Will I Recognize One of My *Mirror Souls?* 228
- Comparing *Twin Souls* and *Mirror Souls* 229
- *LOVEWORK ASSIGNMENT* – My Meditations on *Mirror Souls* 234
- Have We Met in Other Lifetimes? 237
- A *Sacred Trinity* 238
- Historic Examples of a *Sacred Trinity* 238
- Johannes Brahms and Clara and Robert Schumann 238
- Helen Keller, Anne Sullivan Macy and John Albert Macy 240
- *LOVEWORK ASSIGNMENT* – What I Learned from Watching *Casablanca* 242
- Where We Go from Here 244

STEP 8 – HONORING THE FIVE KARMIC PRINCIPLES THAT GOVERN RELATIONSHIPS **245**
- The Five Karmic Principles 245
- The First Karmic Principle 245
- The Second Karmic Principle 246
- The Third Karmic Principle 246
- The Fourth Karmic Principle 246
- The Fifth Karmic Principle 247
- A Pop Quiz – How Karmically Correct Are You? 247
- Leaving a Relationship in a Karmically Correct Manner 249

CONTENTS

CONTENTS

INTRODUCTION

Most relationship books take either the male or female side of the equation, perpetuating the age-old war of the sexes. This book doesn't pit one gender against the other, since to do so would only reinforce the dualistic and separatist ideology of the past millennium. To be granted a higher love, we have to embrace twenty-first century Cosmic Consciousness, which emphasizes the truism that we're eternal spirits housed in a holy, albeit temporary, temple known as the human body.

Although each of us has an essential gender that's either male or female in nature, during our many incarnations we've alternated them as a way of learning to balance the masculine and feminine energies within our own being. This integration of the divine masculine and feminine energy is an integral part of our journey toward healing and wholeness. (Read more about balancing our masculine and feminine energies in STEP 6.)

These 19 STEPS teach the art of loving from your immortal soul. Therefore, this book is written for all human beings who are seeking a higher love, regardless of any superficial or external differences.

Just know that if any of the following genderless statements or questions fits you, then this book is definitely the right one for you.

Are you currently in a relationship that you wish to make better? Have you just gotten out of one that causes you to wonder, "*What went wrong and where do I go from here?*"

Maybe you're in a relationship that seems to be going nowhere fast or one that leaves you wondering every day, "*Should I stay or should I go?*"

Perhaps you keep running from psychic to psychic, trying in vain to find out what your mate is thinking and feeling.

Are you joining the growing ranks of people who've never had a lasting relationship? Are you starting to believe that maybe you never will?

Or could it be that you've had plenty of relationships – bad ones – and you've come to the realization that there's got to be a better way?

Do you have the recurring sense that there's something you're just not getting or seeing that keeps you from having the love you want?

What is it that you haven't learned – or, more correctly, what is it that you haven't been taught – that keeps you feeling lonely, disappointed, and disenchanted even when you're in a relationship?

Why does love always seem to hurt?

Do the following placating lies sound familiar? "I'll find the perfect mate when I lose weight," or "I need to get my career going before I can deal with my love life"? Come on, let's face it: Being rich and famous, or thin and beautiful, doesn't ensure a happy love life, as a glance at any tabloid will tell you. None of these superficial things, in other words, the things that rise and fall, hold the key to love. Your heart, soul, body, and higher consciousness already possess everything you need to have and to hold a perfect love. This book will help you access this innate ability.

By now, we've all seen enough bad marriages and bitter divorce battles to know that being married doesn't necessarily ensure "Happily Ever After." The

very fact that divorce is becoming a commonplace occurrence shows that people are no longer willing to
settle for relationships that aren't working, although
they often remain clueless as to how to make the next
one any better.

If you're currently married with children, are
you proud of what your relationship is teaching your
children? Would you be happy or horrified if they
duplicated your marriage? How about your own parents' marriage? What did their relationship teach
you about long-term relationships?

The answers to the above questions and many
others will be revealed to you as you read this book
and do your written *LOVEWORK ASSIGNMENTS* with
conviction.

For now, just know that this book was written
for any man or woman who wholeheartedly wishes to
love and be loved in return.

The truth of the matter is – we've been taught
very little about love on a conscious level. Much of
what we learned about love and relationships pene-
trated our minds on a subliminal level when we were
very young children. We saw a lot of unhappy marriages and caught the drift that grown-ups in long-term
relationships get to be mean to each other. On the
other end of the spectrum, we were fed fairytales with
our formula, and watched animated versions of these
stories over and over again until we really believed in
"Happily Ever After." Later on, we were influenced
by watching way too many sitcoms, from the old ones
from the fifties and sixties with the perfectly coiffed
stay-at-home mom and totally intact, idealized family;
to the later ones which tried to tackle, in twenty short
minutes, sandwiched in between commercials, the
big issues like divorce, single parenthood, and dys-

functional families. Hollywood's countless romantic comedies and endless string of disintegrating marriage dramas further filled our subconscious minds with more celluloid delusions about relationships. Is it any wonder that so few relationships seem to last, let alone evolve and grow?

So, tell me again – who needs this book? Sad but true, we all do.

My own relationships made me painfully aware that the road to love can be a long, winding, rocky one, overridden with potholes and deadly ravines. At times we may take a giant leap of faith only to find ourselves crash landing in some strange new place, all alone and terrified. At other times, our leap of faith might land us safely in the arms of our beloved.

My own eye-opening experience with fear and the huge part it can play in ending a relationship, no matter how high a love we're given or how long a relationship has been in place, launched me on a painstaking quest to understand the true nature of love. During those angst-filled times, writing a book on the subject was the furthest thing from my mind; I just wanted to put an end to all the heartbreak and make sense of how something so good could turn out so badly.

Before long, it became painfully clear to me that the first thing I really needed to do was to heal myself and come to that inner place of self-acceptance, self-love, and peace, regardless of which person or what relationship was or wasn't in my life. This was a long, heart-wrenching process, but thankfully, I was blessed with much divine guidance. Once I let the universe know that I wanted the whole truth and nothing but the truth revealed to me, the real miracle of healing began.

I read hundreds of books in my journey toward self-knowledge and inner healing. These books covered many topics, including psychology, dream analysis, spirituality, philosophy, mythology, health, religion, and relationships. Much of what I learned from my extensive reading is summarized in this book. Throughout the 19 STEPS, I have recommended many of these books in case you should feel a need to explore a particular topic in greater detail. Be sure to follow your own inner guidance, which may lead you to other books that will assist you in your journey toward healing and love. Never underestimate the amount of knowledge and personal growth that can come from books, audiotapes, and DVDs.

In addition to the insight and knowledge that I acquired from my own studies, a great deal of the information you'll find in this book was channeled to me over the past fifteen years as I read Tarot cards for thousands of people seeking relationship advice. This channeled information came through me from spirit guides, saints, angels, Ascended Masters, and deceased loved ones.

People who have passed on are always eager to share with their loved ones the things they've learned while in spirit, and/or desperate to confess what they should have done or could have done while still on earth to bring more love into their lives and into the lives of others. Most importantly, the deceased come through to compassionately tell those left behind what they can do to bring more love into their lives in the here and now.

As I read people's Tarot cards and witnessed firsthand the devastating consequences that all the misunderstandings and miscalculations concerning love had on their lives, one question plagued me: Why is it that a topic as all-encompassing as love has had so little serious study? It's certainly true that the ancient Greeks took the study of love seriously, but that was light years ago, and not everything they professed about love has proven true, as you will learn in STEP 3, when we discuss ancient Greek philosophy and its impact on modern thinking.

This pressing need to explore the complex workings of the human heart, coupled with my deep-seated belief that all the suffering love inspired couldn't be in vain, planted the seeds from which this book began to take root and grow. The continual promptings from my Tarot card clients urging me to write a book about love and relationships became the fertile ground that nurtured and fed this project every step of the way. Of course, the constant message raining down on me from on high, "You can only help so many people on a day-to-day, one-on-one basis. Get this information down on paper, publish it, and, we don't care how you do it, but just get it out there," further rallied me to this worthwhile cause.

Writing and researching this book proved to be a soul-expanding experience, because it forced me to continually reflect upon and draw from my own personal love life. I've been blessed with more than my share of loving relationships, and I've come to know and greatly appreciate God's brilliant way of giving me real life experience in dealing with every conceivable relationship possibility, including *Cellmates, Razor's Edge Mates,* and every kind of *Soul Mate.* (If you don't know what these terms mean, don't worry – by the time you finish this book, they will have become part of your working vocabulary.)

From leaving my own long-term marriage, I learned how difficult it is to sever the ties that bind, even when a relationship might not be serving our higher good. To enter a marriage we open a door; when we leave it, we have to close (please, no slamming) a thousand doors. Learning how, when, and if to end a marriage is something this book will teach you.

In addition to the wealth of information my own love life provided, the intimate details of other people's love relationships revealed to me from thousands of Tarot card readings filled in any gaps in my knowledge. As I helped my clients through their relationship issues and watched them embrace a higher love, I was given the much needed confirmation and validation that the information being channeled through me was truthful, highly necessary, and practical in its application.

Perhaps the most illuminating concept channeled to me over the years was the idea of *The Ladder of Love*, which classifies the kinds of relationships people have, from the Lowest Rung Love, which is known as First-Degree Brutal Love, all the way to the top tier, which is *Unio Mystica* or the intimate, personal love relationship we're meant to have with God. Once you become aware of the different Rungs on *The Ladder of Love*, you'll be able to see where your love life's been and choose where you want it to go from now on.

Do you know the difference between a *Cellmate* and a *Soul Mate*? Do you know your *Twin Soul* from your *Mirror Soul*? Do you even know there are such things? *The Ladder of Love* has proven to be an invaluable tool, since it provides a working vocabulary of love that makes these often misunderstood terms easy to comprehend. As this terminology of love becomes more commonplace, our level of communication with each other will grow deeper and more meaningful.

As you read this book, be patient with yourself. You're not going to master all this material overnight. Quite frankly, many of us won't get it all right in this lifetime, and maybe not even in the next, but the universe applauds your every effort and will support you every inch of the way.

Go at your own pace. I strongly advise you to work the STEPS in order, starting with the first and ending with the 19th STEP. However, if you're having particular trouble with something say – with the issue of jealousy – feel free to jump ahead and read that information, but then be sure to go back and complete the STEPS in order. Each STEP prepares you for the next one. Trust in the process. It works miracles! I have seen countless numbers of my clients find a higher love by doing this 19 STEP program. Just know and believe that by the time you've completed this book, you'll be well on your way to obtaining the love you want. Keep the faith!

Every STEP will begin with a quote from *A Course in Miracles,* a text that was channeled to Helen Schucman during a seven-year period beginning in 1965. These quotations are from the 1975 Public Domain version available online at http:// acim.home. att.net/. *A Course in Miracles* is a self-help manual that strives to bring its readers to the realization that miracles are merely a shift in our mindset from a fear-based reality into a love-based reality. Anyone embarking on a serious study of love would do well to read and study this text.

Each STEP also features **LOVEWORK ASSIGN-MENTS.** These assignments are designed to help you understand the topics we'll be discussing, and to make this a personalized program for you. In doing your **LOVEWORK ASSIGNMENTS,** you'll be closely examining many aspects of your own life, especially your relationships, both past and present, in order to shed light on many of the obstacles that stand in the way of your getting and keeping the love you desire. If you want to get the most out of this program, I strongly advise you to take your time doing these assignments, and to be brutally honest with yourself when doing them. Operate under The Divine Law of Maximum Effort, and do the best job you can when completing these written assignments. If you want a higher, heaven-sent love, then you have to earn it. The Everyday Law of Minimum Effort will yield only a common love. If you merely skim through this book and ignore the **LOVEWORK ASSIGNMENTS,** then the universe will understand that you really don't want any major changes to take place in your life and will respond accordingly. You really do control the speed with which your love life will change and the level of love you'll receive. Your love life can change in an instant if and when you stop giving the universe mixed messages, such as: "I want a great love, but I don't really want to change myself or my life, nor do I really want to heal my issues." You can't defy The Natural Law of Love, which basically states: Love changes everything. From time to time, review your answers to your **LOVEWORK ASSIGNMENTS** to see how you're progressing in your study of love.

The book itself is divided into two Parts. PART I – UNDERSTANDING *THE LADDER OF LOVE* – will help you understand what love is and what it isn't.

You'll learn the difference between conditional love and unconditional love. You'll gain a deep understanding of the role fear plays in undermining our relationships, and you'll come to know that love is the answer.

We'll also work hard to debunk many of the wives' tales surrounding romantic love, such as the false belief that love is a compromise, or that love is going to rescue us.

We'll study in detail the Five Karmic Principles that Govern Relationships. These principles will tell you specifically how, why, and when you must take positive steps toward healing yourself and your relationship. They'll also show you how to leave a relationship in a karmically correct manner and teach you how to bless it and let it go.

Then we'll go into a detailed explanation of the different Rungs on *The Ladder of Love*, working our way from the bottom up. We'll begin by thoroughly examining Rungs One through Five. These Rungs include *Cellmate* relationships, which tend to bring out the worst in us; and *Razor's Edge Mates*, which can prove to be some of the more challenging relationships we're asked to deal with. Then we'll work our way up *The Ladder of Love* and closely examine Rungs Six through Nine, *Soul Mate* relationships (including *Twin Souls* and *Mirror Souls)*, which tend to bring out the best in us.

In STEP 6, KNOWING THE TRUTH ABOUT *TWIN SOULS,* we'll discuss the life-altering experience known as Enlightenment. Most of what you'll read in this book concerning Enlightenment is based upon my own experiences with this amazing process. In all honesty, if I hadn't become Enlightened, this book would never have materialized.

We'll conclude PART I by examining the two highest Rungs on *The Ladder of Love.* Rung Ten is *Agape* love, or the unconditional love for all humankind which leads to Cosmic Consciousness. We'll then examine Rung Eleven – *Unio Mystica,* or your intimate relationship with God, which is the greatest love of all.

Before proceeding to PART II, you'll take a pop quiz – The Love Test, which will help you review what you've already learned.

In PART II, DEMYSTIFYING LOVE, we'll explore in detail the Eight Golden Rules of Love, and the many obstacles along the path of love that can derail you. The First Golden Rule of Love – Know Thyself, might seem easy enough at first glance, but as you learn the difference between your shadow self and your persona, you'll begin to see just how difficult a task this can prove to be. One of the main objectives of this book is to help you know your true self, since your true self will attract your true love.

The Second Golden Rule of Love – Love Thyself – will get us into some murky waters as we navigate through the Five Deadly Sins Committed in the Name of Conditional Love: narcissism, selfishness, greed, envy, and jealousy.

The Third Golden Rule of Love honors the Sacred Law of Synchronicity and states: The meeting of two people which leads to love is never accidental. This is the part of the book where the moral majority will come and hang me, or, at the very least, publicly tar and feather me, as I hit home with the message: "To God, only love matters." I wish to make it clear from the start that I'm not a person who looks to make trouble or inspire controversy. By my very nature, I'm a peacemaker. Perhaps the most important thing I've learned from delivering thousands of divinely guided message – and, believe me, not all of these messages were necessarily the things my clients wanted to hear – is: I'm just the messenger. Don't shoot me. If any of the things I say don't ring true to you, follow what your heart and higher consciousness tell you. I believe as the Buddha did that you should question everything you read, and everything anyone says, and this goes for all that you read in this book. I've done my best to hear the messages as they were delivered to me, to seek confirmation of their truth, and to search through religious texts to find the elements of eternal truth that exist in every channeled piece of information I've received. I can't stress enough that it's not my intention to rip apart the existing structure known as marriage. It's my intention to help heal this sacred institution, and a careful reading of this book will prove this point a thousand times over. In the twenty-first century, the new archetype of marriage, which is truly a divine state of *Holy Matrimony*, will represent a sacred union between two people who are bound to each other with their entire hearts, souls, minds, and bodies. The glue that holds this *Soul Mate* relationship together is love and not economics, blind fear, or archaic traditions.

The Fourth Golden Rule of Love states: Perfect love asks that we love our *Soul Mate* with our entire heart, soul, mind, and body. In this rather lengthy STEP, you'll start out by exploring the inner workings of your heart and soul. After that, you'll closely examine the complex workings of your mind. You'll learn to recognize the head games people play, and strive to eliminate the psychological defense mechanisms you practice which limit the level of intimacy

you can share with others. You'll also work at paying attention to your dreams so that you can gain access to your subconscious mind. In learning to love
with your body, you'll come to know the difference
between having sex and making love as you explore
Sacred Sexuality and Tantra.

The Fifth Golden Rule of Love states: True
love calls for us to surrender our entire heart, soul,
mind, and body to its power. This short STEP will
show you how to let down your guard and let love
in.

The Sixth Golden Rule of Love states: True
love asks that we commit to our *Soul Mate* with our
entire heart, soul, mind, and body. This crucial STEP
sends us crashing full force into the New Age, collective unconscious fear of commitment, and will help
you recognize and effectively deal with commitment
issues, both within yourself and within your relationship. You'll come to know that without true commitment of the heart, soul, mind, and body there is no
everlasting love.

The Seventh Golden Rule of Love – Heal Thyself – will help you make peace with the undeniable
truth that when we're in a place of love, all of our
unhealed issues will surface. This STEP will teach
you to stay put and resist the instinct to run when the
going gets rough.

The Eighth Golden Rule of Love states: If two
people meet and then separate, know that there were
powerful lessons to be learned in their communion,
and still more powerful ones to be learned in their
separation. This STEP will show you how to pay homage to the ending of a relationship, by reinforcing
this divine truth: There's a time for everything under

the heavens, including a time for holding on and a time for letting go.

As you glance over this book, you'll notice that a great deal of information is given in list form. This book is really more akin to a textbook than a self-help book insofar as it's chock-full of information. As you become more familiar with the information in this book, the lists will make it easier for you to look something up or refresh your memory about a particular topic. The lists also make it easier to repeatedly read over a topic that is particularly relevant or troublesome to you. When you do so, eventually the material will seep deep into your subconscious mind. There, it will work wonders, correcting many of the false beliefs that are still part of your everyday consciousness, so that you can bring your mindset in alignment with the divine state known as Cosmic Consciousness.

To facilitate your learning, use this book as you would use any textbook. Underline key points, highlight passages that hit home, put question marks next to topics that still seem unclear to you, and write in the margins any thoughts that pop up in your head as you read (unless, of course, this is a library book; then please put all your notes and thoughts in a journal). Bear in mind that most people never master everything they read in a textbook, so they keep it handy as a reference tool to use over and over again. Think of this book as a textbook of love, a handy lifelong learning tool and reference guide.

I would advise you to go through the whole book once, and then immediately start over and do the 19 STEPS all over again. You'll readily see how your answers to the *LOVEWORK ASSIGNMENTS* have changed to reflect all that you've learned. Get hold of any of the recommended books that you'd like to read, and then read them! In other words, be active in your studies and watch your entire life transform into one that is filled with love, peace, and joy.

I can honestly say that the thousands of people I've guided through this process have proven to me that when you put these 19 STEPS into practice, you're granted a higher love. More importantly, these STEPS will teach you how to honor and cherish the sacred gift of a *Soul Mate* when it's given to you.

Now that you have some idea of where we're going, time is of the essence, so let's begin. Remember, you're not alone in this journey – I'm with you, angels, spirit guides, saints, Ascended Masters, deceased loved ones, and God follow you as well.

Godspeed!

THE NINETEEN STEPS

1. Learning to distinguish love from fear.

2. Correcting our *Errors in Thinking* concerning romantic love.

3. Recognizing the existence of *Cellmates, Soul Mates,* and *Razor's Edge Mates.*

4. Understanding the different Rungs on *The Ladder of Love* – starting with toxic love and culminating with *Unio Mystica.*

5. Learning to cherish the greatest gift from God – *Soul Mates.*

6. Knowing the truth about *Twin Souls.*

7. Recognizing the existence of *Mirror Souls.*

8. Honoring the Five Karmic Principles that govern relationships.

9. Understanding *Agape* love, which leads to Cosmic Consciousness.

10. Obtaining the divine state of *Unio Mystica,* by having an intimate relationship with God.

11. Understanding The First Golden Rule of Love – Know Thyself

PART I

UNDERSTANDING *THE LADDER OF LOVE*

STEP 1 – LEARNING THE DIFFER-ENCE BETWEEN LOVE AND FEAR

"I have said you have but two emotions, love and fear."
(*A Course in Miracles,* Chapter 13)

The Opposite of Love Is Fear

You're about to embark on the most exciting journey of your life – a mind-awakening, soul-expanding, and body-energizing pilgrimage that will take you deep into the center of your heart. ***Be fore-warned: Once you begin this journey, there will be no turning back.***

The first step in any venture is always the hardest, and just getting your hands on this book and actually opening it, well, that's half the battle! Your thoughts and your actions have already let the universe know that you're on a quest toward a higher love. In accordance with the Spiritual Law of Attraction, your desire for a higher love has led you to this powerful 19 STEP program. Here you will learn everything you need to know to attain your heart's deepest desire.

In STEP 1, we'll begin to tackle the awesome task of understanding the difference between love and fear.

Love? Fear? What's so hard to understand about those emotions? Why, even babies and little children know the difference, right? Sure, we learned an awful lot about love and fear growing up,

but what we learned by observing the oftentimes dysfunctional world around us is far from the truth, the
whole truth, and nothing but the truth.

As we explore together the complex world of
love and fear, please approach this first crucial STEP
with a mature mind, an open heart, and a willing
spirit. You won't grasp all this STEP has to offer in
one reading. You may not grasp all it has to offer
for years to come, but every person you meet and
every circumstance you encounter from this day forward will prove the immutable truths revealed in this
STEP to be self-evident.

In recognizing the subtle as well as obvious
differences between love and fear, you'll find every
aspect of your life gravitating toward the path of love.
This shift in awareness is the miracle you've been
dreaming of.

The first thing we're going to do is to define
and determine what love is and what it isn't. You
might be surprised to learn that a great deal of what
you thought was true love is, in fact, a very watered-
down version of love known as **conditional love.**

**Conditional love is really a manifestation of
fear,** as you'll soon discover for yourself, as we make
our way through this first STEP.

Next, we'll wrestle with fear and reveal the
many masks this omnipotent emotion wears.

By the time you finish this STEP you'll have
learned: **The opposite of love is fear.**

**For now, recognize that we have but two emo-
tions in life – love and fear.**

At this particular time in human consciousness, more of our life's decisions, choices, and actions
are governed by fear than by love. In acknowledging
this fact, and taking the necessary actions to change

this way of thinking, you're taking the first step toward embracing a higher love.

In this STEP, you'll also discover that your desire to seek a higher love is divinely timed. At this very moment, as you sit quietly reading this book, the cosmos is rushing toward a new, higher wave of consciousness which is being ushered in by the Age of Aquarius. (Read more about Cosmic Consciousness in STEP 9.) Together we'll examine what this New Age heralds, but for now, recognize that your need for a higher love shows that you've already been touched by that higher consciousness. The universe rejoices, knowing that you've heard this divine message.

Know that the universe will do its part to bring you a higher love, but you're fully expected to do your share. If you're to draw a higher love into your life, you must first be willing to change your thoughts, behaviors, and actions. Humans, by their very nature, resist change. But if everything were so rosy in your life, you wouldn't be reading this book right now, would you? Begin to view change as an integral part of your journey toward an authentic life. Your authentic life will inevitably guide you to a higher love.

Sometimes these inner and outer changes will occur slowly, and at other times, you'll find yourself taking giant leaps of faith. Actually, your fear level will determine the speed at which a higher love will travel to you. If you're giving the universe a lot of mixed messages, such as, "I want love, but I don't want it to change anything too much," know that the universe will respond accordingly and bring you a lower Rung of Love, one that fits that bill.

Relationships as Mirrors of Ourselves

Before you can change your thoughts, behaviors, and actions, you'll need to learn to view all of your relationships – past and present, personal and professional – as mirrors of who you are, who you once were, and who you wish to be.

By taking the time to stop and reflect on the choices you've made, you'll see how much you already know and what you still need to learn.

As you reflect on your relationships, pay close attention to any emerging patterns. If you realize that you keep getting involved in the same type of dead-end relationships, know that there are important karmic lessons that you haven't learned, and that the universe keeps giving you another chance to learn them. (Read more about these important karmic lessons in STEPS 5, 6, and 19.)

For instance, if you notice that you keep getting involved with people who can't commit to a relationship, know that you secretly fear commitment or you wouldn't keep choosing the same kind of partner over and over again. (Read more on the fear of commitment in STEP 17.)

Another example would be if you keep picking partners who are abusive to you. What would this pattern of behavior be trying to reveal to you? Perhaps you're reliving your parents' marriage, or you have self-esteem issues, or you have a subconscious need to punish or disempower yourself. The good news is that STEPS 11, 12, 13, and 18 will help you to know yourself, love yourself, and heal yourself, so that you can break free of these destructive behavioral patterns.

By following this divinely guided 19 STEP program, you'll come to know why you've made certain choices. This knowledge will free you to choose again, thus ending the vicious cycle of dysfunctional relationships.

The Vacuum Principle, which is one tenet of the Spiritual Law of Attraction, calls for us to let go of the old to make room for the new. This book will teach you how to do this, one STEP at a time. Feel confident knowing that you're moving toward a future in which all of your relationships will mirror the healed person you've become.

Some Things You Need to Know Before We Start

- As you read this book you'll learn to follow your spirit and listen to your heart. You'll come to understand that the heart and spirit never lie, for they always come from a place of unconditional love and truth.
- You must be prepared to unlearn a multitude of false beliefs and *Errors in Thinking* concerning love. (Read more on this in STEP 2.) You'll learn to let go of all that is untrue, allowing room for your new thoughts and beliefs. This thinking is once again in accordance with the Vacuum Principle of the Spiritual Law of Attraction, which tells us that in order to get what we want, we have to let go of what stands in our way.
- The process works best if you allow me to be your guide.

- You must trust in the process and be patient, so you won't get discouraged.
- You must pay attention to the people and opportunities that will be brought to you as you read this book. They'll serve as guides to reinforce what you're learning and to illuminate those places in your being that are still unhealed.
- If real changes are to take place in your life, you must vow to do your written *LOVEWORK ASSIGNMENTS* with conviction. Many times the space allowed in this book won't be enough to complete the answers. Keep a notebook or journal and complete the answers in it. Title your notebook, *My LOVEWORK ASSIGNMENTS.* **Know that the words you write are as important as the ones you read!**

Believe in Divine Timing

- Whatever you are currently doing in your life – is exactly what you are meant to be doing.

- Therefore, you're beginning this journey at the exact right time.

- Every person you've met and everything you've been through has led to this moment. Learn to honor the Sacred Law of Synchronicity. Synchronicity means there are no coincidences. Everything is divinely guided to us at the right time and place. Start paying attention to these divine coincidences and learn to bless them. Be thankful for the divine guidance and opportunities they bring.

- Trust that you'll be guided to learn exactly what you need to learn, exactly when you need to learn it. Learn to believe in the Sacred Law of Synchronicity.

- Although you have reached the perfect time and place in your life to receive this divinely guided information, you must be willing to abandon all of your preconceived notions concerning love to allow this higher consciousness to flow into your being.

- Ask God, your spirit guides, your angels, and those who have passed on to continue to assist you through the challenging days ahead. Write down in your notebook any guidance you receive (including synchronous events) so that you won't forget.

- Take a moment each day to thank the universe for all the divine guidance given and for prayers answered.

Love Relationships in the Twenty-First Century – Welcome to the Age of Aquarius

Every two thousand years or so, we enter a new astrological age which affects human evolution. The shifting from one age to another occurs slowly, so it can be difficult to pinpoint when one age ends and another actually begins.

I believe that the two ages actually overlap and exist at the same time, with some people marching backwards in an effort to keep the old age alive, while others race forward to embrace the new one.

We're currently moving away from the Age of Pisces, which started around the time of the birth of Christ. The Age of Pisces is and was an age character-ized by blind faith, fears, superstitions, false beliefs, *Errors in Thinking*, and dogma. Much dualistic think-ing characterizes the Piscean age, as people violently proclaim their nations, religions, and beliefs as the chosen ones, thus perpetuating the idea of separate-ness and war.

The Age of Pisces represents an age of illusion, in which the self-willed individual tries to play God in a vain effort to control everything. The Piscean age is characterized by the mass delusion that the secular world with all its superficiality reigns supreme.

Even though the advent of Jesus coincided with the Age of Pisces, Jesus, with his emphasis on love and brotherhood, was actually foreshadowing the New Age to come. His earthly mission was to re-veal all the *Errors in Thinking* espoused during this Dark Age of spirituality, laying the groundwork for the major shift in human consciousness that the Age of Aquarius would bring forth. Because the evolu-tionary process in human beings is slow – so slow, in fact, that it takes thousands of years for the entire human race to embrace any major shift in conscious-ness – the love, forgiveness, and universal brother-hood that Jesus spoke of so long ago is finally taking root and growing more widespread now that we've entered the spiritual Renaissance known as the Age of Aquarius.

There's no denying that this New Age is upon us. The evidence of this can be seen everywhere as the mystical and metaphysical make their way into the mainstream. It's commonplace to find Yoga studios in strip malls, and New Age stores featuring Tarot cards, crystals, and candles are popping up in the most unlikely places. You only have to turn on the television to see mediums and psychics appearing regularly on talk shows, and movies and television series featuring metaphysical themes. Twenty years ago most people wouldn't have dreamed of talking openly about angels and spirit guides, or how they believed that people could commune with those who had crossed over, but these days this is common, everyday conversation. Bestsellers like James Redfield's *The Celestine Prophecy* and Gary Zukav's *The Seat of the Soul* are more evidence of this new shift in consciousness. The popularity of *The Oprah Winfrey Show,* with its positive spiritual slant, once again reflects the Age of Aquarius effect.

This New Age calls for us to follow the dictates of our hearts, souls, and higher consciousness. It's a time of "Thy will be done," as opposed to "My will be done."

The Age of Aquarius is an age in which the invisible, spiritual, and ethereal world will take center stage. **It will be a time in which the human race will learn what the universe has been striving to teach – that only love is real and only love matters.**

Alone and collectively, people will slowly come to see that we're all connected and emanate from the selfsame God source. This higher consciousness thinking, this sense of oneness, will create a new world based on love and peace. (Read more about Cosmic Consciousness in STEP 9.)

One of the most fascinating aspects of the Age of Aquarius is the huge number of everyday people, going about ordinary lives, who will achieve Enlightenment on both the personal level and a universal one. (Read more about Enlightenment in STEP 6 and about Cosmic Consciousness in STEP 9.) This is the first time in the history of humankind when God expects us to be monks in everyday life. We're no longer asked or expected to go off to live on a mountaintop and pray, or go live as an ascetic in a monastery, or to renounce our current way of life as was the practice in the Age of Pisces, if we were to seek a spiritual life. Rather, we're asked to be a great beacon of light as we go through our daily life, doing whatever it is we do, wherever we choose to do it.

More and more people, whether they've achieved Enlightenment or not, will begin to receive messages from divine sources, and their powers of telepathy will grow stronger and stronger.

During this New Age, there will be more *Soul Mate* couplings, and the reuniting of *Twin Souls* and *Mirror Souls* will occur in greater and greater numbers as well. (Read more about these relationships in STEPS 5, 6, and 7.)

The Age of Aquarius will be a time of individual spirituality, with much less emphasis on organized religion and the antiquated notion that we need an intermediary in the form of a rabbi, priest, or guru to speak to God for us. The emphasis will be on each of us having an intimate, one-on-one relationship with God. (Read more about your intimate relationship with God in STEP 10.)

This age will further be characterized by greater and greater numbers of people recognizing that they're spiritual beings housed in a physical body. More and more human beings will finally learn how to balance the needs of the flesh with those of the spirit.

From this description of the Age of Aquarius, you can see that your study of love is divinely timed. God has chosen you to be one of the people ushering in this amazing New Age. Feel confident, knowing that you're being called to assist others to take a giant leap of consciousness as well.

The hippie era, back in the late 1960s and early 1970s, gave us the first taste of this New Age. The musical *Hair* sang out the proclamation, "This is the dawning of the Age of Aquarius." The slogan that was popularized during the Viet Nam war, "Make love, not war," humbly bespeaks the sentiments of this New Age. People who love unconditionally don't make war! Never underestimate your quest for a higher love – not only is it important to you, it's important for the salvation of the entire human race!

What all this talk about this New Age is trying to tell you is that you're living in the New Age of Love, and you're not alone in your quest for a higher love. There's a *Soul Mate* looking for you right now. Have faith that your right actions are readying the universe to bring this person to you.

To sum up the difference between the Age of Pisces and the Age of Aquarius, think of the former as the Dark Age of Fear, and the latter as the Light Age of Love.

As We Transition From the Age of Pisces Into the Age of Aquarius More and More of Us Will Find that the Pattern of Our Love Life Doesn't Fit the "Happily Ever After" Formula. The Reasons for this are:

- Our karmic debts, which are basically the intentional or unintentional wrongdoings we have committed over the course of our many lifetimes, weigh heavy on our souls.
- Our souls are racing toward liberation or Enlightenment (if you don't know what Enlightenment is, feel free to jump ahead to STEP 6 to learn more about this amazing process). As a result, we'll meet many *Cellmates* and *Razor's Edge Mates* (STEPS 3 and 4) and many different kinds of *Soul Mates* (STEPS 3, 5, 6, and 7) in an effort to correct the errors of our collective past. These experiences and the karmic lessons we'll learn will help us complete our souls' evolution. (Read more about karmic lessons in STEPS 5, 6, and 19.)

Have faith – out of chaos comes true peace. Remember: You are not going crazy; you are going sane!

What Is Love?

- **Love is the great spiritual force that propels our souls to evolve ever upwards.**
- Love is a beacon of light that emanates from our hearts and souls and vibrates at the highest frequency level.
- Love is the divine energy that unifies heaven and earth.
- Love is the eternal power source that transcends the boundaries that separate heaven and earth. The energy of love allows us to commune with those who have passed on. You don't need to be a psychic to do this. You need to bring the vibrational level of your inner being higher and higher. When you evolve into your higher self, you'll be traveling on the same wavelength (the same plane) as ascended souls, and therefore you'll be able to commune with them.
- **God is love.**
- Love isn't a commodity, nor is it a business transaction.
- Love is pure grace.
- Love is the great healing power of the universe.
- Love makes all things possible.
- Love always comes from God.
- **Love is a miracle.**

Conditional Love versus Unconditional Love

At this stage of human evolution, most of us walking the earth plane right now have a great deal of experience dealing with the very watered-down version of love known as **conditional love,** and very little experience dealing with the pure form of love known as **unconditional love.**

Conditional love is really a form of fear, whereas unconditional love is true love.

Conditional Love

This is the kind of love that's contingent upon behavior, our own or someone else's. As long as we act in accordance with other people's preconceived notions of how we should behave, or they act in the way we expect them to, everything is okay.

In direct response to conditional love, we learn to wear a mask, act out a role, and become increasingly puppet-like. As time goes by, even we don't know who we are anymore.

When children are raised by parents who love them conditionally, they try to be what their parents want and expect them to be, even though those parental expectations may go against the children's own true natures.

When we're involved in a love relationship based on conditional love, it's only a matter of time before we or they will act in some way that isn't considered acceptable and love will be withdrawn. The primal fears of rejection and abandonment are the weapons that those who love conditionally use to control others.

By the time you finish reading this book, you'll have a deep understanding of primal fears and how they manifest. This book will teach you to overcome these fears one STEP at a time, so that you'll no longer be enslaved by the master of deception – conditional love.

Know that conditional love is, in fact, fear-based. When we're loved conditionally, we become afraid to speak our mind, assert our wishes, or demand our God-given rights. We feel the price we will pay for these actions will be too high – the loss of love. The anticipation of the loss of love flings us head on into our two biggest transpersonal fears: the fear of abandonment and the fear of rejection. (You'll read more about these terrifying fears later on in this STEP.)

When we're in a relationship that's based on conditional love, we're always on the defensive, always guarded. It becomes easier in this type of relationship to lie rather than to tell the truth. (Why do we lie? We lie because we fear the person we're lying to can't handle the truth and/or we fear the person's reaction to the truth.)

Conditional love leaves us feeling battered and abused, exhausted and confused. Conditional love is a rocky foundation on which to build a life. It cannot and will not withstand the winds of change that are an inevitable part of life.

Conditional Love Quiz
Am I Guilty of Committing the Sin of Loving Conditionally?

This quiz is designed to help you see if you're guilty of committing the sin of loving conditionally.

You can fail this quiz only if you don't answer the questions honestly, don't learn what this quiz is meant to reveal, and don't take steps to move from loving in a conditional way to loving in an unconditional way.

If you're currently in a relationship, please evaluate your behaviors in this relationship. If not, use your most recent relationship. If you've never had a romantic relationship, evaluate your most intimate relationship, be it with one of your parents, a sibling, or a best friend.

You'll rate yourself by scoring 2 points for each of the sins you feel that you have committed "often" in the name of conditional love. Give yourself 1 point for each of the sins committed "sometimes" in the name of conditional love. Answering "never" scores 0 points.

In your relationship have you been:

1. Judgmental?
2. Intolerant?
3. Critical?
4. Mean or unkind?
5. Selfish and self-centered?
6. Feeling victimized?
7. Feeling guilty?
8. Possessive?
9. Argumentative?
10. Petty?
11. Feeling insecure?
12. Speaking in harsh tones and using harsh words?
13. Compromising on your core values?
14. Unforgiving?

15. Prone to violence or other abusive scare tactics?
16. Lying?
17. Controlling?
18. Demanding?
19. Manipulative?
20. Defensive?

This test is different from most tests, in that, the lower your score, the better. For every point you gave yourself, know that you've committed the sin of loving in a conditional way.

Ideally, none of us would score any points on this quiz. But if we were all perfect and living in an ideal world, none of us would need this book, for we'd already be Ascended Masters dwelling in bliss forevermore.

A year from today, retake this quiz. I will bet you'll be pleasantly surprised to see just how much lower your score is.

Unconditional Love

Unconditional love is a divine gift, freely given, with no strings attached.

This kind of unwavering love fills us with a deep sense of peace and joy and provides a solid foundation to build a life upon. Even under the worst of circumstances, we know our love can survive, since unconditional love fills us with heartfelt feelings of faith and hope.

When we know we're loved unconditionally, we feel safe to express our true self and to become all we were meant to be. (Read more about how to know your true self in STEP 11.)

When someone loves us unconditionally, be it our friends, parents, lovers, whomever, we know love won't be withdrawn if we assert our God-given rights, such as: the right to say what we think and feel; the right to choose our own vocation or avocation; the right to choose our own friends; and the right to choose our own way of expressing our spirituality.

Children who are loved unconditionally are truly blessed, for the life they choose to live is the life they were meant to live, and not the life their parents have chosen for them. The greatest gift any of us can give our children is to love them unconditionally. Children who grow up in this kind of nurturing environment learn to feel free to be themselves and to tell the truth. In turn, they willingly give the gift of unconditional love to everyone they meet. A world full of people who love unconditionally is a world at peace.

Loving unconditionally doesn't mean we allow people to be abusive to us, nor does it give us a license to abuse others. Unconditional love gives us the time and space to work on healing our inner issues, so that we become truly kind and compassionate human beings. (Read more about healing ourselves in STEP 18.)

What Feelings, Emotions, and Traits Characterize Unconditional Love?

- Joy, serenity, generosity, bliss, happiness, humility, excitement, hope, faith, forgiveness, trust, optimism, laughter, endurance, patience, peace, abundance, radiant health, vitality, passion without drama, Sacred Sexuality, tenderness, learning, wisdom, kindness, healing, freedom, creativity, courage, commitment, beauty, caring, personal growth, spirituality, balance, oneness, ecstasy, compassion, empathy, tolerance, being nonjudgmental, spontaneity, fun, healthy pleasure, fulfilled desires, gratitude.

- In other words, all the positive thoughts, emotions, and actions under the sun are characteristic of unconditional love.

Unconditional Love Quiz
Am I Practicing the Art of Loving Unconditionally?

This quiz is designed to help you know if you're practicing the art of loving unconditionally. You can fail this quiz only if you fail to learn what this quiz is meant to reveal, and if you fail to learn how you can move from loving in a conditional way to loving in an unconditional way. Once again, please answer the questions truthfully.

If you're currently in a relationship, please evaluate your behaviors in that relationship. If not, use your most recent relationship. If you've never had a romantic relationship, evaluate your most intimate relationship, be it with one of your parents, a sibling, or a best friend.

Give yourself 2 points for answering "often" and 1 point for answering "sometimes." Answering "never" scores 0 points.

In your relationship have you been:

1. Nonjudgmental?
2. Tolerant?
3. Supportive?
4. Kind?

5. Giving without expecting something in return?
6. Understanding?
7. Feeling secure?
8. Forgiving?
9. Telling the truth?
10. Tender?
11. Joyful?
12. Thankful?
13. Radiating vibrant health?
14. Playful?
15. Laughing?
16. Having passion without drama?
17. Compassionate?
18. Empathetic?
19. Patient?
20. Filled with a sense of hope?

Any score above ten would reveal you've already learned a great deal about loving unconditionally. A year from now, retake this quiz. I will bet you'll be amazed to see just how high your score is.

Now, go back and retake both quizzes, responding with the way you feel your current mate, your previous mate, or the most significant other in your life has acted towards you.

For each quiz, go down the list and ask yourself, "With me, has this person been _____?" If you answer, "often," give yourself 2 points, and if you answer, "sometimes," give yourself 1 point. An answer of "never" would score 0 points.

How did your score for the other person compare to the one you gave yourself? For instance, did your own scores reveal that you're guilty of committing the sin of loving conditionally most of the time, and did the person you rated prove to be guilty of more of the same?   Then this would reveal that you're basically getting what you're giving.

If, on the other hand, you discovered that you're practicing the art of loving unconditionally most of the time, but you feel that most often you're being loved back conditionally, then the STEPS in this book will help you learn how to seek out unconditional love. This may entail lovingly leaving a person who continues to love you conditionally, allowing room for an unconditionally loving person to come into your life. If this is the case, then STEPS 8 and 19 will show you how to leave a relationship in a karmically correct manner.

If the test scores revealed that you're being loved unconditionally, and yet you're guilty of the sin of loving conditionally, then this book will help you to heal those issues that keep you from loving in an open and unconditional way.

Perhaps this quiz revealed that you and your partner are practicing the art of loving unconditionally. Consider yourselves blessed! Say a prayer of thanksgiving for your *Soul Mate* union.

LOVEWORK ASSIGNMENT

Take some time to reflect upon the kind of love you're giving to others, and the kind of love you're receiving from them. Are most of your current relationships based on conditional love? Have you ever had a relationship based on unconditional love? Write down your reflections, and as you progress in this course, go back to this assignment from time to time, noting how you're doing in your quest to love and be loved unconditionally.

Reflections on the Kind of Love I'm Giving and the
Kind of Love I'm Receiving

All fear Based

giving + receiving

I Vow to Love Unconditionally and to Seek Unconditional Love in Return

Everything You've Ever Wanted to Know About Fear but Were Afraid to Ask

Now that you have a better idea about what constitutes unconditional love and what constitutes conditional love, it's time to tackle fear.

Personal Fears versus Transpersonal Fears

All human beings have their own set of personal fears as well as *transpersonal fears* or *collective unconscious fears.* Transpersonal fears are those primal, collective fears common, in varying degrees, to all human beings living within a particular culture. In addition, many transpersonal fears, such as the fear of abandonment, cross the culture line and are inherent at this stage of human consciousness – to some degree – in all human beings.

Now that the Age of Aquarius is upon us, we've come to the stage of human evolution in which God asks that we overcome our own personal fears and conquer the transpersonal ones as well, so that we can walk the path of love.

The first step in our journey toward wholeness is to overcome our own personal fears. After that we can take on the transpersonal ones. Keep in mind that our personal fears are mirrors of our transpersonal ones.

For instance, people who were physically or emotionally abandoned by their parents have been given an opportunity to confront their own personal fear of abandonment. As these people work on their personal abandonment issues, they'll overcome their transpersonal fear of abandonment as they learn that they can never be abandoned since God, their spirit guides, their angels, and their departed loved ones are always with them. For these people, overcoming the personal fear of abandonment and the transpersonal fear of abandonment would be among the primary karmic lessons they've incarnated to learn.

Until we overcome both our personal fears and our transpersonal ones, we'll remain chained to a life that is ruled by our emotions and uncontrollable thoughts. Know that housed within yourself you possess everything you need to overcome these fears. This book will help you to harness those God-given tools.

Your **LOVEWORK ASSIGNMENTS** will help your subconscious mind to recognize and deal with all of your fears so that you can overcome them and begin to live a life that is lovingly guided by your heart, your soul, and your higher consciousness.

And when will this happen? "All in good time" (wise words uttered by the Wicked Witch of the West in *The Wizard of Oz*).

What Feelings, Emotions, and Traits Characterize Fear?

- Pessimism, pity, flight, doubt, arrogance, hubris, violence, lust, jealousy, envy, greed, pettiness, meanness, power struggles, worry, selfishness, narcissism, guilt, feelings of rejection and abandonment, victim consciousness, anger, hatred, prejudice, vengeance, passing judgment, the excessive need to be right, holding a grudge, dogmatic thinking, phobias, obsessions, compulsions, addictions, perversions, feeling sorry for oneself, depression, and anxiety.

- In other words, all the negative thoughts, emotions, and actions under the sun are characteristic of fear.

Go back and read the questions in the Conditional Love Quiz. Can you see that the sins committed in the name of conditional love sound an awful lot like the feelings, emotions, and traits that characterize fear?

From this analysis, can you see for yourself that loving someone or being loved conditionally is, in fact, walking the path of fear? Are you coming to understand how practicing the art of loving unconditionally is walking the path of true love?

Recognizing the inherent truth in the above two questions means that you're well on your way to mastering STEP 1 – Learning the Difference between Love and Fear. Rejoice knowing you're a giant step closer to obtaining your heart's desire – a higher love.

LOVEWORK ASSIGNMENT

Take some time to walk through the bloody alleyways of your heart to remember a time in your life when you needed someone to act out of love for you, and he/she acted out of fear. (You could fill your entire notebook with his one.) For example, when you confessed your deepest feelings for someone, and even though this person felt the same way as you did, he/she was too afraid to act upon these loving feelings and ended the relationship instead.

Or perhaps you were at a crossroads in your life, and you needed advice. Later on you came to realize the advice you were given wasn't at all about what was best for you, but what was best for the person advising you.

Please reread this entire STEP before attempting this assignment. Concentrate on truly understanding the difference between love and fear. **Unless you truly understand what love is as opposed to what fear is, your life will remain unchanged.**

Remembering a Time When I Needed Someone to Act Out of Love, and I Received a Fearful Response Instead

Mom & Dad did not rescue me from Mr. Grey.

Take a Moment to Forgive this Person

LOVEWORK ASSIGNMENT

Now reflect upon a time or times in your life when you acted out of fear and not from a place of love. For example, perhaps you left a meaningful relationship because you listened to what others had to say and turned your back on your heart; or you ended a relationship because you were unable to manage your own jealousy issues; or you ended a relationship because you questioned the package love came in, thinking that the person didn't make enough money or was too old or too young or too whatever.

Remembering When I Acted out of Fear and Not from a Place of Love

Forgive Yourself, For You Knew Not What You Did

Getting the Love We Want

Now that you have a better idea of what love is and what it isn't, let's put your desire to be granted a higher love out there where the universe can hear it.

Close your eyes and repeat these words over and over again until they ring true to you: "Dear God, grant me a higher love."

Remember – love is a miracle.

How Can I Receive the Miracle of Love?

- Ask and you shall receive.
- Pray.
- Tell God what you need. *"I need a miracle."*
- Turn your love life over to God. Admit you don't have a clue as to what you really need. It's definitely okay to draw a word portrait as to what *you think* you might need in a *Soul Mate.* (Your next *LOVEWORK ASSIGNMENT* is going to be just that!)

Is There Anything Else I Need to Do?

- Promise God you won't question the package love comes in. You won't say, "But she's not my type." "But he's too old, too short, too fat, too this, or too that!"
- *To God – only love matters.*
- *Allow me to repeat that: To God, only love matters.*

How Can I Learn Not to Question the Package Love Comes In?

- Learn to see people through God's eyes.
- God sees clear to our hearts, our souls, our higher consciousness, and our intentions.
- God views the human body as a holy temple that houses the immortal soul.

LOVEWORK ASSIGNMENT

To conclude this STEP, you'll do one more *LOVEWORK ASSIGNMENT.* **This one is fun! Write down the traits you wish your ideal *Soul Mate* would possess.** In love, God says, "Be greedy. Be very greedy." For instance, you might write: I want a *Soul Mate* who is trustworthy, kind, funny, passionate, loyal, etc.

Please don't write your request in a negative way such as: I don't want someone who drinks. Instead write – I want someone who is strong and sober. You get the idea. God, your spirit guides, your angels, and those loved ones who have passed on will sort through your writing, and then bring you the love you need.

Your word portrait is a very powerful instrument for bringing love into your life. **So please, take this *LOVEWORK ASSIGNMENT* seriously. Keep adding to your list. Keep revising.**

When you meet your *Soul Mate,* which you most certainly will, you'll be amazed by how many of these traits he/she actually possesses. *If your Soul Mate appears not to possess something that was on your list, you'll soon know that really wasn't what you needed after all.*

If you're currently involved in a less than ideal relationship, write down the traits you feel you need in a life partner, but are lacking in your current mate. Take some time to reflect on whether your partner can, with your help, learn to possess these traits.

If, after careful thought, you come to the conclusion that your current mate could never possess those traits, then this book will help you learn how to leave your relationship in a karmically correct manner.

My Ideal Soul Mate

Trust that God Will Bring You the Love You Need

Making a Vow to God

Promise God that you'll do your best to try and heal your own inner and outer issues. Then turn your love life over to God by saying the following vow daily, until its meaning permeates your entire being.

"Guide me, Lord. I trust in You. I believe You will bring me the love I need. I have complete faith in divine timing. I know You will bring me this miracle when I am truly ready to accept and enjoy it, and for this I am eternally grateful. Thy will be done."

If you don't like these words, or you feel a need to add something, write a vow of your own. (God loves creativity!)

My Vow

Repeat this Vow Religiously

Things You Can Do Immediately to Bring More Love into Your Life

1. Know that if you want love, then you must be love.
2. Radiate love.
3. Give of yourself generously.
4. Smile often.
5. Laugh a lot.
6. See the good in others, and tell them what you see.
7. Be willing to extend the invitation to love first, and await the other person's RSVP.
8. Relax.

Summing Things Up

- There are but two emotions in life: love and fear. Consequently, there are only two roads in life we can travel on. We follow either the path of fear or the path of love.
- Understand that the path of fear is also known as the path of the illusion of safety.
- Know that you'll stand at the crossroads of love and fear every day of your life.
- Learn to choose the path of love. **You'll learn to do this by understanding the difference between love and fear.**
- If you're to be blessed with a higher love, you must first overcome fear.

- You have to be brutally honest with yourself and be willing to ask, "What is it that I fear most?"
- Most people choose to walk the path of fear because at first glance it appears to be the path of least resistance, and therefore the easier one.
- The path of love will often appear to be the more dangerous one at first, because there can be many obstacles to overcome. We must learn to see these obstacles for what they are – mere piles of false beliefs and *Errors in Thinking* that we need to overcome before we can lead an authentic life and walk the true path of love. This initially harder path ultimately becomes the easier one because it leads us to a life filled with love, peace, and joy.
- Never forget – only love matters!

The Ladder of Love Terminology

In STEP 2, we'll begin to debunk many of the wives' tales surrounding romantic love. Before attempting the next STEP, please study the following brief descriptions of some of the terminology used throughout the book.

1. *Karmic Mates* – **Platonic relationships that bring out the worst in us,** causing us to learn most of our karmic lessons through pain and suffering.

2. *Cellmates* – **Romantic relationships that bring out the worst in us,** causing us to learn most of our karmic lessons through pain and suffering. (Rungs One, Two, and Three)

3. *Soul Mates* – **Any relationship, either romantic or platonic, which tends to bring out the best in us,** allowing us to learn most of our karmic lessons through peace, love, and joy. **In this book we're mainly discussing romantic** *Soul Mate* **relationships, and we'll simply refer to them as** *Soul Mates.* (Rungs Six through Nine, including *Twin Souls* and *Mirror Souls*)

4. *Borderline Mates* – **Platonic relationships which show some characteristics of** *Karmic Mate* **relationships and some characteristics of** *Soul Mate* **relationships.**

5. *Razor's Edge Mates* – **Romantic relationships which show some characteristics of a** *Cellmate* **relationship, and some characteristics of a** *Soul Mate* **relationship. At this stage of human development a high percentage of romantic relationships fall into this borderline category.** (Rungs Four and Five) These relationships can go either way. They can move up *The Ladder of Love* and become *Soul Mate* relationships, or they can tumble down *The Ladder of Love* and become *Cellmate* relationships.

6. *Common love* – **The conditional love exhibited by** *Cellmates* **and** *Razor's Edge Mates.* (Rungs One through Five).

7. *Heavenly love* – **The unconditional love exhibited by** *Soul Mates*. (Rungs Six through Nine) *Twin Souls* and *Mirror Souls* are, first and foremost, *Soul Mate* relationships, and therefore considered to be part of heavenly love.

8. *Celestial Contracts* – **These are the pre-birth, divinely guided agreements we make before reincarnating that help determine the people we'll meet, the various circumstances we'll encounter, and the divine calling we'll answer.** Our own level of soul development and our own individual karma determine how much say we have in the creation of these *Celestial Contracts*. Our angels, spirit guides, Ascended Masters, other discarnate beings, including some of our *Cellmates, Soul Mates,* and *Razor's Edge Mates,* and, ultimately, God have tremendous input into the creation of these divine agreements. Basically, these divinely inspired contracts serve as a spiritual map we're asked to follow to ensure our souls' evolution and the soulful growth of others we come into contact with throughout the course of our lifetime. Remember, it's a freewill universe, and whether we honor these *Celestial Contracts* or not is entirely up to us.

Scaling The Ladder of Love

God brings two people together at whatever Rung on The Ladder of Love will best serve their soul growth.

In a nutshell, *The Ladder of Love* postulates that love is like a ladder that has eleven different Rungs.

The bottom Rungs represent what is known as common love, and include *Cellmate* relationships and *Razor's Edge Mate* relationships.

The higher Rungs represent heavenly love and include *Soul Mate* relationships, *Twin Soul* relationships, and *Mirror Soul* relationships.

The two top Rungs on *The Ladder of Love* represent the highest heavenly loves of all: *Agape* love, unconditional love for all humanity which leads to Cosmic Consciousness; and *Unio Mystica,* or our mystical relationship with God.

You've completed the First STEP on your way to a higher love – learning the difference between love and fear.

Please take time to congratulate yourself!

STEP 2 – DEBUNKING THE WIVES' TALES SURROUNDING ROMANTIC LOVE

"Thoughts can represent the lower or bodily level of experience, or the higher or spiritual level of experience."
(*A Course in Miracles, Chapter* 1)

The first wives' tale we need to address is the false belief that love and passion are part and parcel of youth. Let go of that *Error in Thinking* and embrace this truth: At this time in human evolution some of the most passionate and intimate love affairs are happening to people in the second half of their lives. Logic alone should tell you that decades of hard life lessons learned have earned these couples a higher love.

Remember, your heart is a perennial child, your soul is immortal, and true love is eternal.

So, if you've been thinking you've missed your chance for love and passion, this book will help dispel the myth that love belongs only to the young. Start believing with all your heart that no one is ever too old – nor is it ever too late – to be granted a higher love.

What Are *Errors in Thinking?*

Errors in Thinking include remnants of the many false beliefs we've personally acquired in this lifetime or any other one, as well as the multitude of false beliefs that have become part of the human collective unconscious.

Most of our personal *Errors in Thinking* became part of our subconscious mind when we were young children and lacked the skills to differentiate truth from untruth. (Read more about the subconscious mind in STEP 15.)

Your first reaction to the *Seven Errors in Thinking* might be to discount much of what is said in this STEP. You might also find yourself resisting the changes in thinking that are being asked of you.

For this reason, I strongly recommend that you reread this STEP a minimum of three times before proceeding to the next one. I would also advise you to read this STEP over again before beginning any new one. In doing so, you'll begin erasing the many false beliefs that are etched ever so deeply in your mind.

A Pop Quiz
How Many *Errors in Thinking* are Floating Around in Your Head?

To take this quiz you need only think about the main love relationships you've had in your life. Answer each question "yes" or "no." Score 1 point for every "yes" answer.

(If you've never had a love relationship, try imagining how you would behave in one, and answer the questions accordingly; or think about your parents' marriage, and answer the questions from one of their vantage points.)

1) **Have you ever compromised on your core beliefs or values for your mate?** For instance: Did you move in with your mate, even though you believed that cohabitation without mar-

riage was wrong? Or perhaps you don't believe in abortion, but your mate convinced you to have one, even though you were dead set against it. Or, have you ever committed a crime or covered up one for your mate, even though you felt it was wrong to do so?

2) **Have you ever tried to make someone who wanted to leave you feel guilty for wanting to do so?** For instance: Your mate told you he/she was leaving, and you said something like, "God is going to punish you big time for leaving me," or "How could you do this to me after all I've done for you?"

3) **If you answered "yes" to the above question, do you still feel that trying to make that person feel guilty was the right thing to do?**

4) **Have you ever acted in a vengeful way after someone you were involved with left you?** For instance: Did you ever do physical damage to this person's possessions, such as slashing a car tire? Did you ever do something to mess up this person's credit rating, reputation, new relationship, or job?

5) **Did you ever stalk someone who broke up with you or who wanted to break up with you?** For instance: You followed this person to see where he/she was going; or you went online to check up on this person's cell phone calls. Maybe you just kept pumping other people to fill you in on all the details of your ex-mate's activities.

6) **Did you ever make the ending of a relation-ship as difficult as possible for your mate?** For instance: When you got a divorce, did you put your spouse through hell and back? Perhaps you used custody of your children as a weapon to get even with your ex.

7) **Have you ever threatened to physically harm someone who wanted to get out of a relation-ship with you, or threatened another person who you felt was responsible for the break-up?** For instance: Have you threatened to kill someone if he/she tried to leave you? Have you ever threatened to harm anyone this person might get involved with?

8) **Have you ever threatened to harm yourself if someone left you?**

9) **Have you ever threatened to leave someone if he/she does something you don't want him/her to do?** For instance: Your mate says that he/she wants to go away for the week-end with some friends, and you threatened to end the relationship if he/she followed through on those plans.

10) **Do you expect your mate to bail you out of the messes you get yourself into?** For instance: You can't control your spend-ing and expect your mate to pay off your credit card bills; or you have an addiction and expect your mate to support your habit.

11) **Have you ever hated someone because he/she left you?**

12) **Have you ever badmouthed your ex-mate to anyone who'd listen?**

13) **Have you ever given up on a dream because your mate told you to?** For instance: You wanted to be a singer, but your mate told you to get over it and get a day job instead. Or, you really wanted to have children, but your mate didn't want to, so you gave up on that idea.

Add up your score. Every "yes" answer represents an *Error in Thinking*. Ideally, none of us would score any points. Please don't fret if you see that you scored way too many points. This STEP and every STEP in this book will help you correct your thinking!

The *Errors in Thinking* represented in some of the questions are obvious. However, you might respond to others, such as question 12, by feeling that you were perfectly justified in badmouthing your ex-mate, especially since just about everyone you know has done the same thing at one time or another. If you really want a higher love, then you'll have to recognize the fact that just because everyone does something, doesn't make it right.

As you begin correcting your *Errors in Thinking*, you might find yourself at odds with many people who are currently in your life. Bear in mind that marching backwards to keep pace with your friends is never going to get you a higher love. Rather than reinforcing these false beliefs by going along with the status quo, try gently educating your friends as to why their current thinking is incorrect.

Romantic Love and Our Top *Seven* *Errors in Thinking*

(A Quick Overview)

Note: After each *Error in Thinking* I've listed the number of each relevant question from The *Errors in Thinking* Quiz in order to show you which false belief(s) you were guilty of. You might be surprised to see that many of the questions represent more than one *Error in Thinking*.

1. *First Error in Thinking:* **Our romantic mates are meant to be with us forever (questions 2, 3, 4, 5, 6, 7, 8, 11).**

2. *Second Error in Thinking:* **We have to hate our mates before we can leave them (questions 11, 12).**

3. *Third Error in Thinking:* **Love is a compromise (questions 1, 13).**

4. *Fourth Error in Thinking:* **Love is conditional (questions 1, 4, 9, 10, 11).**

5. *Fifth Error in Thinking:* **Love is going to rescue us (question 10).**

6. *Sixth Error in Thinking:* **When two people love each other romantically, it means they own each other (questions 2, 3, 4, 5, 6, 7, 8, 9, 10, 11, 13).**

7. *Seventh Error in Thinking:* **We're capable of loving another even if we hate ourselves (questions 1, 8).**

A Detailed Explanation of the Top *Seven Errors in Thinking* Concerning Romantic Love

First Error in Thinking: **Our romantic mates are meant to be with us forever.**

In Truth:

a) Most of the *Cellmates* and *Razor's Edge Mates* we encounter, as well as many of the *Soul Mates* we meet, are not meant to be with us forever. (Read more about *Cellmates* and *Razor's Edge Mates* in STEPS 3 and 4, and more about *Soul Mates* in STEPS 3, 5, 6, and 7.)

b) These relationships were sent to us from on high as mirrors of ourselves to reveal how far we've come, and how far we still need to go in order to achieve wholeness.

c) Our love relationships have powerful lessons to teach us by coming into our lives at the exact right moment (divine timing), and even more powerful lessons to reveal in their partings. (Read more about paying homage to endings in STEP 19.)

***Second Error in Thinking*: We have to hate our mates in
order to leave them.**

In Truth:

a) This false belief probably causes more pain,
sorrow, and distress than any other false
belief.

b) If we come to understand the ***First Error in
Thinking,*** that not all *Cellmates, Razor's Edge
Mates,* or *Soul Mates* are meant to last forever,
we'll come to understand that there are many
valid reasons for people to separate.

c) Ending a relationship can be an act of love.
Learn to see through the eyes of God. God
sees clear to our intentions. If you're leaving
a relationship because it isn't serving your
higher good or your partner's higher good,
then your intention is not to hurt but to heal,
and in this case you're walking the path of
love. On the flip side, if you're staying in a relationship because you feel guilty about leaving, then see that your intention is fear-based
because guilt is an attribute of fear and not of
love. Therefore, staying in a relationship out
of guilt is walking the path of fear. Sometimes
we might have to leave a relationship despite
the guilt that we may feel, since we can't always
control our fear-based thoughts and feelings.
Just remember to see life through God's eyes.
What this means is to see clear to your intentions or someone else's. If the intention is to
hurt someone, then feeling guilty is justified,
but if the intention is not to hurt but to heal
or grow, then the guilt is unjustified, and feel

free to ask God to remove this unearned guilt from your being.

d) We need to learn to bless our terminating relationships and let them go. If we truly let go of this false belief – in the necessity of hating someone before we separate – we'll stop partaking in the horrific, heart-wrenching divorce dramas that are so prevalent in our culture today.

e) We will then be able to honor our marriage vow – till death do us part – not by remaining miserably married to that partner, but by remaining lifelong friends who are there for each other in times of need. This is particularly important if there are children involved. This positive ending of a relationship via a fair and equitable divorce would change a *Cellmate* or *Razor's Edge Mate* relationship into a *platonic Soul Mate* one, incurring good karma for both people.

f) As you read this book, you'll come to understand the importance of our karmic obligation to end our relationships in a kind, just, and humane manner. (Read more about this in STEP 5 and STEP 19.)

Third Error in Thinking: **Love is a compromise.**

In Truth:

a) Of course we're expected to compromise on the little issues, such as which way the toilet paper goes on the holder, over or under, but not on the core issues.

b) Our deep beliefs, dreams, and unique view-point of life are not issues for negotiation.

c) There can be no compromising on our sense of integrity and honesty. If our partner asks us to do something that we know in our hearts to be wrong, but we do it out of fear of losing that person, know that the relationship is a fear-based one. Also acknowledge that the price we pay to be in this kind of a relationship (loss of peace of mind and a clear conscience, for example) is more than we can bear.

Fourth Error in Thinking: **Love is Conditional.**

In Truth:

a) Conditional love is a very watered-down version of love.

b) Conditional love doesn't allay our fears, but rather exacerbates them.

c) When we're loved conditionally, we never truly feel safe and secure.

d) Know that conditional love will surely fail us.

e) Unconditional love, on the other hand, gives us the strength to face and eventually overcome our fears. Through the power of unconditional love, we heal our old wounds, and then grow to become all we were meant to be.

f) When we love and are loved in an unconditional way, the world begins to feel like a safe place, and we let down our defenses and open our hearts to embrace all God's creatures and creations.

g) Unconditional love never fails us.

Fifth Error in Thinking: **Love is going to rescue us.**

In Truth:

a) Love is not about rescuing someone or having them rescue us. (Read more about this in STEP 3.)

b) Nor is love about us persecuting someone or being anyone's victim. (Read more about this in STEP 3.)

c) Heal thyself. (Read more about this is STEP 18.)

Sixth Error in Thinking: **When two people love each other in a romantic way, it means they own each other.**

In Truth:

a) Love is not about power, possession, or control.

b) People are not chattel; therefore, we can't own them.

c) Love is a life-enhancing force; it's not a weapon used to control another.

d) Love doesn't give us a license to force our personal agendas on those who love us.

Seventh Error in Thinking: We're capable of loving another even if we hate ourselves.

In Truth:

a) Self-hatred leads to all kinds of self-destructive behaviors and addictions. Before long, our out of control behaviors drive the people we love away.

b) Self-hatred makes us feel unworthy of love, and so we either don't seek love, or actively drive love away should it find its way to us.

c) Self-hatred eventually makes you look with disdain at the person who loves you, since it leads you to the false belief that there has to be something fundamentally wrong with that person if he/she could love someone as awful as you.

LOVEWORK ASSIGNMENT

(_Errors in Thinking_ Quiz)

Please answer the following questions **honestly!** (If you've never had a romantic relationship, for the relationship questions you can substitute a friendship.)

1) When my last relationship ended, did I come to hate my mate?

2) Have I ever compromised my sense of integrity or core values in order to be involved with someone?

3) Have I ever expected my partner to rescue me?

4) Have I ever acted like I owned my mate?

5) Am I too hard on myself, beating myself up for every indiscretion?

6) Do I have trouble forgiving myself?

7) Do I have issues with the way I look?

8) Do I put myself down?

9) Do I have trouble accepting a compliment?

10) Do I often feel unworthy?

Every "yes" answer indicates an *Error in Thinking* that you've been guilty of.

Finish this **LOVEWORK ASSIGNMENT** by reflecting on the *Seven Errors in Thinking*. Write down which two *Errors in Thinking* you feel you commit the most often. Write down some things you can do to help youself overcome these *Errors in Thinking*.

The Two *Errors in Thinking* that I Commit the Most

Ask God to Reveal all of Your *Errors in Thinking*

Debunking the Everyday *Errors in Thinking* Concerning the Law of Attraction by Understanding the Seven Tenets of Manifest Destiny

Manifest Destiny means we're granted a higher love because we've earned it via our thoughts, words, and deeds.

By learning the **Seven Tenets of Manifest Destiny** and practicing them on a day-to-day basis you'll be showing God and the universe that you're ready to work towards attaining the love you desire.

The Seven Tenets of Manifest Destiny honor the Sacred Law of Synchronicity, the Laws of Karma, and the Law of Attraction.

Thanks to the enormous success of Rhonda Byrne's *The Secret,* the Law of Attraction is now a household phrase. Even though *The Secret* represents a rather watered-down, overly simplified, slick version of the Spiritual Law of Attraction, there's no denying it does serve a worthy purpose by introducing this all-important spiritual concept to the masses in an easy-to-swallow format.

The first impression you might get from *The Secret* is that it's a "New Age" concept, but remember, "New Age" refers to the Age of Aquarius. If you scratch the surface, *The Secret* and its particular slant on the Law of Attraction sounds an awful lot like, "I want what I want when I want it." This "Me, me, me" and "My will be done" type of thinking is actually very Piscean in nature. Remember, the Age of Pisces represents the age of illusion, where the will of the individual reigns supreme, and man tries to play God in a vain effort to control everything.

As you study the concept of Manifest Destiny, you'll notice the Law of Attraction is certainly at work here, but first and foremost, it calls for you to acknowledge the Age of Aquarius belief in "Thy will be done."

Understanding the Law of Attraction

The Law of Attraction basically boils down to the concept that our feelings and thoughts are forms of energy that vibrate either positively or negatively and draw or attract circumstances, people, or things that vibrate at a current that is the same or similar.

The Law of Attraction further operates on the premise that not only do similar things attract, but opposites attract as well. For example, if you're thinking, "I don't want cancer," you might attract the opposite of what you want because the universe simply can't hear words of negation. So when you say, "I don't want cancer," the Law of Attraction hears, "I want cancer." We need to rephrase our thoughts so they reflect what we mean in a positive way. If you don't want cancer, say, "I want health." In other words, focus your thoughts and attention on what you want and don't dwell on what you don't want. **Remember: The Law of Attraction has a deaf spot and can't hear words of negation, such as "not" or "never."**

You need to comprehend fully that the Law of Attraction operates like a mathematical equation in which our positively charged thoughts, emotions, words, and deeds (the Law of Addition) put us on the plus side of karma, while our negatively charged thoughts, emotions, words, and deeds (the Law of Subtraction) put us on the minus side of karma. When we're operating from a place of positivity, the Lord giveth, and when we're coming from a place of negativity, the Lord taketh away.

If we truly understand that these two powerful magnetic forces, the Law of Addition and the Law of Subtraction, are at work at all times, we'll learn to consciously choose positivity and lose the negativity.

Another *Error in Thinking* that many teachers of the Law of Attraction unwittingly perpetuate is the notion that everything bad that happens to people happens because they have a negative thought. This is absurd, to say the least. Many of our life events were preordained before we were even born as a way for us to learn our karmic lessons. (Read more about these preordained events in STEP 3, when we learn about our *Celestial Contracts.*)

Other life events come as Random Acts of Karma. Sometimes we're just in the wrong place at the wrong time, and we inevitably get broadsided by someone else's karma. For instance, no one can predict the drunk driver who gets in the car in a moment of intoxicated rage and ends up killing a car full of innocent people. No, this was not a case of synchronicity. No divine coincidence conspired to bring about this tragic event. Rather, the freewill actions of an unhealed human being engineered that horrific scenario.

At other times, God may need our particular frequency of light to enter a precarious situation with the hope that we can help heal it. Due to the freewill actions of others, sometimes our light doesn't have that healing effect, and we inadvertently get caught in the crossfire.

So, please, give yourself a break and stop thinking that everything bad that happens to you is a direct result of your negativity. This kind of thinking is juvenile, narcissistic, and self-centered. It completely ignores the fact that the world doesn't always revolve around us.

Additionally, the Law of Attraction doesn't work quite as simply as 1-2-3, the way *The Secret* makes it seem with the "ask, believe, receive" formula. Therefore, if you've been practicing that formula with no luck in getting the love you want, start practicing the Seven Tenets of Manifest Destiny and watch the love you desire materialize.

Watching Our Thoughts, Words, and Deeds

Know that it isn't only our thoughts that control the outcome of a particular situation, but our words and our deeds as well.

People reading most books on the Law of Attraction, or watching *The Secret,* can become filled with angst and guilt because they can't control some or even many of their negative thoughts, and come to fear the sky is going to fall on them. This simply isn't true. This is another example of Piscean thinking, which inadvertently reinforces the disempowering dogma of organized religions that taught us that our thoughts were sins.

Stop punishing yourself for negativity. At this stage of human consciousness a negative mindset is the norm, although this doesn't make it right. In fact, all this global negativity is a massive, collective un-conscious *Error in Thinking*. What this means is that all of us have to work extra hard each and every day to bring our thoughts, words, and deeds into a posi-tive light.

Sometimes our negative thoughts are so in-grained in us that, for the time being, we may not be able to fully control them. In this instance, we're asked to recognize that these negative thoughts are *Errors in Thinking* that need to be eventually over-come. Try not to dwell on these hard-to-master nega-tive thoughts. Don't obsess about them or give them undue attention. Just acknowledge them and move on. In due time, you'll be able to overcome them, bless them, and let them go.

To override the ill effects of any negative thought, make the next two steps – your words and deeds – be positive. Although, you may not be able to fully control your thoughts, you can fully control your words and deeds. Remember the old expres-sion "A slip of the lip can sink a ship"? Use this as a reminder to watch your words. The adage "Actions speak louder than words" reminds you that your deeds are even more powerful than your words in attracting the things you want in your life.

Take comfort in knowing that, although ev-erything begins with a thought, be it a negative or positive one, the universe is compassionate and re-alizes that at this stage of human consciousness we can't guarantee that everything we think will always be positive. We can still ensure a positive result if we practice the art of positive conversation and the art of positive action on a regular basis.

Denying your negative thoughts or pretend-ing they don't exist isn't the answer, either. Learn to acknowledge your negative thoughts and be aware of them, the same way you need to pay attention to a physical pain or symptom you're experiencing, since these are messengers telling you that something is wrong. **Just remember not to take orders, directions, or instructions from your negative thoughts.**

Be patient with your own negativity. As a direct result of World War II and the devastating loss of more than 60 million people, the consciousness of humankind became increasingly negative. The zeitgeist of those nightmarish times brought forth the subconscious mindset that the evil powers of the universe were greater than the good. All of us walking the earth plane right now are asked to alter this devastating *Error in Thinking*, so that all humanity will once again believe and embrace the real truth – the good powers of the universe are so much stronger than the evil.

Remember, God's love is unconditional, infinitely compassionate, nonjudgmental, and kind; therefore, we're not punished for a mere negative thought, or because we say one negative word, or commit one less-than-perfect deed.

Now Is Good

Learn to live the philosophy that **now is good.** Conscientiously work toward the goal of looking back over your life to see the lessons you were meant to learn, but don't waste energy thinking you can change the past. You can't change it, but you can learn from the past, accept it, and work on living life to the fullest today. *Carpe diem!*

Worrying doesn't change yesterday, nor does it take care of tomorrow – it only destroys today. View worrying as the nadir of negative thinking.

Instead of worrying, say a prayer, come up with a plan, do some research on the topic that's causing you so much distress, talk with a friend, and in general be proactive in changing those aspects of yourself and your life that you're not happy with.

Learn to stop thinking that worrying has some magical power to ward off evil. Instead, view worrying as a waste of precious time and energy.

Remember – now is good!

How to Manifest the Destiny You Want – A Higher Love

If you want a higher love to manifest, then remember to be mindful of your thoughts, watchful of your words, and careful with your actions. If you practice the Seven Tenets of Manifest Destiny diligently, the concept of monitoring your thoughts, words, and actions will soon become second nature to you.

The Seven Tenets of Manifest Destiny

I. **Ask and you shall receive. Tell God that you want a higher love, and then be sure to humbly say, "Thy will be done, and I thank you for the gift of love that is about to be received."**

II. **Practice the arts of positive thinking and positive conversation – watch your thoughts and words. Refrain from negativity.** Stop whining, complaining, and bellyaching. If you keep saying, "Men can't be trusted" or "All women care about is money," the universe will keep bringing people into your life who prove your erroneous theories. The universe always assumes the things you think and say are right, or why would you bother thinking them or saying them? This is where all of our *Errors in Thinking* get us into trouble. Understand that you must change your thoughts before you can change your life. Take this tenet very seriously. Further, watch your words by speaking in ways that reflect your unconditional love for all humanity. This means stop gossiping and judging others. Be tolerant and kind in your words. Speak healing words and forgiving words. Be generous with your compliments and praise others often. Say, "please," when you ask someone for something. When you say "please," you're gently asking someone to help you. "Please, put the dishes in the sink" tells the person you're speaking to that you need help. By nature, people like to help others, so your request is willingly honored. By the same token, if you say, "Put the dishes in the sink," what you're saying is, "I order you to do something." As we all know by now, most people don't respond well to orders. Always remember to say a heartfelt "thank you" when someone has honored your request. This lets people know how much you appreciate them and the things they do.

III. **Honor the Laws of Karma. Know that every action has a reaction.** How can you expect your destiny to manifest in a positive way if you respond to every situation in a negative way? Whatever comes your way, assume it's for your greater good. In the eyes of God, it's all good. Everything we encounter and all the people we meet come into our lives to teach us or them something. We can transcend victim consciousness by seeing why God brought this particular person or experience to us. By the time you finish reading this book you'll have a very good understanding of the kinds of karmic lessons you're meant to learn. **The Laws of Karma recognize the concept of free will.** Free will means that we're responsible for our own actions and choices. However, you must also come to understand the concept of **Random Acts of Karma,** which acknowledges that sometimes we are inadvertently broadsided by someone else's freewill actions. We can transcend victim consciousness by acknowledging that we live in a freewill universe in which every human being in this lifetime or any other will be affected by other people's Random Acts of Karma. Sometimes karma, luck, or whatever you want to call it goes our way, but the law of averages alone will tell us that we can't dodge every bullet. Free will in human beings represents the Principle of Uncertainty, which prevails throughout the universe, and sometimes the free will of another can interfere with our destiny and what will manifest. A failure to appreciate the effects free will can have on any relationship or any circumstance is naïve at best. (Read more about the Laws of Karma and free will in STEP 3.)

IV. **Cultivate Clear Vision – We do this by microscopically examining our every thought.** The 19 STEPS in this spiritual program will shake up every thought you've ever had and ever will have. Every human being has to wrestle with the same problem the physicist faces: the participator has a profound influence on the outcome of everything that is happening. We tend to alter and distort and shape and re-shape everything through our own eyes and our own frame of reference. If we don't understand our *Errors in Thinking*, we'll just go on living a distorted and unhappy life that is ruled by a lot of superstitions, mumbo jumbo, hocus pocus, half-truths, and white lies. Know that this book will shatter all your illusions and allow you to see the world through the eyes of truth and clear vision.

V. **The Good Faith Performing of Labors of Love – In reading this book and earnestly doing your** *LOVEWORK ASSIGNMENTS,* **you're letting God know that you're taking the necessary steps to bring your desire for a higher love to fruition.** You can go one step further by making every day and every encounter a Labor of Love. For example: You go to the auto shop to have your car repaired. You find yourself going through all kinds of inconveniences as you wait for two days for your car to be fixed. When you finally pick up your car, you realize it still has the same rattling noise it had when you first brought it in. Your first instinct is to get angry and yell. Remember that anger and harsh words are attributes of fear and not of love. Try to override your gut response and speak kindly, yet assertively, explaining the situation. To be kind is an act of love, and so is effectively asserting your rights an act of love. Chances are the mechanic will appreciate the diplomatic way you dealt with the situation and work to rectify the situation quickly and to your satisfaction. Every time you change the way you behave from a stance of fear to one of love, you're performing a Labor of Love. Your behavior will shout out to the universe that you're ready to embrace a higher love. Acts of charity, goodwill, or effort to do our work or answer our divine calling to the best of our ability are always seen by God as Labors of Love.

VI. **Patiently Wait for a Higher Love to Manifest, for It Is Your Destiny** – The time you spend waiting for romantic love to materialize will seem to pass quickly as you practice the Seven Tenets of Manifest Destiny and surround yourself with positive thoughts, words, and actions. As you begin to manifest loving energy, you'll experience a great deal of loving energy coming back to you from everyone you encounter. By waiting patiently for love to manifest you'll grow psychologically stronger as you learn endurance and fortitude. You're also telling God that you honor the Sacred Law of Synchronicity and have complete faith in divine timing.

VII. **Every Morning When You Wake Up and Every Evening Before You Go to Sleep, Say the Following Prayer:** "God, grant me a higher love. I steadfastly acknowledge the Seven Tenets of Manifest Destiny. I willingly practice the arts of positive thinking and positive conversation. I reverently honor the just and fair Laws of Karma. I honestly seek to cultivate Clear Vision. I graciously offer you my Labors of Love. I patiently wait for my higher love to manifest. My sweet Lord, I have complete faith that Thy will and my will are one. I humbly thank thee, O Lord, for the gift of love that I am about to receive. Amen."

When You Ask For Something Know There Are Three Possible Outcomes:

1. **Your wish is my command** – God gives you exactly what you wished for, exactly when you wished for it. This would represent your will being perfectly aligned with God's will. ("My will be done" and "Thy will be done" acting harmoniously with each other.)

2. **You're granted something different from what you'd originally envisioned, but it fulfills your wish all the same.** This would reveal that God

knew you better than you knew yourself. (In due time you'd come to see how this was, in fact, another example of "My will be done" and "Thy will be done" working harmoniously after all.)

3. **Your wish appears to go unanswered** – Only time will tell what happened to the granting of your wish. The jury could still be out on this one. Here you're asked to honor the Sacred Law of Synchronicity. Maybe it just wasn't the right time for this wish to come true. In this case, God might be testing your faith and in due time your wish may still be granted. It could be an instance of a Random Act of Karma which interfered with your wish. Perhaps God felt that by not granting you your wish, this would better serve your higher good. Trust that as time goes by, the why of it all will be revealed to you, particularly if you ask God to reveal the truth to you. (This would represent a case of "Thy will be done," and you must honor what God has chosen for you. This could still prove to be another case of "My will be done" and "Thy will be done," since God knew what you really wished for in your heart of hearts even though your mind was unwilling or unable to recognize this truth. Cultivate patience and endurance.)

Please, try not to get discouraged if everything you want isn't coming to you at the speed of light. Many times just overcoming our fears speeds up the process; at other times the Sacred Law of Synchronicity or the Principle of Uncertainty may be at work.

You can take great comfort in knowing that your desire for a higher love is one wish God wants to grant you. Trust that God knows how, where, and when to grant you the miracle of love.

If you want to know more about the Law of Attraction, try reading some or all of the following books: *The Law of Attraction*, by Ester and Jerry Hicks; *The Power of Positive Thinking*, by Norman Vincent Peale; *The Magic of Believing*, by Claude M. Bristol; and *The Dynamic Laws of Prosperity*, by Catherine Ponder.

Summing Things Up

This STEP was meant to challenge many of your preconceived notions about love and relationships. If you're going to be granted a higher love, you'll first have to know what stands in your way and keeps blocking that desire. Remember, your fears, false beliefs, and *Errors in Thinking* are keeping you from the love you want, so vow to work hard every day to overcome them.

Where Do We Go from Here?

STEP 3 – *CELLMATE, SOUL MATE,* OR *RAZOR'S EDGE MATE* –WHICH WAY DO I GO? – will explain in detail what *The Ladder of Love* is and how it works.

Remember to read STEP 2 a minimum of three times before proceeding to STEP 3.

Feel confident in knowing that you've taken another step in your journey toward a higher love!

STEP 3 – CELLMATE, SOUL MATE, OR RAZOR'S EDGE MATE – WHICH WAY DO I GO?

"When you meet anyone, remember it is a holy encounter. As you see him you will see yourself…. Whenever two sons of God meet, they are given another chance at salvation."
(A Course in Miracles, Chapter 8)

Relationships as Mirrors of Our Soul

Our love relationships mirror the relationship we have with God. Consequently, if we both love and fear God, our romantic relationships will be love/hate ones, reflecting this duality. If we view God as a distant, silent, or absent figure, we'll continually pick partners who reflect this image. On the other hand, if we know the true nature of God, which is pure, unconditional love, our romantic relationships will be truly intimate, for they'll be based on the giving and receiving of unconditional love. (Read more about having an intimate relationship with God in STEP 10.)

God is love. Housed within each of us is that same divine, loving energy. Each STEP in this book is teaching you how to harness this life- enhancing force.

To receive the gift of love we must first open ourselves to it. The universe responds to this opening of the heart by giving us what *we think we want.*

In other words, the universe gives us the level of love that mirrors our own personal vision as to what constitutes love. When that flawed vision inevitably fails us, God says, *"Think again."*

The 19 STEPS in this book are divinely designed to get you to rethink and reformulate your vision of love.

Nothing New Under the Sun
Ancient Greek Philosophy and Its Impact on Modern Thinking

The idea of a hierarchy of love is nothing new under the sun. Twenty-five centuries ago the Athenians, who took the study of love seriously, had an ascending scale of love.

According to the ancient Greeks, the highest tier on the scale of love occurred between two people (men) who had a purely spiritual relationship and not a sexual one. This non-sensual, idealized vision of love has become part of the human collective unconscious over the millenniums, and its influence can still be felt in the twenty-first century.

Unfortunately, the many *Errors in Thinking* from that long-ago time period make this ancient Greek or Platonic scale of love (named after Plato, who wrote down the philosophical discourses of his great mentor, Socrates) a highly flawed one.

Some Obvious False Beliefs from Ancient Greek Times

- ◆ The ancient Greeks felt that women were inferior to men and were only good for procreation (Ouch!).

- ◆ Because women were considered inferior, and were, as a rule, uneducated, the love a man had for a woman was placed at the low end of the Platonic scale; whereas the love relationship between two men was placed on a higher tier, since they could have both a physical relationship and an intellectual one.

- ◆ Socrates' view of spiritual relationships as the highest level of love was a direct backlash against the highly promiscuous behavior that surrounded those times. Socrates reasoned that all the carnal intercourse men were engaging in kept them from seeking a higher spiritual and intellectual intercourse with one another.

Consequently, this Platonic scale of love is a highly erroneous measurement to use today, although the concept of the levels of love remains a valid one.

Deciphering the Ancient Greek Hierarchy of Love

Once we winnow out the *Errors in Thinking* from the ancient Greek philosophical equation of love, we can come to the grains of truth that are still relevant for us today.

In a nutshell, the Athenians did recognize the difference between common love and heavenly love.

Common love was the name given to the ordinary, everyday kind of love which embraced the flesh and blood of another and dealt with all things visible, while **heavenly love** was thought to be an extraordinary kind of love, for it embraced the spirit and all things invisible to the naked eye.

The ancient Greeks further subdivided love into three categories: *Eros, Philia,* and *Agape.*

Eros **is physical love (sexual in nature) of another,** and the Athenians felt this kind of love was a form of madness showered down upon us from the gods.

Philia **is the non-sexual, brotherly love or friendship we feel for others.**

Agape **is the unconditional spiritual love we feel for all humankind, God, and all the cosmos.** (Read more about *Eros, Philia, and Agape* in STEPS 9 and 10.)

The First Tier of Socratic Love

When we're young, we're drawn to the outward beauty of a person. Since this is a superficial kind of love, or a common love, we will soon get bored and seek out another partner, then another one, and so on and so forth. It is God's hope that as we grow in wisdom, we'll tire of one superficial interchange after another and will therefore seek out a relationship that is based on a soul connection.

This loving of another's soul brings us to the next tier of love.

The Second Tier of Socratic Love

Once we've come to love another's soul, we move beyond the realm of the purely physical world and enter into the sacred realms of heavenly love. Through the blending of two souls, the whole world of spirit begins to open up. Suddenly, one becomes aware of the world of art which represents the beauty of the human soul taking on a physical form. This recognition of the collective soul of humanity as it's manifested through art brings us to the next tier of love.

The Third Tier of Socratic Love

Once we're aware of the collective soul of humankind, our individual souls long to know the eternal beauty that exists in the invisible realm as well. In due time, we come to recognize the collective soul of the entire cosmos (Cosmic Consciousness – more about this concept in STEP 9) and seek to understand the eternal truths. With this divine sense of illumination, we willingly enter into the world of the immortals.

A Summary of the Tiers of Socratic Love

o Basically, the Tiers of Socratic love move us from the physical world to the spiritual world (common love to heavenly love).

o Socrates denounced sexual relations. He believed exercising self-control over our animal impulses to be the highest level of human spiritual evolution.

o One must bear in mind that Athenian men, in their open practice of homosexuality, could be highly promiscuous, and Socrates was really addressing that issue. He felt that all the carnal intercourse men were engaging in kept them from seeking a higher spiritual and intellectual intercourse with each other. This Socratic thinking became the basis for the **Platonic ideal of love** that was later embraced by early Christianity.

o **This erroneous thinking – that a higher love is not a sexual one but only intellectual or spiritual in nature – is still part of our collective unconscious even today.**

o **We must end this collective *Error in Thinking* and come to understand that *Soul Mate* romantic love includes the concept of *Sacred Sexuality,* in which our bodies, hearts, minds, and, most important, our souls blend together in blissful oneness.** (Read more about *Sacred Sexuality* in STEP 15.)

o Let us strive to create a new archetype in the human collective unconscious that recognizes that *Sacred Sexuality* is a great gift from God and definitely a characteristic of the higher levels of love. (Read more about archetypes in STEP 4.)

To learn more about Plato and Socrates, read *Plato for Beginners,* by Robert Cavalier, illustrated by Eric Lurio; *Plato's Thoughts,* by G.M.A.Grube; *Great Dialogues of Plato,* translated by W.H.D. Rouse; or *Five Great Dialogues,* by Plato.

Understanding *The Ladder of Love*

The Ladder of Love is the twenty-first-century hierarchy of love that has been channeled to me over the course of the last decade. It's proven to be an invaluable tool to utilize in the analysis of love.

Before we begin to discuss the different Rungs on *The Ladder of Love* in greater detail, there are some words and concepts you need to understand fully. Please study this STEP often until these words become a part of your working vocabulary.

Understanding Group Souls

Before proceeding further in our discussions concerning *Cellmates, Soul Mates, and Razor's Edge Mates* we need to learn about Group Souls.

♦ Visualize the Group Soul as a huge pie composed of divine energy which emanated from The Godhead.

♦ In the beginning, God made countless numbers of these huge soul pies from divine light and spirit, and then sliced and diced each into thousands of pieces.

♦ Some of these soul slices stayed for a while in the heavenly realms as spirit (discarnate beings) to guide the other soul slices that incarnated on earth in human form. In due time these incarnated souls passed away and returned to spirit, only to return to earth again and again. At different intervals the disincarnate beings also came down to the earth plane, passed away and returned to spirit, only to reincarnate at some later date. (The souls that came down first are considered older souls than those that came down later. However, the lessons we learn while on earth determine how wise a soul we are. Some old souls have learned fewer life lessons than some younger ones!) Thus began the continual cycle of birth, death, and rebirth that the Buddhists refer to as *samsara*.

♦ This chain of rebirths continues until a soul learns all the karmic lessons it was meant to learn; it then attains what is known as liberation. Once the soul is Enlightened or liberated, that soul can stay in spirit for all of eternity to keep watch over the human world, or, if need be, return periodically to earth as a *Bodhisattva*, an Enlightened Master, to help human evolution.

♦ Contrary to popular belief, angels are not part of any Group Soul, for they were never human nor will they ever be human. They have always been a part of the heavenly realm, a kind of spiritual army that protects earthbound bodies and discarnate spirits alike.

- ◆ Over the course of our lifetimes and/or during our times in spirit, we'll meet most, if not all, of our soul group.

- ◆ In the beginning, we were all *Soul Mates* to each other, but through our freewill actions and the freewill actions of others, we began to accrue karma, and as a result some *Soul Mates* became *Karmic Mates* or *Borderline Mates* to us.

- ◆ *Karmic Mates* (remember – romantic *Karmic Mates* are known as *Cellmates*) will come in the form of lovers, coworkers, teachers, acquaintances, strangers, family members, so-called friends, and basically all the relationships in our lives which seem to crucify us or be thorns in our sides. *Karmic relationships* are characterized by the fear (anxiety, worry, depression, violence, guilt, hate, jealousy, envy, etc.) they inspire in us.

- ◆ Our *Soul Mates* will also come in the form of lovers, coworkers, teachers, acquaintances, strangers, family members, and friends. These relationships are characterized by the caring, nurturing, and loving feelings they inspire in us.

- ◆ Some relationships (the most heart-wrenching ones of all) are the borderline ones in which we walk a fine line between *Karmic Mate* and *Soul Mate.* These relationships leave us feeling anxious and insecure, for we never know which way they'll turn out. Couples involved in borderline romantic relationships are called *Razor's Edge Mates.* People involved in platonic borderline relationships are called *Borderline Mates.*

♦ Know that *Karmic Mates, Cellmates, Soul Mates, Borderline Mates,* and *Razor's Edge Mates* are all part of our spiritual family known as the Group Soul.

♦ A good example of Group Souls incarnating in large numbers to help the evolution of all humanity would be all the artists, writers, musicians, and scientists who came down during the Italian Renaissance.

For more information on angels, guides, and Group Souls read *Working with Your Guides and Angels,* by Ruth White. For more information on Group Souls read *Twin Souls: A Guide to Finding Your Spiritual Partner,* by Patricia Joudry and Maurie Pressman, and *The Tenth Insight: Holding the Vision: An Experiential Guide,* by James Redfield and Carol Adrienne. And by all means, read anything that Doreen Virtue, Ph.D. has written.

Know that in the beginning all was one. There was but one God, who split into separate pieces of consciousness. As we grow in our spiritual awareness and blend our souls with those of others, we're working our way back to The Source, to Oneness.

More Insights About Group Souls

1. We all started out as individual souls that were part of a larger family of souls called **the soul group or Group Soul.** Our Group Soul has been with us always, aiding and supporting us,

and it was expected that we would be there for them as well.

2. **Within this Group Soul family reside our** *primary Soul Mates.* Due to freewill negative actions (ours and/or theirs in this lifetime or any other) some of these *primary Soul Mates* became our *primary Karmic Mates, primary Cellmates, primary Borderline Mates,* and *primary Razor's Edge Mates.* Our *Mirror Souls* and our *Twin Soul* are also housed within our Group Soul. (Read more about *Mirror Souls* and *Twin Souls* in STEPS 6 and 7.) **We will refer to all of the above members of our Group Soul as our** *Primary Mates.*

3. These *Primary Mate relationships* are the ones that have had the greatest impact upon our lives, destinies, and souls' growth.

4. When we meet a person who is part of our Group Soul, we'll have a feeling or the sense that we've met this person before. This inner knowing is called **The Recognition Factor.** Sometimes this feeling will come in the form of an instantaneous liking or loving of one another, which means we have a **Soul Mate Affinity** for each other. At other times, we'll have a spontaneous dislike or even hatred for one another, which is called **Karmic Clashing.**

5. On earth, there are countless other Group Souls besides our own. Housed within these other soul groups will be some of our **secondary Soul Mates, secondary Karmic Mates, secondary Cellmates, secondary Borderline Mates, and secondary Razor's Edge Mates. We will refer to these individuals as our Secondary Mates.** Throughout our lifetimes, and while in

spirit, we've met many of these **Secondary Mates** as well, and if this is the case **The Recognition Factor** will be at work here too, giving us the sense that we've met these people somewhere before. Due to negative or positive freewill actions in this lifetime or in any other one, some of these *Secondary Mates* become *Primary Mates* to each other, depending upon how much impact they've had on each other's lives. Think of the blending of individuals from different soul groups in terms of a marriage. When two people marry they blend two different families together. This blending of different soul groups together is part of God's brilliant plan to have us work our way back to oneness via the balancing Laws of Karma.

6. In essence, every human being walking this earth plane, and every disincarnated being in the heavens began this cosmic journey as a *Soul Mate* to every other being. Somewhere along the line we forgot this. Thus began the illusion that physical and ideological differences mattered, and these superficial factors led us to feel separate from each other. We forgot our original nature of oneness, and duality was born. Suddenly there was good and evil, black and white, war and peace, yours and ours.

7. Only through many incarnations, much time spent in spirit, through great trial and error, and Group Soul blending will we, as a species, once again find our way back to the Promised Land of Oneness, ending the vicious cycle of suffering known as *samsara* or the wheel of karma.

8. *Karma represents the law of action.* Every action we take produces a reaction, either a positive or negative one, in this lifetime or in any other. Thus, karma is the sum of our actions and their consequences. Karma serves our soul by helping it grow to completeness. The more complete, the more whole our soul is, the easier it is to attain and maintain love on the higher Rungs of Love.

At this point in the study of love, you're beginning to see that all of us are soulfully connected.

Cellmates, Soul Mates, and Razor's Edge Mates – How Do You Know the Difference?

A. *Cellmate* relationships are characterized by conditional love that tends to bring out the worst in us.

B. *Cellmates* are bound by an unconscious contract *(**Karmic Contract**)* that basically states, "The way we were in the beginning, so shall we be in the end." *Cellmates* tend to do the same destructive dance over and over without learning anything. Consequently, love at the lower end of *The Ladder of Love* becomes more of a war story than a love story. Children raised in these households are not learning how to live in peace – they're learning how to wage war.

C.　On the other hand, *Soul Mates* practice the art of loving unconditionally, and this tends to bring out the best in each. The constancy of *Soul Mate* love heals their souls and helps them to evolve. Children raised by *Soul Mate couples* are learning peace, love, and joy.

D.　Since we're living in a nuclear age, the massive destruction we, as a human race, are capable of is apocalyptic. Hence, the study of love is not just a personal mission, but ultimately a humanitarian one as well.

E.　Karmic law states: Every action produces an equal reaction. Some of our actions are positive and produce positive results. Some of our actions are negative and produce negative results. Know that doing nothing, going into a static state of deep denial, is, in fact, making a choice, and that choice is a negative one. **Negative karma brings us *Cellmates* and *Razor's Edge Mates*, while positive karma brings us *Soul Mates*.**

F.　Whenever we encounter a *Soul Mate*, *Cellmate*, or *Razor's Edge Mate* we'll have lessons to learn.

G.　With *Soul Mates* we'll learn more of our lessons through love, peace, and joy than through suffering. The exception to this rule occurs between *Soul Mates* whose negative, freewill actions drag the relationship down *The Ladder of Love*. At this point they're no longer *Soul Mates*, for they have marched backwards and become *Razor's Edge Mates* or even *Cellmates*. Unfortunately, this couple will then learn most of their karmic lessons through suffering, and only a few lessons will be learned through love, peace, and joy.

H. **When meeting a *Soul Mate,* a *Cellmate,* or a *Razor's Edge Mate,* we'll have a deep inner knowing that we've met them before (*The Recognition Factor*). At this point, our soul takes over and guides us. Logic won't help us. Reasoning means nothing. Our intellect is bypassed. We're at the mercy of spirit.**

I. With a *Soul Mate* we tend to feel safe (although our own fear of intimacy or commitment might rear its ugly head and scare the hell out of us). At other times we may feel as if we're on a roller coaster ride that we can't stop, but we know that we wouldn't want to get off anyway, for the ride is the thrill of our life.

J. With a *Cellmate* we'll sense that the roller coaster will stop only to crash and burn. We only hope we can jump off before we go down with it.

K. *Soul Mate, Cellmate,* and *Razor's Edge Mate* relationships defy reason, and we seem to go from point A to point Z in record time. We have very strong feelings right from the start. Oftentimes this includes a strong sexual attraction which is the tantalizing bait that lures us in the first place. (This is what's referred to as "chemistry.")

L. God brings *Cellmates, Soul Mates,* and *Razor's Edge Mates* together in the great hope that they'll help each other learn and grow.

M. Just as we're not meant to stay with most of our *Cellmates* forever, some of our *Soul Mates* will be with us only for a limited amount of time.

Part of our karmic lesson is to learn when to hold on to a relationship, and when to bless it and let it go.

N. In record time, *Cellmates* bring out the worst in us. We'll learn some of our life lessons while in this karmic relationship, but many of the big lessons will be learned only long after the relationship is over.

O. *Cellmate* and *Razor's Edge Mate* relationships can be the hardest ones of all to break free of because they're based on physical, emotional, psychological, and spiritual bondage and imprisonment. Two people become chained together by the force of fear that has accrued over many, many lifetimes. Breaking free from this karmic bondage can only happen through a great deal of inner and outer work.

P. *Cellmate* and *Razor's Edge Mate* relationships occur more frequently at this stage of human development than *Soul Mate* relationships because many of us alive today are very old souls (having experienced countless incarnations) and have much karmic reckoning to do. We can expect to meet many of our *Cellmates* from past lives, and these encounters give us an opportunity to right the wrongs of the past, both those done unto us, and those we have done onto others. Through karmic reckoning in past lifetimes, some previous *Cellmate* relationships have now evolved into *Razor's Edge Mates*. In this lifetime, positive actions can move these encounters up *The Ladder of Love* to become *Soul Mate* relationships, or negative actions can slide them back down to the level of *Cellmates*. These karmic relationships are

God's way of giving us another chance to learn from our past mistakes by correcting them in this lifetime. *By the time you finish reading this book, you'll have a really good understanding of all the karmic lessons you're on earth to learn.*

What Characterizes Relationships on the Lower End of *The Ladder of Love?*

1) *Cellmates,* as a rule, tend to bring out the worst in each other.

2) The Lower Rungs represent earthbound, fear-based relationships (common love). *Cellmates* reinforce each other's fears rather than helping each other to overcome them.

3) There's a profound feeling of separation and loneliness deep in the heart of each *Cellmate* even when they're clinging to each other for dear life.

4) A great deal of negative karma magnetically draws these *Cellmates* together. Although there can be positive interactions taking place in these relationships, there are more negative interactions going on. God hopes we'll steadfastly work toward understanding why we're trapped in this no-win situation, and either heal the relationship or bless it and let it go.

5) *The basic characteristic of a Cellmate relationship is an unconscious agreement (Karmic Contract)*

made by both partners to stay pretty much the same as they were when they first met. This ***Karmic Contract*** is easy enough to follow in terms of a short-term relationship, but impossible to maintain over the long haul. Of course, if you're a compulsive gambler, a drug addict, or an alcoholic, your *Cellmate* might very well want you to change that aspect of yourself, but the rest of your behavior is expected to stay the same. The problem with this kind of skewed reasoning is that it contradicts the Law of Karma, which basically states that one change will inevitably alter everything. The terms of our relationships must be continually renegotiated if we're to grow, heal, and evolve. Many *Cellmate* relationships won't survive this renegotiation process. The *Cellmate* who refuses to change will feel betrayed by the *Cellmate* who is doing the changing, and will fight tooth and nail to keep the ***Karmic Contract*** alive. Guilt is the weapon the stagnant *Cellmate* uses to control the growing mate. The changing *Cellmate* begins to feel guilty about breaking this unspoken, but very real, ***Karmic Contract***; yet in trying to honor this fraudulent contract, a person is actually being loyal to the wrong cause and to the wrong person. We must be true to ourselves. *It's up to the growing Cellmate to create a new, higher-consciousness, **Sacred Contract** that basically states, "I am a growing, evolving being. It's my greatest hope that you'll grow with me. I'm honestly following my heart, and pray that I can do what is best for everyone, including myself."* At this point, the continuation or dissolution of the relationship depends upon the action (karma) of the stagnant mate. If the stagnant *Cellmate* chooses to abide by the new, higher-consciousness *Sacred Contract*, God bless! If that *Cellmate* can't or simply won't live up to the new contract, then the growing mate is free from karmic obligation to continue the relationship and may move on.

6) *Cellmate* relationships are based on conditional love, and consequently could never lead to *Agape*, the unconditional love for all of humankind and all of the cosmos that is so necessary for the survival of the human race. (Read more about *Agape* love in STEP 9.)

7) It's God's greatest hope that in this new millennium, *Cellmate* relationships will become obsolete, thus ensuring a peaceful, harmonious, and loving future for all humanity.

Keep in mind that although Razor's Edge Mates exhibit many of the negative characteristics of a Cellmate relationship, they also do exhibit some positive characteristics of a Soul Mate relationship. Because these relationships cut both ways, they can be some of the hardest relationships to leave, since there is the ever-present hope that things will somehow get better.

What Characterizes Relationships on the Higher End of *The Ladder of Love?*

1) *Soul Mates,* as a rule, tend to bring out the best in each other.

2) In order to be given a *Soul Mate,* a person must have done an enormous amount of inner homework in this lifetime or in any other.

3) Each partner has already achieved a certain amount of inner soul completion on his/her own, and it is God's hope that bringing together these *Soul Mates* will accelerate the Enlightenment of both.

4) Good karma draws to us a *Soul Mate* who will supply more positive interactions than negative ones. ***Soul Mates are under karmic obligation to honor their Celestial Contract and heal any negative interactions between them in record time.***

5) *Soul Mate* relationships are based on unconditional love. Unconditional love paves the way for the emergence of *Agape* love and Cosmic Consciousness, thus ensuring the survival of the entire human race.

6) *Soul Mate* relationships will ultimately lead us to the highest Rung on *The Ladder of Love.* This is *Unio Mystica,* or an intimate relationship with God.

7) Some older souls might first achieve the top two Rungs on *The Ladder of Love: Agape* love (unconditional love for all humankind) and *Unio Mystica* (having an intimate relationship with God), and as a result of accrued good karma, God will then bring a high *Soul Mate* to them, perhaps a *Mirror Soul* or even their *Twin Soul* to further assist the evolution of their souls.

The Ladder of Love – Going Up and Going Down

Know that any relationship can ascend or descend *The Ladder of Love*. For instance, it's possible, due to the element of free will, for a *Cellmate* to become a *Soul Mate*, if both partners work very hard to resolve their inner issues. This is a rare occurrence, but when it does happen, the universe rejoices. Tremendous amounts of good karma accumulate, and the universe rewards this couple generously.

If a *Karmic Mate* relationship exists between family members such as mother and child, or brother and sister, and these people work to heal their relationship and become *Soul Mates*, once again the universe responds joyfully.

On the other hand, heaven mourns greatly when a high level of love is dragged down *The Ladder of Love* via the destructive power of one or both partners' unchecked fears. We pay a high price for such an *Error in Thinking*, and one can expect life to be a hard battle for some time to come.

Free will – both our own and that of our partner – ultimately determines the positive or negative outcome of any relationship. This holds true no matter how high a *Soul Mate* or how low a *Cellmate* relation-ship you're given.

Never underestimate the power of free will.

Try visualizing love as a sacred vial of energy. If you drink only a drop of this sacred vial, you'll experience only a very watered-down version of love. That watered-down version of love represents the lower Rungs on *The Ladder of Love.*

As we move up *The Ladder of Love,* we drink more of the sacred vial. *Twin Souls* and *Mirror Souls* drink every drop! What the *Twin Souls* and *Mirror Souls* decide to do with this sacred elixir (free will) determines whether it's a restorative love potion or a life-threatening poison. *Mirror Souls* almost always cherish the great gift they've been given. However, at this stage of human evolution, *Twin Soul* reunions, which demand total karmic cleansing and healing, often end prematurely and painfully, because one or both of the *Twins* are unable to handle all the responsibilities inherent in this relationship. (Read more about *Twin Souls* and *Mirror Souls* in STEPS 6 and 7.)

Understand that our relationships are mirrors of the world. If we can't make peace in our own home and in our own hearts, how can we expect the world to make peace?

If we simply leave one relationship without understanding what our soul needed to learn from being in that relationship in the first place, we'll encounter more of the same in the next relationship. Pay close attention to the patterns that keep repeating themselves in your relationships!

LOVEWORK ASSIGNMENT

Reflect upon your current or most recent relationship. Would you say the two of you were *Cellmates, Soul Mates,* or *Razor's Edge Mates?* Write down the reasons why you came to this conclusion. For instance: "My current mate is a *Cellmate* because we bring out the worst in each other, and because he/she puts me down every time I try to change something about myself for the better."

If you've never had a love relationship, then substitute your relationship with a friend, ascertaining whether that relationship brings out the best in you (*Soul Mate*), or the worst *(Karmic Mate),* or is it a little of both (*Borderline Mate*)?

Cellmate, Soul Mate, or Am I Walking the Razor's Edge?

Ask God to Reveal All to You

Looking at All Your Relationships with New Eyes

From this day forward, begin to look at every relationship in your life, however great or small, as a mirror of your soul since all relationships have the power to reveal who you once were, who you now are, and who you would like to be.

Think about your current life. Are there relationships with coworkers, neighbors, or any other people that seem to be particularly negatively charged? Do these people bring out the worst in you? Do you bring out the worst in them as well? Have you seen this pattern in other relationships before?

These people hold the key to your soul. **Even if these people were to leave your life, you would confront these same feelings time and time again with another person until you healed them.**

LOVEWORK ASSIGNMENT

Take some time to reflect upon the one relationship in your current life that's giving you the most distress. Write down the things about this person that drive you crazy. For instance, "He always has to control everything."

After you have listed as many of these examples as you can think of, go over the list and consider whether you're ever guilty of the same crimes. Could this person remind you of yourself? Remember, we only hate that which is part of ourselves.

Then think about whether this person reminds you of someone from the past. For example: Does he/she remind you of your mother, your sister, or your father?

What have you learned about yourself from analyzing this relationship?

A Current Relationship that Drives Me Crazy

I Am Learning to See All Relationships as a Mirror of Myself

Remember, the path of love is rarely a straight one. It's a long and winding road. One moment we may take a giant leap of faith toward love, while the next step might catapult us in the other direction. Even so, if we keep on going, sometimes taking baby steps, sometimes giant ones, sometimes slipping, sometimes falling, eventually, by the Grace of God, we'll find our way to that place of love, peace, and joy. To make the journey easier, we must learn to let our heart, soul, and higher consciousness guide us.

Summing Things Up

This STEP is meant to familiarize you with the terminology used in *The Ladder of Love*. By now, you should have a good understanding of the characteristics that determine whether someone is a *Cellmate, Soul Mate,* or *Razor's Edge Mate.* If you're still confused, please reread this STEP until you really feel comfortable with the material it presents.

In STEP 4, we'll learn more about *Cellmate* and *Razor's Edge Mate* relationships, and how you can learn to recognize and avoid toxic love by mastering the first Five Rungs on *The Ladder of Love.*

Jungian Terms You Need to Know Before Attempting the Next STEP

Collective Unconscious – Carl Jung, the brilliant Swiss psychologist/psychiatrist (1875–1961) believed that the human unconscious mind was divided into two distinct parts: **The personal unconscious,** which is composed of all the information we either forgot, repressed, or suppressed from our conscious mind; and our **collective unconscious,** which is inborn or imprinted in us. The collective unconscious houses primal images called archetypes, and primal fears called transpersonal fears. These primordial images and fears are common in varying degrees to most, if not all, human beings, and they're the closet things to instincts that humans possess. They originally functioned as guideposts and warning signs to help ensure our survival on an individual basis and as a species. However, at this stage of human evolution, our collective unconscious does contain many false beliefs which have been hammered into it over the course of human history. One of the purposes of this book is to eliminate these collective false beliefs and create a new collective unconscious based on higher-consciousness thinking.

Archetypes – These are primordial images that have been deeply ingrained in our collective unconscious. These primal images are like shorthand symbols our subconscious mind uses to communicate with us. For instance, some archetypal images, including the ocean, the stars, the moon, the sun, the desert, or a mountain, convey a mood, a meaning, or an emotion to all human beings just by seeing them.

Archetypes can also be recurring personality types, stereotypical in nature, that are common to a culture, a people, and, to a large extent, to all human beings. These stock characters are stored in our collective unconscious and serve to reveal the different paths and life choices we can make. Some archetypes are positive ones, such as that of the "Hero" and the "Healer," while still others can be negative ones, such as the "Con Artist" and the "Gossip."

These recurring archetypal characters appear in mythology, in our dreams, in fairytales, movies, literature, and artwork, and are easy types for humans to identify with. Some common archetypes are: the "Princess," the "Clown," the "Wise Old Man," the "Hobo," and the "Damsel in Distress," to name but a few.

All of us live out many archetypes during our lifetime, and they serve as the building blocks of our lives. For example, you may be a medical doctor by profession, thereby living out the archetype of the "Healer," but you might also be a mother, and so you're also living out the archetype of the "Matriarch;" and on top of this, you might be a writer, and in that case you're living out the archetype of the "Artist" as well.

Most human beings, at this stage of human evolution, still play out the following two negative archetypes: that of "Master/Slave"and that of "Prostitute."

The Master/Slave archetype is often played out symbolically between men and women. Even today, in this day and age of women's liberation, many women still take on the subservient role in the household, regardless of how powerful they might be in the outside world. The antiquated notion that the man is the king of the castle was continually reinforced throughout human history with its patriarchal societies and has become a part of our collective unconscious. Modern-day men and women both have to vigilantly monitor their behavior to keep this archetype from doing its insidious damage to the relationship. For example, a recent study indicated that in many marriages the man is still the master of the finances, even though women often make as much money as their husbands do, or even more – and then women try to even the score by controlling when the couple has sex.

The Master/Slave archetype is also often re-enacted in the boss/employee relationship and the parent/child relationship.

The Prostitute archetype for most of us plays itself out, not in the literal sense of the word, but symbolically, since most of us can be bought, if the price is right, or if our economic or physical well-being is threatened. In the name of self-preservation, we may find ourselves compromising our values, our sense of integrity, or the truth when money or our sense of security is involved.

The only way to break the hold these negative archetypes have over us is to become consciously aware of them and stop them in their tracks. If you see yourself taking on a subservient role in a relationship, know that you're enacting the Slave archetype. If you see yourself compromising your core beliefs for money, which is an enactment of the Prostitute archetype, meditate on how you can still make money and survive without selling your soul in the process.

To learn more about archetypes and to gain a deeper understanding of how they govern your life, please read *Sacred Contracts,* by Caroline Myss, Ph.D.

This is probably one of the most illuminating books you'll ever get your hands on.

The Head Games *Cellmates* Play (Understanding the Psychodynamics of Dysfunctional Relationships)

Before we begin STEP 4, which will be an in-depth explanation of the first Five Rungs on *The Ladder of Love*, we're going to examine the psychodynamics behind dysfunctional relationships. This will help you to see what keeps *Cellmates* and *Razor's Edge Mates* chained to their destructive patterns of interacting with each other.

Transactional Analysis is a highly effective therapy program created by a California psychiatrist named Eric Berne which teaches people that we are responsible for what happens to us in the future, regardless of what has happened to us in the past. This groundbreaking therapy was later translated into easy-to-understand terms by his disciple, Thomas Harris, in the bestselling book *I'm OK – You're OK.*

A transaction, according to Transactional Analysis, is a social interaction that occurs between people. The first person provides the **transactional stimulus** by opening up a dialogue with a second person. The second person then reciprocates by responding to the dialogue, and this interaction is called the **transactional response.**

Between healed people the transactions are simple and clear-cut. For example: You ask, "Are you hungry?" and someone responds, "Yes." This was a simple and straightforward dialogue in which you began the transaction by asking a question which served as the transactional stimulus and the person's affirmative answer provided the transactional response.

In unhealed and dysfunctional relationships, a simple transactional stimulus such as asking someone if he/she is hungry could be answered harshly with a loaded transactional response, such as, "What's it to you?" This kind of angry remark is called **a hook,** and it can set off a fight. In Transactional Analysis, the fight is the **payoff,** in other words, what the person who answered with the hostile transactional response wanted. If you're a healthy individual, you won't take the person's hook and answer with an angry response. Rather, you'll diffuse the situation by answering the sarcastic response, "What's it to you?" with a simple, straightforward one, such as, "Nothing, really, I was just asking if you were hungry to see if you wanted to join me for something to eat." That cool, calm response would put an end to the fight before it began.

Healthy people learn to answer the questions they're asked – **straight**. They don't load their responses with angry, sarcastic, or attack words.

Cellmates, however, often respond to each other with negatively charged words.

The Transactional Analysis Deadly Triangle

Cellmates have mastered the psychological game that Transactional Analysis refers to as the victim/rescuer/persecutor triangle. In this vicious psychological game, *Cellmates* move around this deadly triangle playing three recurring roles: that of victim, rescuer, and persecutor.

For example: A husband comes home from work and screams at his wife, "The house is a pigsty; the kids are running around like wild maniacs, and why the hell isn't dinner on the table?" (He is the persecutor.) The obviously exhausted wife starts crying. (She is the victim.) Then the husband suddenly acts caring and hugs her. (He becomes the rescuer.)

A moment later the wife starts screaming back at her husband, "You don't give a damn about me. All you care about is yourself. Did you ever stop to think what my day was like?" (Now the wife has taken on the role of the persecutor.) Then her husband gets irate, complaining about how hard he worked all day and how nothing he ever does is good enough for her. (He is now taking on the role of the victim.) He runs out the door, heading to the nearest bar, while his wife starts crying and screaming, "How could you run out and leave me like this?" (Now she's the victim again.) His wife then starts chasing after him, saying she's sorry. (She has taken on the role of rescuer.)

From this all-too-familiar scenario we can see how the husband went from screaming at his wife – in other words, persecuting her – to hugging her or rescuing her, to feeling so victimized (persecuted) and abused by her that fleeing seems the only alternative. The wife went from feeling abused or victimized, to feeling rescued, to becoming the angry persecutor, to becoming re-victimized again as the husband angrily runs out the door, and as she chases after him, she plays the role of the rescuer trying to save the day. Does any of this ring true to you?

Do any of your interactions with people follow this pattern? If so, you have to consciously choose to step out of this deadly triangle and begin to respond calmly. Learn to answer the question *straight*, even if it was a loaded one. A sense of humor goes a long way to diffuse the situation when someone has thrown you an angry hook.

For the next few weeks, pay close attention to the way you habitually respond to people. Nice people seem to think there's nothing wrong with regularly playing the role of the rescuer/martyr. *Just remember that the rescuer might be the nicer part of this deadly triangle, but it's dysfunctional all the same.*

Which role in the deadly triangle are you most often cast in – the victim, the persecutor, or the rescuer?

Before reading the following section, please reread the above section describing the fight between the husband and wife, then close your eyes and envision how this couple could have played out the same situation differently.

Instant Replay

When the angry husband came home screaming, the wife could have answered calmly, "The house is a mess because the children had a lot of fun playing with their toys; and yes, they may seem like wild banshees right now, but this is the witching hour; as for dinner – how does takeout sound?" The wife has not discounted her husband's observations, but instead

addressed them with a sense of calmness and humor –
which are, by the way, contagious emotions – and at
that point the tired husband might have responded
with a simple, "Takeout sounds great!"

Stepping Outside of the Dead-End T.A. Triangle

As long as *Cellmates* choose to stay trapped
within this dead-end triangle, and it is a choice, no
real healing can take place. These negative reactions
keep people fighting and on the defensive all the
time, which ultimately serves to keep them from experiencing true intimacy.

The scary aspect of this deadly triangular way
of interacting is that everybody does it, not just *Cellmates*. This deadly triangle plays itself out at work, in
schools, in courthouses and hospitals, in the military,
in church and temple hierarchies, in families, and
among friends.

All of us are constantly replaying the "old
tapes" we heard as children, as we watched all the
dysfunctional grown-ups playing this deadly triangle
game. If we're to step outside of this no-win triangular transactional pattern, we have to bring conscious
attention to our automatic responses and nip them
in the bud. From this day forward, vow to pay close
attention to your interactions to see how often you
play the triangle game.

I strongly recommend that you read *I'm OK– You're OK*, by Thomas Harris, M.D., to learn more about Transactional Analysis.

Congratulations! You've just completed another crucial STEP on your journey toward a higher love.

STEP 4 – TOXIC LOVE – WE'VE GOT TO GET OUT OF THIS PLACE

Recognizing the Existence of *Cellmates and Razor's Edge Mates*

"It is but the first few steps along the right way that seem hard...."
(*A Course in Miracles,* Chapter 22)

Understanding *The Ladder of Love* (Working Our Way Up from the Bottom Rung)

Couples involved in Cellmate relationships play the "Wounded Mate" game. When they first meet they spend a lot of time talking about the hurts, abuses, and slights of the past, not in the hopes of healing these issues, but with the unconscious desire to reinforce them. The unhealed wounds become the bond, the crazy glue, which holds the relationship together.

Cellmates – Rungs
One Through Three

First Rung Love

First-Degree, Brutal Love...Headline Making Love...Order of Protection Love

Hard-Core Love

The players in these tragically destructive relationships often wind up in the emergency room, courtroom, jail, or morgue. Violence, drugs, alcohol, and/or mental illness often play a big role in these over-the-top, drama-driven relationships.

There are excessive dependency issues, pathological jealousy issues, and fights that rival Chicago's St. Valentine's Day Massacre. (Read more about jealousy in STEP 13.)

In First-Degree love, there's an obsessive need for one or both partners to control the other. First Rung *Cellmates* tend to think they own each other; consequently, there are huge boundary violations committed by one or both of the principal players in these soap-opera-like relationships. For example: invading each other's privacy, spying on each other, and inappropriately interfering in each other's personal and/or professional lives. (Read more about boundary issues in STEP 13.)

Although there are heavy-duty dependency issues going on, when the relationship does come to a crashing halt, these First-Degree *Cellmates* often try to replace each other in record time as an act of vengeance, to save face, and out of the desperate need to find another sparring partner to duke it out with and play co-dependent games with.

Sometimes these *Cellmates* become so burnt out physically, emotionally, and/or psychologically, that they swear off relationships entirely, vowing never to go that route again.

Many of these hard-core *Cellmates* tend to be steeped in sexuality of the lowest chakra level, including sexual perversions, fetishes, excessive need for pornography and/or kinky sex. (Read more about the Chakra System in STEP 15.)

They may love each other (conditionally) with their bodies (sexually); they may love each other with their souls since they do have a karmic relationship going on, but their minds *hate* each other. As far as loving with the heart goes, as a rule, both partners are highly narcissistic; each caring about him/herself far above anyone else.

There's a strong Master/Slave archetype in these relationships, but as soon as the slave starts rebelling, all hell breaks loose. Sometimes these relationships survive because the couple switches roles: the old master becomes the new slave, and the old slave becomes the new master. As long as one partner acts out the role of master and the other plays the part of the slave, the relationship will remain intact.

There's often a playing out of the Prostitute archetype, since one or both of these *Cellmates* stays in the relationship out of fear of financial hardship or ruin should they separate.

First-Degree couples differ from other *Cellmate* couples in the way they move around the Transactional Analysis dysfunctional triangle, since, as a rule, neither of them takes on the role of rescuer. These *Cellmates* are highly narcissistic and rarely comprehend the concept of rescuing another. The rescuer in this dysfunctional triangle usually comes in the form of an outside agency or person, such as the police, the courts, a church, a shelter, a relative, a friend, a Good Samaritan, or a neighbor.

If these couples have children, the children are usually physically, emotionally, psychologically, and/or sexually abused by one or both parents.

The collective unconscious fear of abandonment and rejection are the main tools these couples use to control each other.

These couples are guilty of practicing on a continuous basis the Five Deadly Sins Committed in the Name of Conditional Love – narcissism, selfishness, greed, envy, and jealousy. (Read more about these deadly sins in STEPS 12 and 13.)

An example, of First Rung Love would be Hedda Nussbaum and Joel Steinberg, two highly educated, outwardly successful people. Hedda Nussbaum had been a book editor, and Joel Steinberg was a wealthy lawyer, yet their adopted daughter, Lisa, became the ultimate victim of their destructive love. Unfortunately, the people who tried to come to Lisa's rescue were unable to get the necessary agencies to intervene. In this case, the parents' outward success (personae) hid the monstrous behind-closed-doors scenario (shadow) that was occurring. (Read more about persona and shadow in STEP 11.) From this example you can see that money, education, status, and success don't mean anything, if we don't heal our own inner issues. (Read more about healing our issues in STEPS 11, 12, and 13.)

You need only pick up the newspaper, watch the nightly news, or read the *National Enquirer* to find couples who fit this description. These tragic relationships sell newspapers and are fodder for the "Made for TV Movie" genre.

These First Rung *Cellmates* may or may not have had other lifetimes together. At times, God will bring two *Cellmates* together who have similar life lessons to learn, but who have not actually met on the earth plane before. This couple is brought together for the first time in the great hope that they might learn some very important lessons during the time they are together and/or after they separate.

If they've had one or more lifetimes together, by the balancing laws of karma, you can bet that they must have messed up big time! How these *Cellmates* resolve their issues, both together and when they're on their own, will determine whether they'll meet again in another lifetime for karmic reckoning.

LOVEWORK ASSIGNMENT

Reflect upon all of your love relationships to see if you were ever involved in a First Rung relationship.

Write down what you learned from being in a First-Degree relationship. Write down what you learned from getting out of such a hard-core relationship. (Be grateful you lived to tell.)

If you're currently involved in First-Degree love, is this the first time, or have you done this destructive song and dance before? Are there any patterns involved that you can see? What have you learned from being in this relationship? What is keeping you in this relationship? Usually there's a strong element of self-hatred that plays itself out in this kind of self-destructive behavior. (Read more about learning to love yourself in STEP 12.)

If you've never been involved in a First-Degree relationship, get on your knees to thank God, and then think about someone you know who has. (This can be a real-life person you know or a fictional one.) Why do you think that person got involved in such a hard-core relationship to begin with? Why do you think that *Cellmate* stayed, or what made him/her finally get out?

My Experience with First-Degree Love

Ask God to Help You Know What Fear Is, so that You May Know Love

Second Rung Love

Second-Degree, Brutal Love

Soft-Core Love

As with First Rung Love, there are excessive dependency and pathological jealousy issues going on. Oftentimes, these relationships are still violent, but not quite as life-threatening as those on the First Rung. There are still plenty of threats of violence, curse words, and plates flying. When push comes to shove these relationships can rapidly deteriorate into the kind of violent outbursts we associate with First-Degree love, particularly if there are drugs and/or alcohol involved. There are still lower-chakra sexuality and boundary issues involved, but to a lesser degree than in the First Rung. (Read more about chakras and sexuality in STEP 15.)

These *Cellmates* may love each other (conditionally) with their bodies, perhaps even with their hearts and souls, but their minds wage guerilla warfare with each other.

There's still a playing out of the Master/Slave archetype and the Prostitute archetype in Second-Degree love.

These *Cellmates* are also adept at playing the Transactional Analysis deadly triangle game of victim/rescuer/persecutor. What distinguishes the Second Rung from the First Rung is that sometimes one or both of these partners play the rescuer role, and this can serve to keep both their own relationship and their relationship with their children in check.

For instance, a woman might tolerate her husband beating her, but she'll leave him if he begins beating the children or sexually abusing them, since she will feel a need to rescue her children from the situation. Or a woman could have her husband arrested for beating her, and then go to the jail to rescue him by bailing him out.

Both of these *Cellmates* are guilty of practicing on a regular basis the Five Deadly Sins Committed in the Name of Conditional Love – narcissism, selfishness, greed, envy, and jealousy. (Read more about these deadly sins in STEPS 12 and 13.)

Cellmates involved in Second Rung relationships may or may not have had other lifetimes together. How they resolve their issues, both jointly and separately, will determine whether they'll meet again in another lifetime for karmic reckoning.

An example of a modern-day couple that epitomizes the scenario of the Second-Degree, Soft-core love would be Tommy Lee and Pamela Anderson.

LOVEWORK ASSIGNMENT

Once again, take some time to reflect upon your relationships. Did any of them fall into the Second-Degree love category? If so, what did you learn from being in that relationship?

If you're currently involved in a Second-Degree relationship, reflect upon lessons learned, lessons you still need to learn, and what keeps you locked into this relationship. From time to time, review your answer to see if you're learning more lessons from this relationship through your study of love.

Have you ever been in a relationship that started out good, yet ended as a Second-Degree relationship?

If you've never been involved in a Second-Degree relationship, think about your friends, coworkers, or family. Have any of them been involved in such a relationship? What lessons do you think they were meant to learn? What did you learn from observing this couple?

My Experience with Second-Degree Love

I'm Beginning to Know the Difference Between Love and Fear

Third Rung Love

Third-Degree Love

Interchangeable Love

Countless numbers of people settle for Third-Degree love. It's what I call the "Donald Trump syndrome," where one physically attractive and/or outwardly successful person is interchangeable with another.

Third-Degree love is a very superficial level of love based on external elements such as looks, money, and status. Third-Degree love is all about ego, power, and trying to impress the world with a trophy mate.

In Third-Degree love relationships the *Cellmates* have no intention of healing any of their personal issues, mainly because they're too egotistical to realize they have any. Unconsciously, they decide to project all the relationship problems onto the other *Cellmate.*

When the going gets rough, the *Cellmates* often bail out of the relationship, and then go after each other's jugular. On its way out, Third Rung love can disintegrate quite rapidly into Second Rung or even First Rung love, for these couples are still guilty of practicing the Five Deadly Sins Committed in the Name of Conditional Love – narcissism, selfishness, greed, envy, and jealousy. (Read more about these deadly sins in STEPS 12 and 13.) They're also adept at playing the Transactional Analysis deadly triangle game.

This love can be highly sexually charged at first, but before long these *Cellmates* get bored with each other. In the beginning, there can be an illusion of loving each other (conditionally) with the heart, mind, body and soul, but reality soon sets in, and both *Cellmates* become well aware that it's all about ego.

Think Donald Trump and blah, blah, blah, or many celebrities and blah, blah, blah.

The archetypes involved here are: "Gigolo," "Femme Fatale," "Prostitute," and "Eternal Child" (think Peter Pan and "I'll never grow up").

These *Cellmates* may or may not have had other lifetimes together, and in the balancing laws of karma, their actions both together and separately will determine if they'll meet in another lifetime.

Relationships in these first Three Rungs on The Ladder of Love may have passion, but it's passion with a high price tag and a lot of drama.

LOVEWORK ASSIGNMENT

Once again, take some time to reflect upon your relationships. Are you now, or have you ever been, involved in a Third-Degree love relationship? Take some time to reflect on the superficial aspects of that *Cellmate*. What drew you to that *Cellmate*? Was it all about looks, sex, money, power, or all of the above?

If you've never been involved in such a relationship, think about friends, fictional characters, or celebrities who have. What do you think draws these people together? What do you think tears them apart?

My Experience with Third-Degree Love

I'm Learning to Look at Love Through the Eyes
of the Soul

Razor's Edge Mates

Fourth Rung Love

"The Old Ball and Chain Thing"

For Better, but it's Usually for Worse

As we move up *The Ladder of Love* to Rung Four, these *Razor's Edge Mates* will meet more of each other's basic needs, such as the need for companionship, economic survival, and the primal impulse to perpetuate the human race.

A high percentage of Fourth Rung couples marry. Once the honeymoon is over, however, Fourth Rung married couples tend to take each other for granted, treat each other without respect, and in general, they act much nicer to everyone else in the world than they act with each other. Before long, these marriages become "the old ball and chain thing."

These couples don't have to deal with healing their relationship issues because they operate under the false belief that this is the way it is: "It's a male thing," or "You know how women are." They buy into a lot of the cliché expressions about the war of the sexes, and go into a state of deep denial about having any real issues of their own. These *Razor's Edge Mates* have a middle school mindset and take a "like it or lump it" attitude with each other.

Fourth Rung couples can remain functional alcoholics, control freaks, etc. Basically, the holes in one *Razor's Edge Mate's* head fit the points in the other's.

There may be little physical contact in or out of bed, or they may have a decent sex life, but there isn't a lot of affection expressed outside of the bed-room. For cheap thrills they might turn to pornog-raphy to add some needed spice to their otherwise ho-hum sex life.

If one partner has a life-awakening experience (a near-death experience, a full-blown midlife crisis, or life-threatening illness) the status quo will be bro-ken and all hell will break loose. The other partner will anxiously wait for the day when things "get back to normal."

A Rung Four love is usually a relationship which is a very socially acceptable arrangement as far as the whole "tribal thing" goes. To the outside world it may appear to be a match made in heaven because they're both of the same race, religion, social status, etc. From the start there are few obstacles to over-come in being together. Even if both *Razor's Edge Mates* were unhappily married when they first met, with divorce becoming easier and more acceptable, this is not considered a daunting obstacle that they had to overcome. And in fact, it's becoming increas-ingly prevalent for couples involved in Fourth Rung marriages to divorce.

They love each other (conditionally) with their hearts, and perhaps with their souls. They may or may not love with their bodies, and as far as their minds go, for the most part, it's all their dysfunctional thinking that keeps them together. These couples are still guilty of practicing the Five Deadly Sins Commit-ted in the Name of Conditional Love – narcissism, selfishness, greed, envy, and jealousy – but to a lesser degree than in the first Three Rungs on *The Ladder of Love.* (Read more about these Five Deadly Sins in STEPS 12 and 13.)

Many of these marriages will last a lifetime, since these couples took the vow for better – unconsciously knowing it would mainly be for worse. Oftentimes, one or both partners are too lazy, insecure, or depressed to change their lives. The usual modus operandi for these couples is to play the victim/rescuer/persecutor game on a moment-to-moment, day-to-day basis. In fact, without these petty transactions there probably wouldn't be any interaction at all.

You need only think of Marie and Frank Barone on the sitcom *Everybody Loves Raymond* or Fred and Ethel Mertz from *I Love Lucy*.

Many of the same archetypes that play themselves out in the First Three Rungs of love are present here, but with the addition of some of the more pleasant archetypes, such as: the nurturing "Matriarch" and "Patriarch." We still have the Master/Slave archetype at work here, but it might be a more watered-down version, such as the Parent/Child archetype, where one partner is always serving, protecting, and coddling the other.

Fourth Rung *Razor's Edge Mates* may or may not have had other lifetimes together, and once again, the actions they take in this lifetime, both separately and together, will determine if they meet again in another one.

LOVEWORK ASSIGNMENT

Once again, reflect upon your love relationships. Have you ever been involved in a Fourth Rung relationship? Were your parents involved in this type of marriage, or your grandparents, or aunts and

uncles? List as many couples as you can, real or imagined (TV characters, movie characters, cartoon characters, etc.), that fit this mold. You can stop when you
have named one hundred such couples. Believe me,
it's not all that hard, since Fourth Rung couples are
everywhere!

My Experience with Fourth Rung Love

I'm Beginning to Understand What a Razor's *Edge Mate is*

Fifth Rung Love

Old Archetype of Marriage

Everyday, Garden-Variety Love

When you think of many of the marriages you've seen over your lifetime, you'll probably be thinking of the Fifth Rung of Love.

This Rung of Love is very similar to the Fourth Rung in that there are no great obstacles to overcome in order for this couple to be together. It's a very socially acceptable arrangement, but, unlike Fourth Rung Love, these *Razor's Edge Mates* would never consciously plan on leaving each other. They meant it when they vowed, "Till death do us part," and for the most part, there are enough positive reinforcements to keep this relationship going. These can include a nice home, stability, a comfortable lifestyle, and the respect of friends and of the larger community.

Yet, there are many unhealed issues swept under the carpet, and whole areas of discontent. These couples deal with their differences by thinking, *Well, I made my bed, so now I have to sleep in it.* Over the years, they may have fewer and fewer interests in common, and their children and grandchildren become the cement that really keeps them together.

Fifth Rung couples often have a series of unresolved, petty arguments going on, but no one pays much attention to these anymore. It's just the way it is. These couples are quite adept at playing the victim/rescuer/persecutor game. If they have children, the children may be relegated the job of rescuer in an effort to end the parental bickering quickly.

These couples still practice the Five Deadly Sins Committed in the Name of Conditional Love, but to a much lesser degree than in the first Four Rungs of Love, and they can, at least some of the time, transcend these negative emotions.

Both partners complain about being taken for granted. This chronic feeling of being neglected can lead one or both of these *Razor's Edge Mates* to have an occasional extramarital affair, with the hopes that these shenanigans won't be discovered. The marriage usually won't end even if the infidelity should come to light, although the cheated-on partner will make the unfaithful partner pay dearly for his/her straying.

They may or may not love each other with their bodies, and most often they do love each other with their hearts, and even their souls, but their minds are not so sure. And keep in mind – the kind of love they practice is *conditional.*

The archetypes involved here are basically the same ones found in Rung Four.

Think Lucy and Ricky in *I Love Lucy,* or Ray and Debra Barone in *Everybody Loves Raymond.*

At this level of love, these *Razor's Edge Mates* have had at least one lifetime together and possibly many more. It's God's greatest hope that these couples will evolve together enough in this lifetime to bring their love up *The Ladder of Love* to a blessed Sixth or even Seventh Rung. More often than not, these marriages descend *The Ladder of Love* and become a Rung Four relationship.

If you're involved in a Fifth Rung marriage, vow to bring your marriage up *The Ladder of Love.* The universe needs the two of you to become beacons of love and light.

Rung Four and Rung Five love represent borderline relationships that have some characteristics of Cellmates, and yet they also possess some characteristics of Soul Mate relationships. For example, some nurturing and support is usually present.

For this reason, Rung Four and Rung Five relationships tend to be the kinds of long-term relationships that are the hardest to actually leave because they do have the potential to ascend The Ladder of Love, if both Razor's Edge Mates would be willing to work together. It's this hope for some kind of positive change that keeps Razor's Edge Mates hanging in there.

LOVEWORK ASSIGNMENT

Once again, review your love relationships. Have you ever been involved in a Fifth Rung relationship? List as many real and fictitious marriages as you can that fit this mold. (You can quit when you get writer's cramp or when your pen runs out of ink, whichever comes first!)

My Experience with Fifth Rung Love

I'm not Willing to Settle for a Good-Enough Relationship. I Want a Higher Love

Possible Outcomes of Cellmate and Razor's Edge Mate Relationships

1. **One or both of the *Cellmates* or *Razor's Edge Mates* learn their lessons and move on.** (This is a positive ending in which there is karmic closure.) They won't have to meet each other in another lifetime to do the same destructive dance again. They may, however, meet the next time around as *Soul Mates,* depending upon whatever karma the two of them incur separately. **Remember, you're only responsible for your own behavior.** We're not expected to, nor can we, control anyone else's behavior. For instance, if you've learned your karmic lessons and choose to move on, you won't have to meet up with this *Cellmate* or *Razor's Edge Mate* in another lifetime, unless while in spirit you choose as part of your life plan to do so. In this lifetime, as a result of the good karma you've accrued through learning your karmic lessons, you'll move up *The Ladder of Love* and obtain a higher love. The *Cellmate* who hasn't learned the lessons will be given either no relationship or perhaps another *Cellmate* in the great cosmic hope that this time he/she might get it right. **(This accrues positive karma for the person who learns the karmic lessons and negative karma for the one who doesn't.)**

2. **One or both of the *Cellmates* or *Razor's Edge Mates* don't learn their lessons, but move on regardless.** They may or may not meet again in another lifetime, depending upon the positive

or negative karma they separately incur. During this lifetime, these people might not be given another relationship, or they could be given other *Cellmates* or *Razor's Edge Mates* and start the same destructive pattern over again, until someone wakes up and changes. So, if you see a recurring negative pattern in your relationships, stop blaming the other person. Take responsibility for your actions. Learn and heal. Then bless your relationship and move on. **(This accrues positive karma for the person who learns the karmic lessons and negative karma for the one who doesn't.)**

3. **Neither *Cellmates* nor *Razor's Edge Mates* learn their lessons, but they still don't move on.** They just whine and complain endlessly about each other to anyone who'll listen. It soon becomes clear to everyone, except the couple themselves, that they'll be together for the duration. This is the saddest of all of the outcomes because no one learns anything. They'll meet up in subsequent lifetimes until one or both of them get it right. **(This "moving sideways" relationship incurs negative karma for both.)**

4. **Each of the *Cellmates* or *Razor's Edge Mates* learns their karmic lessons and chooses to stay with the other. (This positive outcome or positive karma allows these couples to ascend *The Ladder of Love* to become *Soul Mates*.)** This moving up *The Ladder of Love* rarely happens to First-Degree, Second-Degree, or Third-Degree *Cellmates*. More often, this happens to couples who began their relationship

on the Fourth or Fifth Rung of *The Ladder of Love*. These couples are already walking the razor's edge between *Cellmates* and *Soul Mates*, and choose to take a quantum leap of faith upward, rather than spiraling down or staying in stasis. These *Razor's Edge* relationships are often the most challenging of all relationships, because there's the ever-present sense of hope that our mate will learn and grow and become the *Soul Mate* we so desperately desire. **But a person is expected to evolve in a timely manner, and the universe doesn't expect us to wait forever for someone to come around.**

What Does Evolving in a Timely Manner Mean?

It means two things. First, both partners need to learn patience and give each other enough time and emotional space to grow into deeper and deeper intimacy; and second, each mate is in fact taking positive steps toward intimacy in a reasonable amount of time.

For the most part, it's up to you to determine if your mate is moving toward greater intimacy in an acceptable and timely fashion.

Soul contracts between *Cellmates, Razor's Edge Mates,* and *Soul Mates* have various time structures depending upon karmic reckoning. (Read more about Karmic Relationship Cycles in STEP 8.)

Know that if you're involved in a First-Degree brutal relationship, the sooner you learn your lessons and move on, the better.

In fact, any acts of violence between *Soul Mates,* *Cellmates,* or *Razor's Edge Mates* make any soul contracts immediately null and void. The universe doesn't expect you to stick around and learn your lessons while someone is beating the hell out of you. The instant violence is perpetrated upon you is the moment God says, "All bets are off. Move on." If your mate takes positive actions to show he/she has changed and will never do this again, it's up to you to exercise your better judgment before entering back into any kind of relationship with this person.

Some Terms You Need to Know Before Taking the Next STEP

Kundalini Energy – This is the Goddess energy of our soul or of higher consciousness which is stored in the base of our spine. When activated through prayer, meditation, Yoga, dance, Sacred Sexuality, or in countless other ways, Kundalini energy can assist us in our journey toward individuation and Enlightenment. In ancient times this energy was known as the serpent force. (Read more about Kundalini energy in STEP 15.)

The Chakra System – For now, suffice it to say that it's an energy system which exists within our body. The word "chakra"comes from the Sanskrit word for "wheel." A chakra is one of the vortexes of energy that starts at the base of our spine and continues spiraling upward toward the crown of our head. The upward rising of Kundalini energy is the potent force that activates the Chakra System, and this propels our soul to take a quantum leap of faith toward Enlightenment. (Read more about the Chakra System in STEP 15.)

Enlightenment – This is the spiritual awakening that allows us to see the world through the tolerant, compassionate, and nonjudgmental eyes of God. (Read more about Enlightenment in the next STEP.)

Congratulate yourself on having finished the first Four STEPS in this book. You're that much closer to attaining your heart's desire – a higher love.

STEP 5 – CHERISHING THE GREATEST GIFT FROM GOD – SOUL MATES

"When you want only love you will see nothing else."
(*A Course in Miracles,* Chapter 12)

Our Romantic *Soul Mates* – Rungs Six through Nine
(You Must Have Been Heaven Sent)

Most of us will have many platonic *Soul Mate* relationships during our lifetime. These *Soul Mate* relationships are characterized by the close bonds we have with each other. Platonic *Soul Mate* relationships can take place among friends, relatives, neighbors, coworkers, etc. These relationships tend to bring out the best in us, and they make our journey through life a lot easier and much more pleasant.

In this STEP, however, we'll mainly be discussing **romantic *Soul Mates,*** and we'll simply refer to these couples as *Soul Mates.*

Why God Brings a *Soul Mate* to Us

A. When we're given a *Soul Mate* relationship, God expects us to learn how to love unconditionally. If we continue to love in a conditional manner, the *Soul Mate* relationship will descend *The Ladder of Love*, resulting in a *Cellmate* or *Razor's Edge Mate* relationship.

B. At this stage of human consciousness, many couples walk the razor's edge between *Cellmates* and *Soul Mates*. You've already learned that Rung Four and Rung Five couples fall into this borderline category (*Razor's Edge Mates*). From the outset, these relationships, which are based on **conditional love**, exhibit some characteristics of *Cellmates* and certain traits of *Soul Mates*. For instance: One moment the relationship brings out the best in us, and the next thing we know, it's bringing out the worst. God hopes we'll heal our issues and bring these borderline relationships up *The Ladder of Love*, becoming *Soul Mates*. More often than not, at this stage of human evolution, these borderline relationships tend to move down *The Ladder of Love*.

C. *Soul Mate* relationships are characterized by **unconditional love** that tends to bring out the best in us. God wants us to evolve and brings us this wonderful experience to assist us on our soulful journey. Once we learn what it feels like to love another unconditionally, the universe expects us to bring this same kind of love to all of our relationships and experiences.

D. Eventually, this love for our *Soul Mate* will evolve into *Agape*, the unconditional love of humanity, which is the Tenth Rung on *The Ladder of Love*. (Read more about this in

STEP 9.) The very existence of the human race depends upon our recognition of the oneness of all humankind.

E. In due time, a great love has the power to lead us to a profound relationship with God which is called *Unio Mystica*. This personal, intimate relationship with God is the ultimate Rung on *The Ladder of Love* – The Eleventh Rung. (Read more about this divine experience in STEP 10.)

F. It's God's hope that a great love will cause our heart to expand and grow to embrace the metaphysical truth that everything in the universe has a spirit (*anima mundi*). With this profound understanding of the universal spirit, we'll return to that place of reverence and respect for the earth and its resources.

G. Unlike *Cellmates,* who are bound by an unconscious contract (**Karmic Contract**) to remain the same, *Soul Mates* are bound to each other by a **Celestial Contract** that supports the spiritual, intellectual, emotional, psychological, and physical well-being of both partners.

Are you beginning to see how your personal journey toward a higher love is the most important journey you can ever embark upon? The universe recognizes your noble efforts and willingly assists you every step of the way. Keep up the hard work, knowing that it's God's great pleasure to grant you a higher love.

How Can I Bring Forth a Soul Mate Union?

To bring forth a Soul Mate union, you must wish with all your heart to be given this experience.

❖ You must also earn the right by working on your own inner issues.

❖ When you learn, you earn, so it really is up to you.

❖ Please stop giving the universe mixed messages such as, "I want love, but I'm afraid to go there."

❖ Tell the universe that you don't want any more *Cellmates* or *Razor's Edge Mates*. You've been there, done that. You're ready for the real thing – a *Soul Mate*.

❖ Turn your love life over to God.

❖ Work on your ability to love unconditionally. Start with those relationships that already exist in your life. Try loving your children, parents, friends, or siblings unconditionally. Most of us love our pets unconditionally, so try transferring that kind of love to human beings. It's easy to love our dogs unconditionally, since they always greet us with enthusiasm and love. We should learn to embrace each other as warmly as our pets greet us, and as we greet them.

❖ Know that the Age of Aquarius is upon us and *Soul Mate* unions are rapidly occurring.

❖ A *Soul Mate* relationship represents a blessed, sacred, and highly intimate union. In a romantic relationship it embodies the blending of the body, mind, heart, and soul. (Read more about this concept in STEP 15.)

❖ **Know that true love and sacred marriage (*Holy Matrimony*) are possible only between two people who are working toward being all they were meant to be. In other words, both are striving toward individuation. Individuation is the process of becoming whole or becoming one's true self through self-realization and self-actualization. This long and painful process toward understanding and knowing ourselves leads us back to the original state of oneness. (Read more about how to know ourselves in PART II, DEMYSTIFYING LOVE.)**

How Will I Recognize My *Soul Mate?*

♦ *Soul Mates* are spiritual partners. Your soul houses a memory of all the *Soul Mates* you've ever met while on the earth plane or in spirit (*The Recognition Factor*). Because a *Soul Mate* reunion stimulates our awareness of the immortal life of our soul, it helps us to awaken spiritually.

♦ Additionally, the memory of our *Soul Mates* is a cellular one. This cellular memory stimulates our wise inner being to wake up and pay attention. Every fiber of our being vibrates with a deep knowingness that something extraordinary has occurred.

♦ This inner radar helps ensure that *Soul Mates* will recognize each other.

◆ When you meet a *Soul Mate,* you'll have a gut feeling that you've always known each other.
◆ Somehow you just know you're in a safe place, and you instinctively trust each other.

What Are the Possible Outcomes of a *Soul Mate* Relationship?

1. *Soul Mates* may choose to stay with each other and learn their karmic lessons together. Some of these lessons will be learned through suffering, for each *Soul Mate* does have some karmic reckoning to contend with (in other words, each *Soul Mate* has his/her own issues); however, most of the life lessons can and should be learned through peace, love, and joy. (**This accrues positive karma for both *Soul Mates,* if they choose to remain together and learn their life lessons.**)

2. Sometimes, one or both of the *Soul Mates* becomes frightened and flees from the relationship. (**This accrues negative karma for one or both *Soul Mates* depending upon who did the running and how the other responded.**) The blessing in disguise from this scenario is the possibility that we can still learn many of our karmic lessons as a result of this deep wounding to our hearts. Sadly, these lessons will be learned via the immense suffering the untimely ending of that relationship brought forth. The untimely ending of a *Soul Mate* relationship is called a ***Sacred Betrayal.***

3. Through words and deeds, one or both of the *Soul Mates* drag the relationship down *The Ladder of Love*. Through negative actions, these *Soul Mates* become *Razor's Edge Mates*, or even *Cellmates*. If *Soul Mates* should regress to *Cellmates*, they'll learn most of their life lessons through suffering, either together or when the relationship falls apart. **(This accrues negative and/or positive karma for each person, depending upon lessons learned and his/her individual actions and reactions.)** These couples might also choose to continue the dance of destruction as *Cellmates*. In these cases, neither partner seems to learn much of anything. **(This would incur negative karma for both.)** The best-case scenario would be for this couple to learn from their errors and bring their love back up *The Ladder of Love to Soul Mates*. **(Once again, resulting in positive karma for both.)**

Basically, the outcome of a *Soul Mate* relationship depends upon the freewill actions of each *Soul Mate*. **Remember – we're responsible only for our own actions.** We cannot, nor should we even try to, control the actions of others. **Our own actions and reactions determine the positive or negative karma we incur.**

Understanding Our Celestial Contracts

Celestial Contracts, or pre-birth contracts, are divinely guided agreements we make while we're still in spirit. Our own level of soul development and our own individual karma determines how much say we have in the creation of these *Celestial Contracts*.

To help you better understand the concept of these spiritual contracts, try visualizing yourself in spirit appearing before a heavenly grand jury composed of spirit guides, angels, ancestors, saints, Ascended Masters, and God. In front of this divine jury, you'd plead your case concerning the *Celestial Contracts* you'd be expected to honor in your upcoming lifetime. This heavenly grand jury would hear your case and take into consideration your wishes for your overall life plan.

Basically, these divinely inspired contracts serve as maps or guides that we're expected to follow. Remember, it's a freewill universe, and whether we honor these contracts or not is ultimately up to us.

The *Celestial Contracts* we make while still in spirit are many, and they concern different aspects of our lives – for instance, which *Cellmates, Soul Mates,* or *Razor's Edge Mates* we'll meet; what divine calling as far as avocation or vocation we'll follow, and a host of other tasks and services we'll need to perform to learn our life lessons.

Honoring Our *Celestial Contracts* with Our *Soul Mates*

♦ As previously stated, prior to incarnating on earth, *Soul Mates* engage in a *Celestial Contract* with each other in which they vow to meet, love, and grow. When *Soul Mates* meet, the unconscious memory of their *Celestial Contract* begins to re-surface. We may never have conscious awareness of our contract, but our spirit begins to take on a life of its own. We begin to follow our hearts, even though our minds might not agree. This experience can be harrowing to people who are habitual "control freaks." Suddenly they can't control everything, nor can they wish or will love away. Their first response might be to flee in fear rather than to stay in love. This kind of situation calls for courage. Courage is the ability to do something in spite of fear. If you're given love, always remember that love comes from God. Rather than follow the impulse to run, stand still and surrender to the healing power of love. (Read more about surrendering to love in STEP 16.)

♦ We're under karmic obligation to honor these *Celestial Contracts,* since we vowed to do so while we were still in spirit.

♦ When we break our *Celestial Contracts,* we begin to navigate through life without a compass, and we lose our bearings.

♦ The *Celestial Contracts* we make are divine maps guiding us along the path of love. When we walk the path of love, we begin living the authentic life we were meant to live. We then become capable of accomplishing the personal and transpersonal goals we've incarnated to attain.

♦ Each time we break a *Celestial Contract,* we walk the path of fear. This is why honoring these divinely inspired contracts is a great cosmic responsibility.

♦ One reason our world seems to be falling off its axis is that people are breaking these *Celestial Contracts* in record numbers. This causes the fear in the world to grow to epidemic proportions and the love to diminish. People then begin to believe the destructive illusion that the evil forces of the world are more powerful than the good ones.

♦ Love reverses this negative mindset, and we begin to see the world once more as a safe place – one in which the good powers of the universe are far more powerful than the dark forces.

♦ But take heart, when *Soul Mate Celestial Contracts* are broken, those individuals who are brave enough to look beyond the obvious hurt will learn the multitude of powerful lessons inherent in this **Sacred Betrayal.**

♦ The brokenhearted *Soul Mate* who does the inner homework, and who stays in the inevitable state of suffering long enough to learn these all-important karmic lessons, will be rewarded by being brought another *Soul Mate* – one who is ready to embrace love.

♦ On the other hand, if the brokenhearted *Soul Mate* chooses not to learn the lessons inherent in the untimely separation, but rather escapes from the pain through drugs, alcohol, gambling, promiscuity, excessive work, or mindless, neurotic worry, etc., that person will then be given either no relationship or, more likely, a relationship on the lower end of *The Ladder of Love*. This is consistent with the balancing Laws of Karma.

♦ One main tenet of our *Soul Mate Celestial Contract* states that we're under karmic obligation to love each other with our entire heart, soul, mind, and body, but sometimes our fear of abandonment is so great that we try to limit the depth of our love for our *Soul Mate*. Even though our *Soul Mate* says he/she will love us forever, our terrifying primal fear that he/she could die and leave us alone and abandoned can greatly inhibit our ability to love fully. What God asks of us is to overcome our fears and consciously choose to love intimately and passionately without worry about outcome. Take great comfort in knowing that if *Soul Mates* love each other with their entire hearts, souls, minds, and bodies, should one of them pass away, the deceased *Soul Mate* will search the universe, along with the help of God, the spirit guides, angels, and disincarnated Group Soul members, to find the living partner a new *Soul Mate*, if that is what is needed to further advance that earthbound soul, or if that is what the remaining partner desires. (Read more about loving with the heart, soul, mind, and body in STEP 15.)

A Sacred Betrayal

Because of their *Celestial Contract* and the instinctual trust *Soul Mates* feel for each other, nothing disrupts their psychological, emotional, spiritual, and physical well-being so much as as the untimely ending of this relationship. This ending is called a **Sacred Betrayal.**

When *Soul Mate* relationships fail, we feel a profound sense of loss. We know in the very core of our being that there were many powerful lessons to be learned in our being together, and now that opportunity for soul growth has been temporarily truncated. All alone, we must face the hard reality as to why we or our *Soul Mate* were unable to live up to that God-given task.

Eventually, we'll come to know that there were powerful lessons to be learned in the ending of that relationship as well, and we're under karmic obligation to learn them. (Read more about honoring the endings of relationships in STEP 19.)

After all the suffering and angst, if we later come away with wisdom and deep inner truth, we'll know that this **Sacred Betrayal** was a blessing in disguise.

What Lessons Would God Expect You to Learn from a *Sacred Betrayal?*

♦ You'd learn that only love matters.

♦ You'd learn to tell the truth and to be your true self.

- You'd learn to act out of love and not fear, because you'd know the difference between the two.

- You'd learn to endure.

- You'd learn patience.

- You'd learn courage.

- You'd learn the difference between dogmatic morality, which was hammered into your head from outside sources from the time you were born, and true inner morality dictated from your own heart, soul, body, and higher consciousness. You'd then begin your own personal journey out of the Age of Pisces and into the Age of Aquarius.

- In the physical absence of your *Soul Mate*, you'd learn how to commune with this person on a soul plane level (telepathically). This communing would open your other soul channels so that you'd be able to commune with your spirit guides, angels, those who have passed on, and, ultimately, with God.

- You'd learn to forgive others and yourself as well. (Forgiving ourselves is the most challenging lesson of all.)

- You'd learn to love unconditionally, despite everything, for you'd learn that true love never dies.

♦ You'd learn that revenge is not the answer.

♦ You'd learn compassion.

♦ You'd learn to stop blaming others and take responsibility for your own choices.

♦ You'd learn fortitude.

♦ You'd learn to be nonjudgmental.

♦ You'd learn serenity.

♦ You'd learn that you're responsible only for your own behavior.

♦ **Besides these big, universal lessons, you'd learn many other lessons that pertain to your own personal karma. Remember, the road not taken often affects our soul more than the road taken.**

LOVEWORK ASSIGNMENT

Take some time to reflect upon your relationships. Have you ever been in a *Soul Mate* relationship that ended? What lessons did you learn from this *Sacred Betrayal?* Please list them. Then go back and think more deeply about this relationship. What other lessons do you think you were meant to learn, but didn't? Please list them. **It's these previously un-learned lessons that hold the key to your meeting and keeping your *Soul Mate*.** Meditate upon these unlearned lessons. Continue to read over this assignment daily until you feel that these unlearned lessons begin to feel like lessons learned.

Lessons Learned from a *Sacred Betrayal*

I Bless this *Sacred Betrayal* for the Many Lessons
Learned

Understanding *Kairos* Time

The ancient Greeks had two words for time – *kronos and kairos.*

Kronos was the word coined for time as measured by sundials and schedules and that which we never seem to have enough of; while *Kairos* was used to define those divine moments in life that seem to transcend the restraints and demands of ordinary day-to-day time.

While *kronos* time is measured by seconds, minutes, and hours, *kairos* time is measured by the care, growth, and nurturing an experience has brought to our soul. Since the soul is immortal and of the divine, *kairos* time can't be measured by the clock or the calendar, which are man-made instruments.

Kairos time represents those transcendent, unforgettable moments in life when time seems to stand still, or those sacred moments in which time doesn't matter, for it ceases to exist. *Kairos* moments are those extraordinary times that stay with us all of our life, and, in fact, define its quality.

Know that whether a relationship lasts a day or a lifetime, its true value is measured by the impact it has had on our soul's growth.

The Difference Between Our Major-League and Minor-League Soul Mates

1. Throughout our lifetimes and during our times in spirit, we'll continuously meet up

with *Soul Mates,* both our *Primary* Ones and our *Secondary* Ones. (Remember, *Soul Mates* are not just those people we become romantically involved with.)

2. Some *Soul Mates,* including some *Secondary* Ones, will have a **major impact** on the course of our life, while others will only have a **minor impact** upon us.

3. Our *major-league romantic Soul Mates* are not necessarily just those people we spend the most time with. We measure *major-league Soul Mates* by the impact they've had on our psychological, emotional, and spiritual growth, not by the duration of the relationship. Thus, we could meet a *major-league Soul Mate,* and due to life circumstances, only spend a week together out of an entire lifetime, but the impact of this meeting lasts forever (*Kairos time*). Think *The Bridges of Madison County,* by Robert James Waller.

4. On the other hand, a *minor-league Soul Mate* can be someone who's in your life for a very long time, and yet the impact upon your soul growth is minimal.

Now that you have a better understanding of what constitutes a *Soul Mate,* let's explore the higher Rungs on *The Ladder of Love.*

STEP 5 - *SOUL MATES*   175

Sixth Rung Love

New Archetype of Marriage - Holy Matrimony

Till death do us part

Sixth Rung Love represents the new archetype of marriage, in which *Soul Mates* unconditionally love each other and commit to each other with their entire hearts, souls, minds, and bodies

These couples consciously try to eradicate the Master/Slave archetype and view each other as equals.

Sixth Rung Love is similar to Fifth Rung Love insofar as there are no major obstacles for this couple to overcome in order to be together, although they may face all kinds of traumas over the course of their lifetime together. Initially, there are no age, race, religious, or social class issues to overcome; or they may come from extended families that are already racially or religiously blended and these differences are seen as inconsequential.

What differentiates this Rung of Love from the previous one is the simple fact that these couples truly know they belong together, and if they could go back and live their lives over, the one thing they wouldn't change is their marriage.

One or both of the *Soul Mates* in a Sixth Rung relationship are easygoing and have a kind of "live and let live" attitude. As a rule, these *Soul Mates* are not overly jealous or possessive. They tend to live in gratitude for what they have. Money, having it or not, has little impact on this relationship because the real wealth of their lives is measured in the love they have for each other.

Infidelity is rarely a problem for these couples, for most of their primary needs are met within the relationship. Because these couples are totally committed to each other, they meant it when they vowed, "Till death do us part."

One or both partners could, however, have issues that remain unhealed throughout their lifetime together. This inability to heal certain issues keeps these couples from ascending *The Ladder of Love* to the next level – the Seventh Rung.

At times, one or both of these *Soul Mates* could be guilty of practicing the Five Deadly Sins Committed in the Name of Conditional Love, but they're not proud of that fact, and they will openly acknowledge that they have issues they need to work on.

They can, under times of stress, play the Transactional Analysis deadly triangle game, but the biggest crime they are guilty of is trying to rescue each other, which is at least the kinder part of the dysfunctional triangle.

These couples can have a great sex life together, but they might not be aware of the concept of Sacred Sexuality. (Read more about Sacred Sexuality in STEP 15.)

The archetypes they exemplify are many of the positive ones such as: the loving "Mother" and "Father," the "Guide," and the "Mentor." Consequently, people enjoy visiting this couple's home, and they have the kind of household that neighborhood children tend to gravitate to.

These *Soul Mates* seem to be adept at handling sticky situations with grace and a sense of humor, and these are the powerful weapons they use to keep any dysfunctional elements in check.

Since they unconditionally love each other with their hearts, minds, souls, and bodies, they treat each other with kindness and respect, and would find it inconceivable to do otherwise.

They like to work together or be involved in joint projects, and often one of these *Soul Mates* could be "the wind beneath the wings" of the other. For the most part, they work hard together to benefit their family and the community in which they live.

Think of George and Mary Bailey in the beginning of the movie, *It's a Wonderful Life.* Although they're both people of integrity and high moral standards from the start, it's only after George's life-altering experience with his guardian angel that God becomes an integral part of their relationship. By the end of the movie, George and Mary have become Seventh Rung *Soul Mates.*

When God takes center stage in an already healed relationship, couples ascend *The Ladder of Love* to become Seventh Heaven Love.

Rung Six *Soul Mates* definitely have had other lifetimes together in which they've perfected their act!

LOVEWORK ASSIGNMENT

Once again, take some time to review your love relationships. Have you ever been involved in a Sixth Rung relationship? Do you know any couple who has a Sixth Rung marriage? How does it feel to be around this couple? Think about a fictional couple on television or in a movie or novel that made you wish you could have been born into their family.

What thoughts and feelings come to mind? Write them down. For example: "If George and Mary Bailey had been my parents, I would have grown up feeling loved and safe. I would have felt proud to be a member of that family. I know that I would have talked openly about what was bothering me, and that they would have protected me from harm."

My Experience with Sixth Rung Love

I Do Know Real Love When I See It

Seventh Rung Love

Healing, Holy, Happy Love

Seventh Heaven Love

The *Soul Mates* involved in Seventh Rung Love are very blessed indeed! They not only have an intimate relationship with each other, but they have an intimate relationship with God as well.

These couples unconditionally love each other, and they truly respect and appreciate each other as well. They're totally committed to each other with their entire hearts, souls, minds, and bodies.

This blessed couple enjoys great passion, but without all the drama because they're both remarkably healed human beings.

From the outset, there may or may not be external obstacles for this couple to overcome in order to be together. There could be big age differences, or they could be of different races, but no matter how daunting the obstacles may be, they somehow manage to overcome them. **In fact, the chief characteristic of Seventh Rung Love is the ability of both *Soul Mates* to deeply understand that only love matters. Therefore, they both do everything possible to ensure that their love flourishes.**

These *Soul Mates* see eye to eye on most important issues, and they agree to disagree on others with no ill effects. They have a great many interests in common, and this makes them not only lovers, but best friends as well.

Seventh Rung *Soul Mate* relationships can withstand the winds of change. These couples seem to be able to face every situation in life, no matter how harsh, with grace and courage. For this reason, people tend to look up to them for inspiration.

Infidelity rarely plays a part in these relationships, simply because their most important needs are met within the relationship. These *Soul Mates* experience a great deal of affection in and outside of the bedroom. They have come to understand that sex is a sacred act. They've learned to mesh in oneness with each other, and their lovemaking is a form of prayer and meditation as they live in the now, fully experiencing the wonder of the moment.

Over time, they learn to blend their essences in intercourse of the mind, the heart, the soul, and the body as well. (Blending is the free flow of energy between people. Blending of energies occurs between people on many levels. We can blend our energies on a creative, spiritual, emotional, psychological, or sexual level, or any combination of the above. You'll know that blending has occurred because after you've exchanged energies with another soul, your spirit will feel renewed and recharged. It's as if your soul and the soul or souls you have blended with have all been realigned.)

Seventh Rung *Soul Mates* tend to have passionate relationships, not only with each other, but with the rest of the world. They're active and passionate participators in life. Oftentimes these couples join forces to fight for a cause they believe in, and this benefits not only their local community but the larger world as well.

The archetypes they live by are varied. They can epitomize the "Mentor," the loving "Mother" or "Father," the "Activist," the "Artist," "Dancer," "Writer," "Seeker," or "Mystic," to name just a few.

They can communicate telepathically with each other, and usually do so without questioning the why of it. More than likely, they have had many lifetimes together, and consequently, they've earned the right to enjoy the love, peace, and joy this blessed union of souls brings.

At the end of their lives, they'll feel they have accomplished almost everything they really wanted and needed to do, and they know they have each other to thank for this. As long as both *Soul Mates* are alive, no one on earth could take the place of the other.

By the end of the movie *It's a Wonderful Life,* George and Mary Bailey have moved up *The Ladder of Love* from a Sixth Rung, *Holy Matrimony Soul Mate* relationship to a Seventh Rung, *Seventh Heaven Soul Mate* relationship.

For more information about blending, oneness, and essence contact, please read *Loving from Your Soul: Creating Powerful Relationships,* by Shepherd Hoodwin.

The wonderful part about this Rung of Love is that even if your relationship didn't start out as a Seventh Rung Love, you and your mate can choose to bring your love up The Ladder of Love to this Blessed Rung. Mind you, it won't be easy, but it can be and has been done, and all the knowledge that you're acquiring by reading this book can help make this heartfelt desire become a reality.

Why the World Needs a Higher Love

What the world so desperately needs now is *Soul Mate* love, for children who are raised in homes where there is peace, love, and joy, won't grow up to wage war.

There's no denying that we're living in a time in which technology is evolving in quantum leaps. Unfortunately, these advances include the making of even more powerful weapons of mass destruction.

Consequently, the universe is working frantically to help our collective soul evolve rapidly so that we may know how to use our "new toys" for the collective good of all humanity, and not for its ultimate destruction.

Understand that your journey on this sacred path to knowing the true nature of love serves not only your higher good, but the higher good of the entire planet.

If you learn nothing else from reading this book – learn that only love matters.

Unconditional love has the power to solve every problem you or the world will ever encounter.

LOVEWORK ASSIGNMENT

Before attempting this assignment, reread The Seventh Rung of Love, and then close your eyes and chant quietly, "Dear God, grant me a higher love. Thy will be done." If you're already in a relationship, chant, "Dear God, help me bring my relationship higher and higher. Thy will be done." After a minute of chanting, meditate for five minutes. Then write down, in a stream-of-consciousness way, the feelings and thoughts that came to you.

Stream-Of-Consciousness Thoughts on the
Meaning of Higher Love

What the World Needs Now is Higher Love

Soul Mates and Karmic Accountability

- ◆ If we're given a higher love, but are unable to heal our own issues, or if we turn to drug or alcohol abuse and bring our relationship down *The Ladder of Love*, we'll personally incur negative karma as a result of our actions.

- ◆ The *Soul Mate* who is responsible for the destruction of the relationship won't usually be given another High Rung *Soul Mate* anytime soon, but will eventually be given a *Cellmate* or *Razor's Edge Mate*. Sometimes a person who messes up a *Soul Mate* relationship may choose to spend the rest of his/her life alone rather than heal any inner issues or chance facing that kind of pain ever again. (Remember, doing nothing incurs negative karma.)

- ◆ The *Soul Mate* who tries to heal the relationship, but because of the freewill negative actions of the other *Soul Mate* finds this to be an impossible task, can take comfort in the knowledge that the universe will reward those noble efforts by bringing him/her another high *Soul Mate* – this time, one who is ready, willing, and able to love.

- ◆ *Remember, we're responsible only for our own actions.*

To learn even more about *Soul Mate* relationships, please read *Soul Mates: Honoring the Mysteries of Love and Relationship*, by Thomas Moore. This book will help you understand how our souls speak to us in subtle and not-so-subtle ways, and will furnish you with additional insights into the complex nature of spirit.

By now you're beginning to know what a *Soul Mate* is. In STEP 6, we'll be moving up *The Ladder of Love* and discussing the *Sacred Duad* known as *Twin Souls*.

Now that you know what a Soul Mate is, you've taken another giant STEP on your journey toward a higher love!

STEP 6 – KNOWING THE TRUTH ABOUT *TWIN SOULS*

"Opposites must be brought together, not kept apart."
(*A Course in Miracles*, Chapter 14)

Eighth Rung Love

The Stormy *Sacred Duad*

Twin Souls

Ancient Greece and the Myth of the Halved Soul

The idea of *Twin Souls* is as old as man, and every age and era seems to have its own legends, myths, and stories that bespeak this concept.

If we were to time travel to ancient Greece and stop back at that famous drinking party known as the Symposium, we'd grab a glass of wine and listen spellbound as the comic playwright Aristophanes told, in mythological terms, the origins of love.

Since this is an ancient Greek tale, there would have to be a vengeful god in the story, in this case, Zeus. There'd also be mortal beings known as humans, and they, by their very nature, would be willful and defiant.

Aristophanes would tell us how Zeus got angry one day and decided to take things into his own hands and diminish the power of these arrogant mortal beings by cutting them in half. The comic playwright would conclude his tale by saying, "Ever since then, humans have been roaming the earth in the great hope of finding their other half."

From this ancient myth you can see that the idea of *Twin Souls* has intrigued people throughout history.

The Divine but Difficult Gift of Twinsoulship

The most important thing you can do right now is to let go of any preconceived notions you have about *Twin Souls.*

A *Twin Soul* coupling forms what is known as a **Sacred Duad.**

The first thing you need to know is that a *Twin Soul* reunion isn't always the "Happily Ever After" stuff of fairy tales, although it can be, and in the not-so-distant future, as we evolve and grow in the knowledge of love, it will be a blessed and joyful event. Sadly, at this stage in human consciousness, it's a difficult course lined with obstacle after obstacle, and *Twin Soul* reunions can bring more pain than bliss.

Therefore, if you have been wishing for a *Twin Soul* reunion, be forewarned: Be careful what you wish for. Sometimes the gods punish us – they give us what we wished for.

The next thing you need to know is that each of us houses deep within the knowledge of our missing half, our *Twin Soul,* sometimes referred to as "Twin Flame" or "Twin Ray."

Twin Souls are actually one soul housed within two separate physical bodies – one male and the other female. A *Twin Soul* reunion is always an earth-shaking experience. A great love is apt to bring forth a great fear, and there is no greater love than that which exists between *Twin Souls*. Therefore, a *Twin Soul* reunion is as terrifying as it is exhilarating.

You must also come to realize that no relationship on this earth is as extraordinary and as heart-expanding as a *Twin Soul* one. Remember, the deeper the relationship, the more we'll be challenged to heal and grow, and there is no relationship as all-encompassing as a *Twin Soul* one. In fact, the most intimate and intense relationship that exists for human beings occurs between *Twin Souls*. Great intimacy is a gift, but it's also a great burden, for it asks that we burn away all that's untrue. Sometimes the soul is willing, but the ego isn't. Remember: the soul's essential nature is composed of love, but the ego's essential nature is composed of fear.

Relationship Percentages at This Time in History

♦ *Twin Soul* relationships on the earth plane are very rare, comprising <u>less than one percent</u> of all relationships. As we go further into The Age of Aquarius, this percentage will increase. How fast this percentage rate increases depends upon free will and on how willing people are to heal and grow.

♦ *Mirror Soul* relationships are also rare. However, they are less rare than *Twin Soul* relationships, because each of us has many *Mirror Souls,* but only one *Twin Soul.* (STEP 7 will explain *Mirror Souls* in great detail.) Additionally, a *Twin Soul* relationship will always be a romantic one even if, due to life circumstances, the divine couple can't act upon it. *Mirror Souls,* however, can be either a romantic *Soul Mate* relationship or a platonic *Soul Mate* relationship, thus giving us more chances to be blessed with such a wondrous encounter. About <u>five percent</u> of all romantic relationships are *Mirror Soul* ones.

♦ All other *Soul Mate* relationships account for approximately <u>thirty-four percent</u> of romantic relationships.

♦ *Razor's Edge Mates* comprise <u>forty percent</u> of romantic relationships.

♦ *Cellmates* comprise the remaining <u>twenty percent</u> of romantic relationships.

These percentages will change in the future as we enter deeper into the Age of Aquarius. More people will meet their *Twin Souls* and romantic *Mirror Souls.* More relationships will be *Soul Mate* ones, and fewer will be *Razor's Edge Mate* and *Cellmate* relationships. By reading this book, you're working toward making this positive change possible!

Historically, at any one time on earth, there were only a few thousand couples reunited as *Twin Souls.* In this new millennium, the reuniting of the **Sacred Duads** will take a quantum leap.

A Brief Overview of *Twin Souls*

◆ In a nutshell, *Twin Souls* share the same soul. Your *Twin Soul* would possess the other half of your own soul housed in the body of a person of the opposite sex.

◆ *Twin Souls* are like male/female Siamese twins attached at the soul, who were separated at birth and then raised apart from one another.

◆ *Twin Souls* rarely meet on earth.

◆ Sometimes they incarnate at the same time, but don't meet during that lifetime.

◆ In other lifetimes, one *Twin* may be in spirit while the other is on the earth plane. The *Twin* in spirit would watch over the earth-bound one.

◆ Because they spend so many lifetimes apart, *Twin Souls* accrue individual karmic debt.

◆ This individual karmic debt can cause havoc in the relationship when they are granted a *Twin Soul* reunion.

When Are We Granted a Twin Soul Reunion?

A. *Twin Soul* love happens to very old souls who are in their last incarnations, or in one of their last incarnations.

B. It's our higher self, our higher consciousness, that searches for the *Twin*.

C. We carry within us the seed of knowledge that in order to achieve the liberation of the soul, we must meet our *Twin*. It's our desire to achieve Enlightenment that prompts us to seek a *Twin Soul* reunion.

D. Each *Twin* would have learned many of life's **karmic lessons** alone, and finally they are ready to learn the rest of their **karmic lessons** through a *Twin Soul* reunion.

Some of the Karmic Lessons We're Here on Earth to Learn

1. We're here to learn compassion, unconditional love, forgiveness, patience, endurance, trust, hope, and faith.
2. We'll learn that the world is an abundant place.
3. We'll learn to be nonjudgmental.
4. We'll learn that we're spiritual beings living in temporal bodies.
5. We'll know that the good powers of the universe are greater than the evil ones.
6. We'll learn to take responsibility for ourselves and for our actions.
7. We'll learn courage, and to be kind, fair, and just.
8. We'll learn to care for our bodies diligently, for we will discover that our physical bodies are the holy temples which house our souls.
9. We'll learn humility.

10. We'll learn temperance.

11. We'll learn to be disciplined beings.

12. We'll learn to live and let live.

13. We'll learn to live in peace, harmony, and joy.

14. We'll learn the difference between external power (money, status, and physical appearance – in other words, all the things that can be taken from us) and authentic power, the power that is generated within us, from our heart, soul, and higher consciousness.

15. We'll learn to be generous and caring.

16. We'll learn to live in a state of gratitude.

17. We'll learn to be happy for the success of others.

18. We'll learn how to commune telepathically with other earthbound spirits, with disincarnate spirits, and with God.

19. We'll learn that God is love.

20. We'll learn that life is a gift.

21. We'll learn that we're all soulfully connected and that everything has a spirit.

22. We'll learn to honor the earth and its resources.

23. We'll learn how to answer our unique calling, *the big why*: "God, why was I born, and what is it that you want me to do?"

24. We'll learn to seek wisdom.

25. We'll learn serenity.

26. We'll learn to embrace our own power, and not fear it, for we know we'd never abuse it.

27. We'll learn to speak the truth with great tenderness.

28. Basically, we've incarnated to overcome fear, and to learn that only love matters.

Twin Souls on Earth and in Heaven

◆ Throughout many of your lifetimes, your *Twin Soul* has been in spirit, guiding you.

◆ The times when you've been in spirit and your *Twin Soul* has incarnated, you've been one of your *Twin's* guides.

◆ Sometimes *Twin Souls* may be on earth at the same time, but never meet during that lifetime. During these lifetimes, they'll have a profound sense of alienation, feeling as if they've lost their guiding light. As we grow in knowledge of the way in which the soul communicates, we'll be able to commune with our *Twin* telepathically no matter where he/she might be, and this will lessen our feelings of loneliness during these lifetimes.

◆ In some lifetimes, *Twin Souls* may have met briefly. This relationship will have had a great influence upon both people, although they might not understand the how and why of it *(Kairos* time experience*)*.

◆ If *Twin Souls* have met in another lifetime, but were unable to make the relationship work, they'll have unhealed issues (karma) to work out when they're reunited, and these reunions can be particularly trying ones.

◆ At this stage of human consciousness, *Twin Souls* usually have many obstacles to overcome to be together. Surmounting these obstacles will teach the two greatest karmic lessons of all: **only love is real** and **only love matters.**

◆ Once again, keep in mind the wild card – free will. Let me state once more: Not every *Twin*

Soul reunion will lead to nirvana or to heaven on earth. The success or failure of this relationship rests with the two individual souls and their ability to accept the awesome responsibility this relationship brings forth.

A Visualization of the Heavenly Decision to Reunite *Twin Souls*

1. Know that a divine conspiracy of heaven and earth must take place for such a synchronistic reunion to occur.
2. Visualize a kind of Grand Jury in heaven composed of angels, spirit guides, saints, Ascended Masters, and deceased loved ones, with God as the ultimate judge. The pros and cons of reuniting the *Twin Souls* are tossed about.
3. More often than not, each *Twin* gets to testify as to whether the reunion should or shouldn't take place.
4. If one of the *Twins* is on earth already and is in desperate need of help, the *Twin* in spirit can appeal to God and the heavenly Grand Jury to let him/her return to earth to assist the other. This explains why there can be a considerable age difference between *Twin Souls*.
5. Ultimately, the free will of both *Twin Souls* will decide the success or failure of the relationship.
6. Regardless of the final outcome, just the alchemy of these two souls encountering each other will cause an internal spiritual revolution. Whether it's to be a revolution characterized by the love, peace, and joy it brings, or

one characterized by the turmoil, suffering, and pain it brings is determined by what the *Twins* choose to do with the divine gift they've been given.

7. Sometimes the odds are overwhelmingly in favor that when the *Twin Souls* do reunite – their souls will rapidly evolve.

8. At other times the odds are slim, but God still feels the internal revolution is a necessary one. God is fully aware that these unfortunate *Twins* will learn most of their karmic lessons through their unbearable separation. Through this great suffering, a kind of trial by fire, many of the final karmic lessons will still (ideally) be learned. God hopes that at least one of the *Twin Souls* will go on to complete the God-given task inherent in their reunion. As the one *Twin* evolves, the other will benefit regardless of the physical distances that separate them, due to the great power of telepathy that exists between them.

9. As the *Twin Souls* grow and heal, the entire Group Soul of which the *Twins* are a part of will likewise evolve.

10. In due time, all humanity will benefit from the reuniting of *Twin Souls,* as they accomplish the sacred task that is part of their joint calling.

What Kinds of Obstacles Could Twin Souls Face?

The obstacles could come in the form of external obstacles or internal ones – in other words, man versus the world, or man versus himself.

External Obstacles

1) The *Twin Souls* may have big age differences between them, anywhere from seven years to twenty-plus years. (Think Collin Higgins's *Harold and Maude.*)
2) They may be of different races, religions, or classes. (Think Cathy and Heathcliff in Emily Brontë's *Wuthering Heights.*)
3) One or both of the partners might be married. (Think Tom Wingo and Dr. Susan Lowenstein in Pat Conroy's *The Prince of Tides.*)
4) They live far away from each other or are parted. (Think Homer's *Odyssey* and Odysseus and Penelope.)
5) Their countries or families may be at war with each other. (Think Shakespeare's *Romeo and Juliet* or Puccini's *Madame Butterfly.*)

Internal Obstacles

1) Although the reuniting of *Twin Souls* is considered to be a great gift, one or both partners may be unable to heal their own inner issues and may run away from the relationship.
2) Inherent in the reuniting of the **Sacred Duads** is the remembrance of the *Celestial Contract* made between each other and with God. One or both of the *Twin Souls* may become frightened when this pre-birth memory is ac-

tivated, thinking he/she is incapable of living up to the tenets of that divine contract. This fear could drive the couple apart.

3) *Twin Souls* instinctively feel each other's pain. When one *Twin Soul* can't live up to the responsibilities inherent in this union and realizes the pain he/she is inflicting upon the other, to spare the beloved *Twin* any additional pain, the offending *Twin* may leave, truly believing that this is the kindest thing to do.

4) Because *Twin Souls* have had other lifetimes separate from each other, one of them may have acquired a heavier amount of karmic debt to reconcile, and the task proves overwhelming. This karmic overload may result in a need for that *Twin* to flee.

5) The reuniting of *Twin Souls* carries the karmic obligation to heal the mental, physical, emotional, psychological, and spiritual self. The tremendous weight of this can prove to be too much for both of the *Twin Souls*. When this occurs, neither of them can take the giant leap of faith necessary to stay together.

Notice that all the internal obstacles represent an inability of the *Twin Souls* to fully comprehend the divine truth that **only love matters.** They begin to get caught in the quagmire of great fear that a great love inspires, and they simply cannot or will not heal enough to remain together.

Some of the Healing Issues that Can Wreak Havoc on the *Twin Souls'* Ability to Be Together

o   The terrifying fear of commitment may rear its ugly head. (Read more about this gigantic fear in STEP 17.)

o   When we meet our *Twin Soul,* we're expected to answer our divine calling. In answering our divine calling, we might have to leave the world we've always known behind. This is the world built on the false beliefs and *Errors in Thinking* of the ego. We'd then be expected to embrace a new world created from love and our higher consciousness. The all-too-human fear of change can sabotage our soulful journey.

o   One or both of the *Twin Souls* fears their own power. Branded into these old souls is the memory of other lifetimes in which they've abused power. Coming to terms with power, both internal and external, is a big karmic lesson for all of us.

o   One or both of the *Twin Souls* may fear that he/she is not up to such a daunting challenge and flee.

The Wounded Healer

The upside to the failure of the *Twin Souls* to make their love work on the earth plane is that one or both of them may come to embrace the archetype of the "Wounded Healer."

The loss of the *Twin* is an exquisite and profound wound, and the only cure for that pain lies in the source of the suffering in the first place – the return of the beloved *Twin Flame.*

If the *Twins* are not reunited on the earth plane, the prolonged agony rips open the heart to deep levels of compassion. God hopes the *Twin(s)* learn to endure this pain, and transcend it, knowing full well that the two of them will inevitably be reunited in this lifetime, in another one, or in spirit.

If one or both of the *Twins* manage to learn their karmic lessons through the experience of this deep suffering, he/she becomes a powerful instrument for healing others, epitomizing the archetype of the "Wounded Healer."

By the way, any failed *Soul Mate* union (*Sacred Betrayal*) can lead the way for a person to become a "Wounded Healer," if he/she learns the lessons revealed by such a painful parting.

Some Things *Twin Souls* Have Said After Separating

"When we met years later, it was as if time had stopped only to start again. The divine music of my heart had paused only to begin again without missing a beat. It was as if I were a dancer that long ago leaped, staying in midair all this time, waiting to land safely in his arms."

"Although he was long gone, I still knew he loved me. He came to me in starlight visions as I slept. He spoke so softly and told me of his love for me. I swore he was there, and then I was never sure if I had really been dreaming, or if I had been awake."

"I came to accept the nightly visitations and fleeting moments that she came and went like a ghost. She would inhabit my home, rattling around demanding to be heard. This did not drive me mad, no, not at all. It was what kept me sane."

"I had spent most of my life in the wading pool of love, only allowing it to touch my feet, but with her I felt the depth of love, and I thought surely I would drown in it. When the love first touched my knees, they quaked. When it reached my groin I ached with longing. Suddenly, my heart tore open, and as the love reached the depth of my very soul, I couldn't breathe. When the waters of her love covered my head, I was drowning till I managed somehow, godlike, for one brief moment to walk on that divine water with her. Then I let go of her, and watched helplessly as she sank to the bottom. Alone, I made it to dry land, to the desert, where I searched endlessly for what I once had and abandoned."

"Part of why I had run so far, so fast – was in the deepest recesses of my soul, I knew something not of this earth had transpired, and it had scared me as completely as if I'd seen a ghost. I had ridden to eternity with him, and eternity scared me to the bones."

Why Can a *Twin Soul* Reunion Take Place Only Between Members of the Opposite Sexes?

Unlike the other Rungs on *The Ladder of Love*, a *Twin Soul* relationship can only take place between members of the opposite sexes because inherent in

Twinsoulship is a balancing of the male and female energies.

Remember that each individual soul is a fragment of God, and contained within God is the male-female essence. It's this *Yin-Yang* principle, the interaction of the male-female energies, that is the creative force of the universe.

Throughout our many incarnations, although we have spent some lifetimes in a male body and others in a female one, each of us has an essential gender that is either male or female. In other words, we're truly, in the deepest part of our being, either a man or a woman. The knowledge of our true gender is carried within our energy body, which is the blueprint of our being that stays with us from life-time to lifetime. (Read more about our energy body in STEP 15.)

In the lifetime in which the *Twin Souls* meet, they'll each be in the physical body, either male or female, that represents their true essential gender.

Before reuniting, the female *Twin* would have mastered her inner masculine energies (animus) on her own during this lifetime as well as in the many previous lifetimes when her soul was housed in a male body. Additionally, she'll be very in touch with her feminine energies (anima), or goddess en-ergy that Hindu mythology refers to as Shakti, when she meets her male counterpart. The male *Twin* in turn would have mastered his inner feminine ener-gies (anima), and be very in touch with his mascu-line energy(animus), or god energy known as Shiva. This reconciliation of the opposite energies we pos-sess is part of the balancing nature of karma. It ends the duality, the war between the polar opposite male/female energies, within us.

Twin Soul relationships are the quintessential reuniting of the primal male and female energies, and this joining of opposites becomes the strong magnetic pull that draws the *Twin Souls* together.

After the *Twin Souls* meet, the woman will become more in touch with her essential goddess energy, and the man will become much more in touch with his god energy. This coming to terms with our own gender essence is a vital step in our ascension toward wholeness.

Twin Soul reunions are, no doubt, the stuff of great fiction, not only because of the irresistible passion that takes place between them, but because of all the obstacles and drama that accompany this sacred reunion. (Think Wagner's opera *Tristan and Isolde* or Shakespeare's *Romeo and Juliet* to understand the passion, obstacles, and drama that go hand in hand with *Twin Soul* love.)

In essence, *Twin Souls* are the living embodiment of the powerful attraction that the opposite sexes have for each other.

When Do *Twin Souls* Meet?

1) They are very old souls who have already learned most of their karmic lessons separately.

2) They are both in their last or one of their last incarnations.

3) The individual balancing of the male/female energies is a prerequisite for the sacred reunion.

4) As each of the *Twins'* individual souls evolves toward wholeness and becomes conscious of the need to complete this inner journey, his/her spirit guides, angels, saints, Ascended Masters, God, and, most of the time, the *Twin Souls* themselves will decide if it's the proper lifetime for a *Twin Soul* reunion.

5) Both *Twins* must also come to the profound realization that there's no "Prince" or "Princess" who's going to come and rescue them. Although they may still be victims of these subconscious archetypes when they meet, on a conscious level, the *Twins* know they have to, first and foremost, rescue themselves.

6) Furthermore, God feels, in reuniting these *Twin Souls,* that all of humanity will benefit from the project or service they will accomplish either individually or jointly. This is the most important reason for the reuniting of the **Sacred Duads.**

Before such a blessed reunion can take place, each Twin would have healed a great deal of his/her own inner issues individually through countless incarnations on the earth plane.

Why Does God Bring Twin Souls Together?

♦ God reunites *Twin Souls* in hopes that they'll become a beacon of light for others to see the true nature of unconditional love.

♦ **God reunites *Twin Souls* because they have an important project, work of art, scientific discovery, or some other service to perform, either jointly or individually, that will benefit all of humanity.** God feels that the rapid soul growth and consciousness raising effect of the *Twin Soul* meeting is necessary for this project to be completed. Think of the *Twin Souls,* Elizabeth Barrett and Robert Browning, and the poetry they created; or the accomplishments of the *Twin Soul* chemists, Marie Curie and Pierre Curie. Note: Sometimes the great project(s) that are expected from the *Twins* can only be accomplished if the *Twin Souls* are reunited and then separated. This meeting and then agreeing to separate would be part of the *Celestial Contract* they made with each other. This **Sacred Betrayal,** with its painful ripping open of their hearts, is absolutely necessary for the completion of one or both of their divine calling(s). Think of Beethoven and all the beautiful music he created in the absence of his "Immortal Beloved."

♦ Whether the *Twin Soul* reunion lasts or not, each *Twin* is still expected to try and answer his/her divine calling and accomplish whatever great work of art, science, or humanitarianism that was supposed to be created because of their meeting. Angels, spirit guides, and earthbound souls will be sent to the separated *Twins* to assist them in their projects.

♦ God reunites *Twin Souls* to help advance their entire Group Soul. As the *Twins* achieve Enlightenment, they help others within their soul group to do the same.

♦ Basically, God reunites *Twin Souls* to benefit all humankind. Know, then, that this reunion, this gift from God, carries the weight of the world with it.

How Would I Recognize a Twin Soul Reunion?

A *Twin Soul* reunion is so revolutionarily life-altering, and so overwhelming an experience, that you'd instinctively know – only a divine conspiracy of heaven and earth could have produced this.

You would have some kind of prophetic experience forewarning you that something extraordinary is about to happen. It may come in the form of a dream, through a psychic reading, or through some thought of your own that you can't explain. Just know that the universe will alert you to keep your eyes open and pay attention.

You'll suddenly feel that you're being divinely guided. You'll begin to recognize the awesome power of love, and you'll find yourself surrounded by synchronistic experiences.

From the second you meet, you'll feel that you've always known each other. Very early on, your *Twin* will say or do something that registers deep within you, activating the memory of your *Celestial*

Contract. From that moment on, you'll feel like your souls are conspiring with each other. For instance, you'll find that you're able to communicate telepathically with this person, even though you have never had this power before.

After you meet your *Twin,* you'll feel differently about yourself and about your world. Because the *Twin Soul* reunion always results in a complete transformation of both humans, each of you begins to see life through entirely new eyes.

This new vision is the first step toward *Enlightenment.*

What Is Enlightenment?

Enlightenment is spiritual awakening. It's seeing the universe with a new perception – a very clear vision in which you recognize the light of God is not only within you, but within everyone and everything else as well.

Although the first flashes of Enlightenment can feel like a sudden, explosive shift in your awareness or consciousness, it's really more of a long, continuing process in which you burn away all that is untrue.

Much of what I've written in this book about the process of Enlightenment comes from my own experience with this life-altering experience. What I've discovered is that many people resist Enlightenment because they instinctively know that once they've experienced this heightened sense of awareness, they can no longer deceive or delude themselves, or go into a deep state of denial. An Enlightened being sees things as they truly are, without all the smoke and mirrors, and most people at this stage of human consciousness aren't quite ready for this all-too-real view of the world.

Understanding the Enlightenment Experience

1. Basically, Enlightenment is seeing the world through the tolerant and compassionate eyes of God.
2. This clear vision illuminates that secret place deep within each and every one of us which has been and always will remain untouched and unscarred by any and all experiences we've ever encountered in this lifetime or in any other.
3. Enlightenment is the deep inner knowing that all experiences are good as long as we learn from them. "It's all good."
4. To be an Enlightened being is to know and radiate unconditional love.
5. An Enlightened mind is a positive one that strives to heal all and see all in a concerted effort to end *samsara* or the vicious cycle of rebirth.
6. An Enlightened being asks and expects to see the truth, the whole truth, and nothing but the truth.
7. Enlightened beings know that what they bring forth from the depths of their being will heal them, and what they keep hidden will destroy them.
8. Enlightenment can sometimes come as a sudden release of Kundalini energy that shoots

through your body and opens all your chakras, so that energy flows freely throughout. After the initial jolt, it once again becomes a long, slow process. (Read more about Kundalini energy and chakras in STEP 15. If you don't know anything about the Chakra System, jump ahead to STEP 15, and read about it, before proceeding with this study of Enlightenment.)

9. For some people, Enlightenment does come slowly, bit by bit, until one day they wake up and realize they have become totally transformed.

10. Regardless of whether Enlightenment comes like a bolt of lightning from the heavens, or as a slow chiseling away of all that is untrue, it still is, as Buddha stated, "the final nightmare," because we must walk through the bloody alleyways of our hearts and minds to heal all our issues. We can sometimes become afraid and wish we could go back, but we can't, unless we abuse drugs or alcohol or turn to other addictions.

11. To become Enlightened is to become awakened.

12. Enlightenment is a total life-transforming experience.

13. It's a spiritual rebirth, an awakening to profound realization that we're a spirit temporarily housed in a body. It's our own personal resurrection.

14. After Enlightenment, we'll still be human. We'll still be flawed sometimes, but we'll be fully aware that we've behaved in ways we're

not proud of, and we'll strive to never act that way again.

15. An Enlightened life is a compassionate one.
16. An Enlightened life is one that has respect for all life.
17. An Enlightened person knows that kindness is the highest evolution of a human being.
18. An Enlightened being is not a perfect human, but is perfectly human.
19. It's a long, slow process. Be patient!

A Visualization of Enlightenment

o Visualize the path to Enlightenment as a spiral staircase that begins on earth and ends in heaven.
o For many lifetimes you'll be circling around the bottom step.
o Eventually, you get to the second step.
o For several lifetimes you circle around that step, then the next, and then the next.
o After countless incarnations you finally get closer to the top of the spiral staircase.
o Eventually, you get to the top of the staircase and become terrified as you see before you a long, dark tunnel that appears to be endless.
o Now you have to crawl on your hands and knees with only the light of your Enlightenment to guide you toward the end of the tunnel.
o Every once in a while you get stuck and can't go any further, and then you feel this great big cosmic kick (with your angels, spirit guides,

saints, Ascended Masters, *Twin Soul,* deceased loved ones and/or God doing the kicking) forcing you to go a little further in spite of your trepidation.

o   At this point, you'll need to muster up courage to keep going despite your fears.

o   When you finally get to the end of the tunnel you'll know, see, and feel the unconditional love of God, who was waiting patiently for you all along.

o   Whether *Twin Souls* stay together or separate, the experience, the alchemy of their souls, will, in due time, bring both partners to Enlightenment and to God.

o   We're all here on earth on a journey. The destination is love – pure, unlimited, unconditional love. That is Enlightenment.

Remember, there are only two paths in life: the path of love and the path of fear. Sometimes, people become so afraid when they're given a great love that they run. They pull a geographic and move far away from their beloved, or they simply end the relationship.

But if you run away from a *Soul Mate* – or, worse yet, if you run away from a *Twin Soul* – you'll be a haunted being. No matter how fast or how far you run, how hard you work or how much you drink, your *Twin Soul* remains forever etched into your heart and soul. If you deny your *Twin* by day, he/she will come to you at night in your dreams. Your *Twin* will always be there in the back of your mind, but more likely, your *Twin* will be in your every thought.

If there were many obstacles for you to overcome to be together, then you'll know you took the easier, yet ultimately harder, path in running. Instead of learning your karmic lessons through love, peace, and joy, you and your *Twin* will have the painful task of learning those same karmic lessons through great suffering.

Twin Souls and Enlightenment

A. When *Twin Souls* meet there will be an intense alchemy between their hearts, minds, souls, and bodies, as if their entire beings are about to spontaneously combust.

B. If they meet and circumstances permit them to make love, it will epitomize Sacred Sexuality. They will release tremendous amounts of Kundalini energy as they merge their entire beings in this great cosmic dance known as lovemaking. (Read more about Sacred Sexuality and Kundalini energy in STEP 15.) Through this experience, the two of them will catapult with blazing bodies into that long tunnel known as Enlightenment. If, due to life circumstances, they're unable to make love, they'll still achieve Enlightenment via the immense learning, healing, and growing the reuniting of their souls brings forth.

C. The free will of each *Twin Soul* will determine how far into the tunnel of Enlightenment each one will go. With any luck at all, they'll help pull each other through to the end of the tunnel, where they'll come into the blazing light of God.

D. One or both *Twin Souls* could get frightened and choose to go no further forward on this long path toward the liberation of the soul. This will make life extremely difficult, because the frightened *Twin(s)* begins living a splintered life. The terrified ego refuses to let go, and the half-enlightened soul feels tortured. At times, a *Twin Soul* may turn to drug or alcohol abuse to escape the pain of knowing he/ she could not live up to the challenge.

E. The experience of Enlightenment leads to Cosmic Consciousness, which is our collective sense of affection and affinity for all creation. (Read more about Cosmic Consciousness in STEP 9.)

To further your understanding of Enlightenment, please read *Enlightenment is a Secret: Teachings of Liberation,* by Andrew Cohen.

LOVEWORK ASSIGNMENT

Reflect upon all your love relationships. Do you think you've met your *Twin Soul?* If not, do you feel you're ready to meet your *Twin Soul?* Knowing what I've told you about all the obstacles *Twin Souls* have to overcome, do you even feel that you'd want to meet yours in this lifetime? Do you feel you know any couples who could be *Twin Souls?*

My Meditations on *Twinsoulship*

I Understand the Awesome Responsibility Inherent
in a *Twin Soul* Reunion

Some *Twin Souls* throughout History

Clara and Robert Schumann
Marie and Pierre Curie
Petrarch and Laura
Jeanette MacDonald and Nelson Eddy

LOVEWORK ASSIGNMENT

Pick one of the abovementioned couples and do as much research as you can on this couple. Look on the Internet, read a book, or watch a movie that depicts this couple. Do you see why they should be considered *Twin Souls?*

Then think of a movie in which you think the lead characters were *Twin Souls.* Please list as many reasons as you can to justify your choice.

A Screen Couple that Epitomizes *Twinsoulship*

From This Day Forward I Will Send My *Twin Soul*
Wherever He/She May Be, Love and Light

Recommended Reading

To learn more about **Sacred Duads**, read *Twin Souls: A Guide to Finding Your True Spiritual Partner,* by Patricia Joudry and Maurie Pressman, M.D., and/or *Soul Mates and Twin Flames,* by Elizabeth Clare Prophet.

Bear in mind that I may not agree with everything said in the books I recommend, particularly as far as *Twin Souls* goes. In fact, some of the information I've given in this book might contradict some of the information in the abovementioned books, but I still feel you'll benefit from reading them. Just keep in mind, as you're doing your soul work that you must filter everything you read and hear – including everything you read in this book – through your own higher consciousness to draw your own conclusions. On the path of Enlightenment you must question everything you see, hear, or read.

What You Need to Know Before Taking the Next STEP

In STEP 7, we'll be exploring Ninth Rung Love – *Mirror Souls.* To truly understand *Mirror Souls* and their relationship to *Twin Souls,* we must fully understand what a Group Soul is.

In STEP 3, we discussed Group Souls in detail. Please go back and reread the sections titled *Understanding Group Souls* and *More Insights About Group Souls* before proceeding to STEP 7.

Now that you have a true understanding of what comprises a Twin Soul relationship, take a moment to congratulate yourself, because you've just taken another STEP toward a higher love.

STEP 7– RECOGNIZING THE EXISTENCE OF *MIRROR SOULS*

"Think what a holy relationship can teach!"
(*A Course in Miracles*, Chapter 22)

NINTH RUNG LOVE

Serene Soul Mates

Mirror, Mirror on the Wall, Who Are the Fairest Loves of All?

Why, Mirror Souls, of Course!

In the last STEP, we explored many aspects of a *Twin Soul* reunion. One of the things we learned was that a *Twin Soul* reunion can only take place between members of the opposite sexes. We further learned that *Twin Souls* will always have passionate romantic and sexual feelings between them, although due to life circumstances the **Sacred Duads** may not be able to act upon those feelings.

Mirror Soul relationships, on the other hand, are *Soul Mate* relationships which have much more flexibility and a greater range. For instance, *Mirror Soul* relationships can be same-sex or opposite-sex unions, and these relationships can be either romantic or platonic in nature. In fact, *Mirror Soul* relationships can run the gamut from a great and passionate love affair, to a lifelong friendship, to a particularly close bond between siblings, or to a tight bond between a parent and child, to name but a few.

Mirror Soul relationships are characterized by the joy, peace, and harmony they bring to our lives. *Mirror Souls* love each other unconditionally, and for many people this will be the first time they've ever loved or been loved that way.

If *Mirror Souls* do have a love affair, there's great passion without all the drama inherent in a *Twin Soul* reunion.

The term for this serene, joyful, and unconditionally loving experience that takes place between *Mirror Souls* is called the **Magic Mirror Effect.**

Group Souls and the *Holy Alliance*

In STEP 3, you learned that we all began our journey on this earth plane as individual beings who were part of a larger family of souls known as the Group Soul.

The **Holy Alliance is the smallest unit of your Group Soul.** Visualize your Group Soul as your extended family, and your *Holy Alliance* as your immediate family.

Your *Holy Alliance* would include you, your *Twin Soul*, and five other sets of *Twin Souls*. All six sets of *Twin Souls* who comprise a *Holy Alliance* are also *Mirror Souls* to each other. This means that you and your *Twin Soul* are *Mirror Souls* to each other and to the other five female and five male members who comprise your *Holy Alliance*.

A good metaphor to help you understand the concept of the *Holy Alliance* and the *Twin Soul/ Mirror Soul* relationship would be to visualize six sets of fraternal male/female twins born into one family. In this family (*Holy Alliance*), each of these twelve individuals (*souls*) would be siblings (*Mirror Souls*) to each other, and a twin (*Twin Soul*) to one of the others.

Since *Twin Souls* are also *Mirror Souls* to each other, as humankind evolves in Cosmic Consciousness, reuniting the *Sacred Duads* will result in passionate relationships minus all the drama. At this stage of human evolution, however, although *Twin Souls* are in fact *Mirror Souls* to each other as well, these *Sacred Duads* provide the exception to the rule that states: *Mirror Soul* relationships are characterized by the immense sense of peace, unconditional love, and joy they bring. As you learned in the previous STEP, *Twin Soul* reunions demand total karmic cleansing, and for most people walking the earth plane right now, this daunting cross to bear far outweighs many aspects of the *Magic Mirror Effect*. However, *Twin Souls* will always love each other unconditionally regardless of the outcome of the relationship, simply because this aspect of the *Magic Mirror Effect* is too strong for either of them to will away, wish away, or deny.

Reuniting *Holy Alliances*

Although a *Twin Soul* reunion represents a reuniting of only the smallest fraction of a *Holy Alliance*, it is by far the most powerful karmic reunion in all of the cosmos. By the time *Twin Souls* meet, they've already learned a great many of their karmic lessons on their own, and their reunion catapults each of them toward Enlightenment. God and the universe fully expect all of humanity to benefit from the reuniting of a *Sacred Duad,* as the *Twins* separately and jointly answer their divine callings.

During the Age of Aquarius, as we, as a species, continue to evolve spiritually, God will begin to reunite on the earth plane several members of a *Holy Alliance* (including *Twin Soul* reunions), and in some rare instances, entire *Holy Alliances,* in an effort to accelerate the Enlightenment of the human race. When these wholly or partially reunited *Holy Alliances* are brought into alignment with other wholly or partially reunited *Holy Alliances,* they will join forces and become a tremendously powerful instrument for harnessing the good powers of the universe in a concerted effort to rapidly advance the evolution of all humanity. Let us pray for such a blessed day!

Each of us is blessed with a Twin Soul, five female Mirror Souls and five male Mirror Souls, and these Soul Mates form our Holy Alliance.

Our Twin Soul and our Mirror Souls represent the closest soul ties any of us will ever encounter on earth or in spirit.

Similarities and Differences Between *Mirror Soul* Reunions and *Twin Soul* Reunions

A *Mirror Soul* reunion is a gift from God with no strings attached. The universe lovingly reunites

Mirror Souls to help each other in their journey through life. God doesn't ask that we heal all our issues when we meet a *Mirror Soul,* and we aren't necessarily expected to accomplish great things as a direct result of this reunion, but with any luck at all, this extraordinary relationship will show us the way.

Although a reuniting of *Twin Souls* is also a great gift, it does come with serious strings attached. These strings are the source of much angst and the reason so few *Twin Soul* reunions work out at this stage of human evolution. The reunited *Twins* are asked to heal all their issues, both personal and transpersonal. Just trying to perfectly balance their male-female energies can prove to be a daunting task. Basically, these attached strings demand a learning of all life's karmic lessons. Regardless of the *Twin Soul* relationship outcome, God fully expects the *Twins* to answer their individual divine calling(s) – completing the great work of art, science, or humanitarianism which is meant to lift humankind another step toward Cosmic Consciousness. (Read more about Cosmic Consciousness in STEP 9.)

Keep in mind that *Twin Souls* are also *Mirror Souls* to each other. *Mirror Souls* by their very nature are *serene Soul Mates.* For this reason, it truly is the birthright of *Twin Souls* to have a peaceful and joyful relationship. As human beings grow, heal, and evolve they'll come to readily accept the gift of *Twinsoulship* as the holiest of holy relationships.

The Many Faces of *Mirror Souls*

Since we're blessed with many *Mirror Souls,* both male and female, we can encounter our

Mirror Souls in the form of friends, lovers, parents, children, or any other assortment of relationships, depending upon the balancing karma the souls need to grow spiritually. Thus, a *Mirror Soul* relationship can be either platonic or romantic, and these relationships can be either same-sex or different-sex unions as well.

The Magic Mirror Effect

A *Mirror Soul* relationship helps us to know what a good relationship is all about. It allows us to understand what it means to love and be loved unconditionally. Unlike so many other friends and lovers we encounter during our lifetime, our *Mirror Soul* has no personal agenda when they give us advice. *Mirror Souls* genuinely want what is best for each other. Rare, indeed! *Mirror Souls* are like having our own spirit guide on earth, loving us, supporting us, and guiding us. *Mirror Souls* can practice tough love with each other when necessary, but in their heart of hearts, both parties know that this stern behavior is what was absolutely needed at the time.

The two reunited *Mirror Souls* may be guilty of practicing the Five Deadly Sins Committed in the Name of Conditional Love on a regular basis in the rest of their lives, but when they're together, the *Magic Mirror Effect* takes over and only rarely are *Mirror Souls* selfish, greedy, narcissistic, envious, or jealous with each other. When they're apart, they may see the other person objectively and fully realize how flawed he/she really is, but when they're together the *Magic*

Mirror Effect once again kicks in to bring out the best in both of them. Think of *Mirror Souls* as two people who look at each other with magic mirror eyes.

The *Blessed Platonic Duad*

The deep friendship which develops between two *Mirror Souls* forms what is called the **Blessed Platonic Duad.** A *Blessed Platonic Duad* can involve two members of the same sex or two members of the opposite sex.

Oprah Winfrey's close-knit relationship with her longtime friend, Gayle King, would be a good example of a *Mirror Soul* relationship. Oprah herself has stated that there isn't a definition (up until now) for the kind of bond she and Gayle have with each other, and she has referred to their relationship as "otherworldly," believing that a hand greater than her own designed it.

The *Serene Sacred Duad*

A reuniting of two romantic *Mirror Souls* is called the *Serene Sacred Duad*.

While a *Sacred Duad* (the romantic union formed by reuniting *Twin Souls)* can take place only between members of the opposite sex, a *Serene Sacred Duad* can be either a same-sex or opposite-sex union.

In this STEP, we'll concentrate on the **Serene Sacred Duad,** the reuniting of two *Mirror Souls* which results in a romantic love affair.

For now, keep in mind that while we have only one *Twin Soul,* God has blessed each of us with ten additional *Mirror Souls.* Unlike the reuniting of *Twin Souls,* which is a rare occurrence and usually happens toward the end of our countless incarnations, we can be granted a *Mirror Soul* relationship(s) anytime.

How Will I Recognize One of My Mirror Souls?

1. *Mirror Souls* may not have met on the earth plane before, but they've definitely been with each other in spirit, thus ensuring that *The Recognition Factor* will be activated when they meet.
2. *Mirror Soul* relationships are characterized by fierce loyalty, true friendship, peace, joy, and deep, unconditional love. Even if your *Mirror Soul* is your lover, you're first and foremost true friends to each other, incapable of betraying or intentionally hurting each other. *Mirror Souls* are eternal friends, "Immortal Friends."
3. *Mirror Souls* commune telepathically with each other. If one of our *Mirror Souls* were to pass on before us, we'd still be able to commune with each other because of the tremendous telepathy that exists between *Mirror Souls.* In fact, *Mirror Souls* have been spirit guides for each other since the dawn of time.

Comparing *Twin Souls* and *Mirror Souls*

- Because *Mirror Soul* relationships are characterized by unconditional love, peace, joy, and trust, these *Soul Mates* do not incur much, if any, karmic debt from each other. Consequently, if they've had other lifetimes together, they won't have much karmic reckoning to do. This is a unique characteristic of *Mirror Souls.* Regardless of how flawed the two *Mirror Souls* may be in relation to everyone else in the world, and how much karmic debt they have incurred with others, they will act in a highly evolved manner when dealing with each other. Of course, we live in a freewill universe and there can and will be exceptions to every rule, but *Mirror Souls* rarely betray each other, and if they do, they almost always reconcile their differences in record time.

- *Twin Souls* rarely meet on the earth plane more than one, two, or perhaps three times. Therefore, each *Twin* has incurred a great deal of karmic debt, not so much from their other lifetimes together, but as a result of all the other relationships they've encountered during their separate lifetimes. This separate karmic debt can and usually does affect the quality and outcome of the *Twin Soul* relationship at this stage of human evolution.

- Although *Mirror Souls* can have great obstacles to overcome in order to be together, these obstacles appear to melt away because the alchemy of *Mirror Souls* is one of fierce determination, peace, serenity, harmony, joy, and unconditional love.

- *Twin Souls* will often have tremendous obstacles to overcome before they can be together, and at this time in human consciousness, they're often unable to overcome them.

- Because of the peaceful nature inherent in a *Mirror Soul* reunion, fear doesn't factor all that much into the equation. However, fear can have a huge detrimental impact upon the *Twin Soul* relationship due to the separate karmic debt each *Twin* has incurred. With *Twin Souls, The Recognition Factor* contains the additional knowledge that they're both expected to heal all their issues and learn all their karmic lessons now that they've been reunited. Among all other reunited *Mirror Souls, The Recognition Factor* does not contain that fear-provoking knowledge.

- The peace and harmony that exists between *Mirror Souls* allows both individuals to realize what a great gift they've found in each other.

- At this stage of human evolution, *Twin Souls* often separate rather than heal their issues. This path is superficially easier but ultimately the harder path in life, since they'll suffer greatly as they long unceasingly for each other.

- *Mirror Souls*, for the most part, take the initially harder path and face together the daunting obstacles. Ultimately, this becomes the easier path.

- Remember: *Mirror Souls* don't necessarily have great obstacles to face, but if and when they do, they most often manage to face them with courage.

- In the future, as humankind grows in spiritual knowledge and karmic reckoning occurs, *Twin Souls* may be so blessed as to come together without all the obstacles; or, at the very least, they may come better armed with the courage to face whatever life may throw their way.

- During the Age of Aquarius, *Twin Souls* will be working their way back to the primal remembrance that they're also *Mirror Souls* to each other. This recollection will help them embrace the serene simplicity a *Mirror Soul* relationship embodies.

- All *Soul Mate* relationships transcend *kronos* time. This means that if we didn't see our *Soul Mate* for twenty years, it wouldn't matter. In reuniting, it would be as if no time had passed between us. This is particularly true of either a *Twin Soul* or a *Mirror Soul* relationship.

- *Mirror Soul* relationships are characterized by the joyful, unconditional love and support they give to each other. Conflict is rare, and both *Mirror Souls* will feel a need to bring their differences to a rapid resolution. (Exceptions to this rule occur if one or both of the *Mirror Souls* are abusing drugs or alcohol or suffering from severe mental illness.)

- At this stage of human evolution, it's highly unlikely that you'll meet more than one or two of your *Mirror Souls* in any one lifetime. In many lifetimes we won't meet any of our *Mirror Souls.* Through our good karma – our good thoughts, words, deeds, acts, and works – we earn the right to be given a *Mirror Soul* relationship.

- If you meet your *Twin Soul,* you'll most likely meet at least one more of your *Mirror Souls.* At this stage of human consciousness, the experience of meeting a *Twin Soul* is often so traumatic that another *Mirror Soul* is sent down to help one or both of the *Twin Souls* accomplish their life missions.

- When you meet a *Mirror Soul,* you might also be made aware of another *Mirror Soul* who is already in spirit and who has helped guide the two of you together. The two of you could learn to commune with the discarnate *Mirror Soul* as well.

- As humankind evolves, more and more *Mirror Soul* reunions will take place. At any one time, three or more *Mirror Souls* could be reunited. If God were to reunite three or more *Mirror Souls* at one time, it would be to accomplish a divine purpose. This partially reunited *Holy Alliance* would be a very powerful one indeed, since it would harness the collective powers of those *Mirror Souls* reunited on earth and those still in spirit. If one or more sets of *Twin Souls* were involved in this reunion, the sacred calling they'd all be expected to answer would be of epic proportions.

- Whereas a *Twin Soul* reunion dictates that the two individual souls already be highly evolved, anyone at any stage of evolution can be brought a *Mirror Soul* as long as they have accrued some good karma.

- Both a *Twin Soul* relationship and a *Mirror Soul* relationship will cause rapid ascension of the souls involved. However, the *Twin Soul* ascension will influence not only the way the *Twins* interact with each other, but all their other relationships as well. *Twin Souls* achieve Enlightenment and soon learn to be nonjudgmental, forgiving, and compassionate. This affects the way they deal with everyone they encounter, from a stranger to a *Soul Mate,* even if the *Twins* themselves were unable to heal fully enough to remain together. Remember, the element of freewill is always at work. If a *Twin Soul* turns to drugs or alcohol in an effort to block the pain of separation, or becomes totally incapable of healing the traumas of the past, all bets are off as to how that *Twin* will respond to the rest of the world. This negative behavior incurs heavy karma for the unhealed *Twin.* (Think of Heathcliff in Emily Brontë's *Wuthering Heights.*) Highly evolved beings who are given a *Mirror Soul* relationship will also ascend as a result of this reunion and could possibly achieve Enlightenment as well. The interactions they'll have with the rest of the world will reflect this. However, less evolved beings who are given a *Mirror Soul* relationship will find their behaviors altered only in the way that they deal with each other. Due to the *Magic Mirror Effect,* when they're together they find themselves in a blissful state of peace, unconditional love, and joy, but they may still be negative and petty with everyone else in their lives.

- God brings a *Mirror Soul* into your life to show you how all relationships, particularly love relationships, should be. Therefore, you could be married to a *Cellmate* and fight like cats and dogs, and yet have a best friend who is a *Mirror Soul,* with whom you never speak a harsh word. God is trying to show you how splintered a being you are. Your actions can be highly evolved one moment and hellish the next.

- The nature of the *Twin Soul* reunion, because it's a catalyst for rapid soul growth, is stormy. In contrast, a *Mirror Soul* relationship is peaceful and serene.

- Know that there can be any combination of *Twin Souls* meeting one or all of their *Mirror Souls,* but at this stage of human evolution, it would be rare, even for *Twin Souls,* to meet more than two or three *Mirror Souls* in one lifetime.

LOVEWORK ASSIGNMENT

Reflect upon your relationships. Do you think someone in your life was or is a *Mirror Soul?* Remember, a *Mirror Soul* can be a romantic partner, but it could also be a platonic relationship. What characterizes a *Mirror Soul* relationship is a close kinship in which there is a lot of support, little or no conflict, unconditional love, and a feeling of safety and great joy whenever you're together. Your *Mirror Soul* thinks, feels, and experiences life as you do. You understand each other in the very depths of your being.

If you haven't had such an experience, think of two people you know, either in real life or in fiction, who have had this experience. Then take some time to write down your reflections on *Mirror Souls*.

My Meditations on *Mirror Souls*

My Knowledge of Soulful Relationships is Growing Every Day

Have We Met in Other Lifetimes?

♦ *Cellmates* have usually met in previous lifetimes and are trying to right the wrongs of the past.

♦ *Soul Mates* have usually met in other lifetimes. They have worked out many of their past issues, but they could still have some karmic settling to accomplish.

♦ Every now and then we may be given a brand-new *Soul Mate* or *Cellmate.* We may or may not have met this *Soul Mate* or *Cellmate* in spirit, but we have definitely never been with them on the earth plane before. God is giving these couples a clean slate. If healed individuals are given a brand-new *Soul Mate,* this would prove to be a very blissful relationship, occupying the Seventh Rung on *The Ladder of Love.* God will bring a brand-new *Cellmate* relationship to two people in the hope that the alchemy of their meeting will teach the two of them many karmic lessons, albeit the hard way. We might still have a feeling that we've met these brand-new *Cellmates* or *Soul Mates* before, if they're part of our Group Soul. When we encounter any member of our Group Soul, *The Recognition Factor* is always present, regardless of whether we've met these people in another lifetime or not.

♦ At this stage of human development, *Mirror Souls* have almost always met in other lifetimes.

♦ *Twin Souls,* at this point in history, are meeting on earth for the first, second, or – extremely rare – third time.

A Sacred Trinity

A **Sacred Trinity** is the reuniting of a **Sacred Duad** **(Twin Soul Reunion)** and one **Mirror Soul.** Remember that all three of these beings are also *Mirror Souls* to each other, so in essence a *Sacred Trinity* is really a reunion of three members of a *Holy Alliance.*

In the future more *Twin Soul* reunions will take place, and they may meet as many *Mirror Souls* as necessary to further their earth mission.

What a wondrous life we'd have if we were reunited with not only our *Twin Soul,* but all ten of our other *Mirror Souls.* We can only imagine the love, peace, and joy that such a reunion would inspire, not to mention the great personal and humanitarian accomplishments that would emerge.

Historical Examples of a Sacred Trinity

Johannes Brahms and Clara and Robert Schumann

An historical example of a *Sacred Trinity* involved the pianists/composers Clara Schumann, Robert Schumann, and Johannes Brahms

The Schumanns were *Twin Souls* and their reflecting *Mirror Soul* was Johannes Brahms.

Clara and Robert's *Twin Soul* relationship is an apt example of the less-than-storybook-perfect romance inherent in a *Twin Soul* reunion. From the outset, there was the daunting exterior obstacle that

Clara's overbearing father provided with his vehement opposition to their relationship. Still, this divine couple managed to overcome this.

The Schumanns were brought together to heal their inner issues, evolve spiritually, and create musical works of art that would benefit humanity. Another joint task they were given was to advance the art and career of their *Mirror Soul* Johannes Brahms.

Robert's severe mental illness provided the daunting internal obstacle which separated these *Twin Souls*, particularly after he became confined to a mental institution.

Over time, Brahms proved to be a dear and loyal friend to both Robert and Clara. Because of her husband's institutionalization, Clara had to support her children by going on concert tours. While she was away, it was Brahms who kept in touch with her, informing her about the doings of her children and husband. He corresponded with Robert on a regular basis as well, to keep him informed of the activities of Clara and the children.

From this example of a *Sacred Trinity*, you can see that a *Mirror Soul* relationship can take place between members of the same sex, as was the case with Robert and Johannes. This would be an example of a *Blessed Platonic Duad*. But *Mirror Souls* can also be of the opposite sex, as was the case of Clara and Johannes, and these relationships can be either platonic or romantic in nature.

As can often happen between *Mirror Souls*, Johannes fell in love with Clara. When Robert died, Brahms wanted to marry Clara, but she refused. (What happened behind closed doors between them is a matter of speculation.)

Helen Keller, Anne Sullivan Macy and John Albert Macy

The long and fruitful relationship between Helen Keller and Anne Sullivan represents a reuniting of two members of a *Holy Alliance*, in which one *Mirror Soul*, Anne, instinctively knew how and when to exercise tough love with another *Mirror Soul*, Helen. Their extraordinary relationship would be another example of a *Blessed Platonic Duad.*

Anne Sullivan, a visually impaired woman herself, was hired to be a teacher to Helen Keller, a defiant seven-year-old deaf, blind, and mute child. The young Helen had been spoiled by her well-meaning but uninformed parents and, as a result, was prone to violent outbursts and temper tantrums. Anne knew she had to be strict and unyielding to break the willful spirit of her young charge.

Eventually, Anne was able to gain Helen's trust and love. Their early experience together was brilliantly captured in William Gibson's award-winning stage play and film *The Miracle Worker.*

Over the course of nearly half a century these *Mirror Souls* spent together, many people saw these two remarkable women as almost one being. People often wondered how much of Helen Keller was really Anne Sullivan and how much of Anne Sullivan was really Helen Keller.

While attending Radcliffe College (despite her severe disabilities, Helen graduated *cum laude*), Helen wrote her autobiography, *The Story of My Life*, with the help of Anne and a young Harvard instructor named John Albert Macy. As John and Anne worked closely together on Helen's autobiography, these *Twin Souls* inevitably fell deeply in love.

John and Helen, being *Mirror Souls,* naturally formed a close friendship known as a *Blessed Platonic Duad.*

Eventually John and Anne married and set up a household with Helen.

A careful analysis of John and Anne's troubled but passionate love affair reveals the many difficulties inherent in a *Twin Soul* reunion. They certainly had many external obstacles to overcome, including Anne's own physical disabilities, and the fact that John was eleven years younger than Anne. Additionally, the constant care that Helen needed drained them both of energy, and their precarious finances further strained the relationship.

However, the most daunting obstacle our *Twin Souls* faced was the internal obstacle of Anne's horrible childhood traumas and the terrible toll they took on her. Besides having witnessed the deaths of three siblings and the early death of her mother, she suffered unspeakable abuse at the hands of her alcoholic father. When he later abandoned her, she was placed in a state poorhouse where she saw and experienced every atrocity known to humankind.

This haunting legacy filled Anne with unrelenting rage and eventually ate away at her relationship with her husband. During these trying times, Helen was the only person capable of dealing with Anne.

Much to Helen's dismay, John and Anne eventually separated, but these *Twin Flames* never divorced. Anne lived out her remaining days with Helen, her beloved *Mirror Soul.*

The world will be forever blessed by the re-uniting of this *Sacred Trinity*, since their joint effort to document this incredible story of courage and perseverance opened the way for humanity to see, not the limitations of a person, but the amazing heights one can reach with determination and love.

LOVEWORK ASSIGNMENT

Watch the movie *Casablanca*, starring Humphrey Bogart, Ingrid Bergman, and Paul Henreid, and pay attention to the relationship that emerges around the trinity of characters: Rick Blaine, Ilsa Lund, and Victor Laszlo.

Do you think they're a *Sacred Trinity*? Who do you think are the *Twin Souls*, and why? Who are *Mirror Souls*, and why?

How was humanity supposed to benefit from the reuniting of this *Sacred Trinity*?

What I Learned from Watching *Casablanca*

I Can See Why the Entire World Benefits from a Higher Love

Where We Go from Here

Now that we understand the different kinds of love relationships we can have, in STEP 8, we're going to study the Five Karmic Principles that Govern Relationships to learn how we can behave in a more loving and karmically correct manner.

You've just taken another STEP toward a higher love. Feel confident that you're partaking in a spiritual quest and all the divine forces of the universe are rallying behind you.
Keep the faith.

STEP 8 - HONORING THE FIVE KARMIC PRINCIPLES THAT GOVERN RELATIONSHIPS

"Let me recognize the problem so it can be solved."
(*A Course in Miracles*, Lesson 79)

On first glance, this STEP will look like a relatively short, easy one. But don't let its diminutive size fool you. In actuality, it's one of the hardest of all, for it asks you to deal on a day-to-day basis with your partners in a kind, considerate, and karmically correct manner. This, as we all know, is easier said than done.

These Five Karmic Principles will also help you understand when to hold on to a relationship and when to let it go. If you're currently debating whether you should stay in a relationship or leave it, you might want to reread this STEP several times and then jump forward to STEP 19. After doing so, if you're still undecided about which way to go, I would seriously advise you to complete all 19 STEPS before making a decision. Of course, if you're involved in an emotionally abusive relationship, then there's no time like the present to move on. And, please, if you're involved in a First or Second Rung *Cellmate* relationship that has turned violent, get out now!

The Five Karmic Principles

<u>The First Karmic Principle</u> – From the moment *Cellmates, Soul Mates,* or *Razor's Edge Mates* meet and

become involved, they're under karmic obligation to begin taking positive steps toward healing their issues both individually and mutually.

The Second Karmic Principle – We're asked to tell our mates in a clear, calm, and honest manner what we need. What we say in anger, screaming and shouting, doesn't count. Cultivate a sense of humor. Humor disarms people. When our guard is down, a true dialogue can take place. When you bring your sense of humor to the table, your mate won't feel attacked and will stop being on the defensive. Your efforts to get your point across in a lighthearted way, rather than a hurtful way, will be greatly appreciated. Besides, sharing a good laugh with someone can be one of the most soulful and healing experiences.

The Third Karmic Principle – We're asked to demonstrate through words and deeds our intention to work on our relationship. I can't stress enough the healing power of carefully chosen words. Be kind and respectful when you talk to your mate. Then put your money where your mouth is and act upon some of the changes your mate is requesting. For instance: If your mate keeps complaining that you don't help around the house, then start helping. Or, if your mate says you're spending too much money, and you know that you really are, then stop spending excessively.

The Fourth Karmic Principle – Our mates are under karmic obligation to hear and evaluate what we have to say, and we're under karmic obligation to do the same for them. If you want your mate to stop discounting everything you have to say, then stop discounting everything your mate has to say. Try to see the other point of view. Walk a mile in your mate's shoes so that you may become less judgmental, more tolerant, and infinitely more compassionate.

The Fifth Karmic Principle – Before leaving a relationship, we're under karmic obligation to put into practice the first Four Karmic Principles. If, after a reasonable amount of time, nothing changes, then you're karmically free to move on. A reasonable amount of time is determined by several factors, such as how long you've been together, whether you're married, whether there are children involved, and whether you're dealing with a *Cellmate, Soul Mate,* or *Razor's Edge Mate* relationship. The bottom line is that you must follow your heart to determine if and when to throw in the towel.

A Pop Quiz
How Karmically Correct Are You?

To take this quiz you need to think about your current or most recent love relationship and answer the following questions honestly. If you've never been involved in a romantic relationship before, then think about the most significant relationship in your life, be it with a friend, a parent, or a sibling. Answer each question "yes" or "no." Remember, honesty counts!

1) When you want to get your point across, do you tend to raise your voice?

2) Do you wait until things get out of hand before speaking up, and then find yourself crying or

having a temper tantrum to try and express all of your pent-up feelings?

3) Do you only half listen when this person talks to you?

4) Do you discount a lot of things your significant other has to say?

5) Do you keep a great deal of what you're thinking and feeling inside?

6) Are you afraid to tell this person what you need or want?

7) Do you continually threaten to leave this person if he/she doesn't do what you want?

8) Do you practice deep denial when it comes to your own healing issues? For instance: You abuse drugs and alcohol, but refuse to go to rehab, or see a therapist, or attend a twelve-step program.

9) Do you expect this person to read your mind and know what you need even if you don't actually say it?

10) Do you find yourself nagging or screaming at this person in a vain effort to get him/her to change?

11) Do you hate saying you're sorry to this person even when you've intentionally hurt his/her feelings?

Every "yes" answer reveals an instance when you've acted in a karmically incorrect manner.

Now go back and reread each of the Five Karmic Principles. Can you see why your behavior has been karmically incorrect?

In a nutshell, we're acting karmically incorrectly when we scream at our partners, discount what they say, don't listen to what they have to say, don't say what we mean or mean what we say, keep too much bottled up inside, continually threaten to leave them when we have no real intention of doing so, refuse to work on the relationship, and refuse to do something about healing our own issues.

Part Two of this book, DEMYSTIFYING LOVE, will help you deal with many of your unhealed issues. Have faith that by the time you finish reading this book, you'll know how to act in a more unconditionally loving and karmically correct manner, and this way of behaving will come quite naturally to you.

When you've completed all 19 STEPS, revisit this quiz. I guarantee you'll be astounded by how much of your old way of interacting with people has changed.

Leaving a Relationship in a Karmically Correct Manner

A. If you want to end a relationship in a karmically correct manner, you're expected to practice the Five Karmic Principles for a reasonable amount of time before packing up and leaving.

B. If and when you honestly feel you've been prac-
    ticing the Five Karmic Principles, and you've
    done all you feel you can do, and nothing of
    significance has changed, you're karmically
    free to move on.

C. If there's no need for you to have any further
    dealings with this person, then you're free
    from karmic obligation to be involved with
    him/her in any way, shape, or form.

D. If, however, there are children involved or
    some other long-term financial partnership
    or commitment that forces you to still come
    into contact with each other, then you're un-
    der karmic obligation to find a way to deal
    with each other, if not in a friendly manner, at
    least in a civil one.

E. If you find that after practicing the Five
    Karmic Principles you see positive chang-
    es occurring in your relationship, you may
    choose to stay and continue working on the
    relationship.

F. As time goes on, if things revert back to the
    way they were or stop progressing, you're
    under karmic obligation to try once again
    with all your being to move the relation-
    ship forward. If after a reasonable amount
    of time and effort on your part nothing
    changes, you're once again karmically free to
    move on.

Karmic Relationship Cycles

Long-term *Cellmate, Soul Mate,* or *Razor's Edge Mate* relationship karmic cycles tend to run in five-year periods. Keep in mind that this five-year cycle is only one of many cycles, but it's the most common one.

The basic karmic relationship cycle in which people get involved, issues emerge, issues resolve or remain, and the relationship ends or continues, can happen on an hourly, daily, weekly, monthly, or yearly basis, but we're analyzing long-term relationships here, and they tend to follow a five-year plan.

An Example of the Karmic Five-Year Cycle

Let's use a fictionalized couple named Jane and Bob to illustrate the karmic five-year cycle.

Jane and Bob met in college when they were both eighteen years old. There were a lot of unhealed issues between them from the start that made them want to leave each other time and time again. They even broke up several times in the first year, but they always got back together because they couldn't find a replacement fast enough, and neither of them could stand to be alone.

Time passed quickly as the relationship veered along on its stormy path, and then they both graduated from college.

At this point, Jane and Bob decided to move in with each other (it seemed like the logical thing to do), and then they both began focusing on their careers. All the same issues that were there in the beginning were still there, and living together only made this more apparent. Behaviors that might be acceptable at eighteen are no longer acceptable at twenty-three, but neither Jane nor Bob bothered to do anything to improve the relationship. Yet neither of them had the courage to move on (negative karma for both). And so, at the close of the first five-year point, things ended pretty much the same way they started, with two people who each had one foot in the relationship and one foot out the door.

However, at this point they'd reached the age when people tend to marry. So, rather than working on their issues, Jane and Bob swept them under the carpet, and spent the next two years distracting themselves from the problems of their relationship by obsessing about the wedding – an event that lasts but one day. They were twenty-five when they said, "I do."

After they tied the knot, they spent the next few years setting up a "real" home. When that project was finally completed, the problems between them started surfacing big time. Jane and Bob began fighting constantly, and both of them started wondering if they should get a divorce.

Then fear set in as Jane started thinking that she wanted to start a family, and she wasn't getting any younger, and Bob started worrying about what everyone else would think if he decided to get a divorce. And so, Bob and Jane decided to stay together, opening up another five-year karmic cycle.

Bob and Jane saw all their friends starting families, and they, too, started trying to have kids. Two years later, Jane had a baby. At this point, they were so busy with the new addition to the family that they were able to distract themselves from their un-healed issues for a while. But before long, Bob and Jane began fighting once again, realizing they had different ideas about childrearing. Just as their third five-year karmic cycle was finishing, reality set in, as our couple realized they were too in debt and too overwhelmed with parenting to move on, and so they just did what they had always done and stayed put. Just to ensure that nobody went anywhere, Jane had another baby.

You can see how easily a relationship that wasn't supposed to last for more than a few years can go on for decades.

Basically, the five-year karmic relationship cycle corresponds to the natural progression of human existence.

LOVEWORK ASSIGNMENT

We've all watched David Letterman and laughed at his Top Ten List, haven't we? If you haven't, or if you're not sure how to go about this assignment, Google David Letterman's Top Ten List and get a much-needed laugh and some how-to ideas.

If you feel that in your relationships, you haven't been acting in a karmically correct manner, then sit down and write a Top Ten List telling why you need to start acting in a karmically correct way.

Start with the number 10 and work your way down the list.

Use the following Top Ten List as an example.

Top Ten Reasons Why You Need to Start Acting in a Karmically Correct Manner

10. Your preschooler got in trouble in school today for screaming at the top of her lungs at her teacher, "You never listen to a word I say!"

9. You told your husband for the twelfth time this week that you're going to divorce him if he doesn't start picking up his socks, and he said, "Good, I'll go pack your bags."

8. Your neighbors called 911 eight times this week because they kept hearing you scream bloody murder.

7. Your four-year-old says, "You and daddy need a time out!"

6. Your neighbors signed a petition to have you and your husband thrown out of the building because your fights scare the hell out of their pets.

5. You've maxed out your credit cards going to psychics trying to figure out what your husband is thinking.

4. Your kids think their father's first name is Butthead.

3. If and when you and your husband sit down for a meal together, it has to be "sushi and chopsticks" since neither of you can be trusted near the other with sharp objects.

2. Your children's friends say, "When your mom talks to your dad, she reminds us of Cruella De Vil."

1. Your husband spends more time on the Internet in one week than he's spent with you all year.

Top Ten Reasons Why I Need to Start Acting in a
Karmically Correct Manner

I'm Beginning to See a Better Way to Communicate My Feelings

The Big Picture

Try putting into practice what you've learned in this STEP by dealing with everyone you meet in a karmically correct manner. Remember to speak in kind and compassionate words. Say what you mean and mean what you say. Try to really listen when someone is talking to you. Share a heartfelt laugh with others whenever you can.

This karmically correct manner of dealing with others will lead you to the Tenth Rung of Love – *Agape* and Cosmic Consciousness, the unconditional love we feel for all humankind and all the cosmos. In the next STEP, we'll be discussing these concepts in great detail.

The remembrance of *Agape* love and Cosmic Consciousness are buried deep within each of us in our collective unconscious, just waiting to be activated. At this stage of human evolution, Cosmic Consciousness is a higher level of consciousness than most people walking the earth possess. This, of course, will change as we enter more and more into the Age of Aquarius. By taking the study of love seriously, you're stirring up the memory of this higher consciousness.

Every STEP you're taking in your personal journey toward a higher love is reverberating throughout the universe. If each of us were to scale *The Ladder of Love* in this lifetime and attain Cosmic Consciousness, the world would be heaven on earth - - utopia. Humanity would transcend the dualistic and separatist thinking that has led to war. All humankind would be united as one family under God, and the entire universe would be treated with reverence and respect. During our lifetime, unfortunately, this utopian dream will not manifest. But we can all look forward to witnessing this amazing event in our lifetimes to come. How many generations must live and die before we, as a species, achieve this level of consciousness largely depends upon each and every one of us, right in the here and now, doing all we can to advance our own soul's evolution.

Your personal, heartfelt quest for love will ultimately lead you to the transcendent realization of the absolute oneness of the universe, and to the great secret our Creator wants each of us to discover for ourselves – that love is the principal guiding force of the cosmos.

As a species we're destined to achieve this great spiritual evolution, one person at a time. I can't stress enough the importance of your desire to seek a higher love. In the past, this experience of Cosmic Consciousness was a very rare occurrence. But the Age of Aquarius is a time when great numbers of people will experience this heightened sense of awareness. It's God's great hope that you will be one of them.

This is the divine illumination the universe is waiting for.

You've just completed another STEP in your quest for a higher love. Feel confident knowing that the universe wants to grant you your heart's desire.

STEP 9 - AGAPE AND COSMIC CONSCIOUSNESS - HAVING A PERSONAL LOVE AFFAIR WITH THE ENTIRE UNIVERSE

"The peace of God is shining in me now."
(A Course in Miracles, Lesson 188)

TENTH RUNG LOVE

Altruistic, Unconditional Love for All God's Creations

Love is patient and is kind; love doesn't envy;
Love doesn't brag, is not proud, doesn't behave itself inappropriately, doesn't seek its own way, is not
provoked, takes no account of evil, doesn't rejoice in
unrighteousness, but rejoices with the truth, bears all
things, believes all things, hopes all things, endures
all things.
Love never fails. (1 *Corinthians* 13: 4-8)
    (A special thanks to *The World English Bible*
(WEB), a public domain modern English translation
of the *Holy Bible,* for the Biblical quotations used in
this book.)

Replace the word "love" with the word
"Agape" in the passage from Corinthians, and
you will have a very good understanding of the
nature of Agape love.

What is Agape?

Agape (pronounced "ah-gah-pay") is uncon-ditional love for humankind and for all God's cre-ations.

Agape gives reverence to all things. *Agape* love is the type of love that's most often spoken of in the traditional religious texts. *Agape* love is kind, patient, tolerant, and nonjudgmental.

To love this way one has to relax the body, ex-pand the mind to access higher consciousness, open up the heart, and delve deep into the recesses of the soul.

The kind of love God has for us is also *Agape* love. God waits. God is patient with our *Errors in Thinking*. God allows us time to reconsider these er-rors and to correct them. God doesn't judge us, but rather instructs us. God is filled with unconditional love and affection for all the cosmos. So in practicing *Agape*, you'll become more and more Godlike in your behavior.

Agape asks – not, "What you can do for me?" but "What can I do for you?"

Characteristics of Agape Love

Agape love is selfless.
Agape love is characterized by deep humility.
Agape love is overflowing with heartfelt compassion and understanding.

Agape love is given freely without asking, "What's in it for me?" In other words, one loves simply for love's sake without fear or worry related to outcome.

Agape love is kind.

Agape love is tolerant.

Agape love is compassionate.

Agape love waits, for it is infinitely patient.

Agape love is truthful.

Agape love is nonjudgmental.

Agape love is endlessly forgiving.

Agape love is unconditional and all-encompassing.

Agape is the way of peace. When humankind evolves to understand Agape love, and puts this understanding into practice, we'll see a blissful world without war.

Time Traveling to Ancient Greece Once Again

The ancient Athenians, in trying to explain the true nature of love, divided the concept of love into three categories: *Eros, Philia, and Agape.*

Eros

Modern man tends to think of *Eros* as passionate devotion or love that is sexually driven, hence the word erotic.

But Plato and Socrates thought of *Eros* as a desire to seek transcendent beauty by the act of loving another. These ancient philosophers believed that humans came to discover the transcendental beauty of the cosmos by first discovering the beauty inherent in their beloved.

Eros is love given in the great hope that it will be reciprocated. If the object of our affection doesn't return the same kind of feelings, we're devastated. (Most popular songs are based on this type of love and the yearning, longing, and angst that goes hand in hand with the emotionally charged experience of *Eros.*)

Eros is a selfish form of love, for we really need and desire to be loved in return. *Eros* is a way of loving someone with an eye toward the outcome of that love.

Eros asks, "What's in it for me?"

Philia

Philia denotes a fondness for others, a warm, heartfelt devotion, and a loyal friendship and appreciation of another.

Philia friendship is not selfless, for it's often driven by what is best for both parties involved. *Philia* is a two-way street, and therefore, a rather transactional form of love.

In business, *Philia* makes the interactions between individuals pleasant, for one hand readily washes the other.

Philia is referred to as "brotherly love."

Philia asks, "What can we do for each other?"

Agape

Agape is the unconditional love we show toward someone and toward all humankind that doesn't have the quality of, "What's in it for me?" It's an unselfish form of love because it's chiefly concerned with meeting the needs of others.

Agape is a much more abstract kind of love than either *Philia* or *Eros,* since the object of our affection can often be an individual or a group of individuals that we've never met personally.

Agape is a very egalitarian way of loving, for we're *not* supposed to find some people more lovable and worthy than others. For example: in our Judeo-Christian culture, it seems perfectly acceptable to find Muslims unlovable. In practicing *Agape,* we come to realize that the external differences are inconsequential. All paths lead to God. We come to love all human beings regardless of race, color, or creed. Therefore, *Agape* can be seen as the noblest kind of love.

You experience *Agape* love when you willingly help unknown victims of a natural or manmade disaster. There's nothing in this charitable act for you personally, but your heart, soul, body, and God consciousness tell you to do it all the same.

Agape love fills us with inner warmth, an elevated feeling, an inner knowing that we've acted the way God would have wished us to. It's the mindset of, "What would Jesus, Buddha, Moses, or Mohammed do?"

Since *Agape* love asks that we love all humanity, this implies that we must love our enemies as well. *Agape* love is patient, so patient that it waits to win over our opponents, and it allows us to be tolerant, kind, nonjudgmental, merciful, and forgiving in the meantime.

Agape understands that love waits. *Agape* love is always optimistic. *Agape* love believes it has the power to alter the world for the better. This kind of love isn't easily discouraged because, by its very nature, it's patient and enduring.

Agape is love filled with devotion for all humanity. *Agape* love embodies hope, trust, and faith.

Agape asks, "What can I do for you?"

In summary, *Eros* is the romantic love we feel for someone with the great hope and desire that this individual will feel the same way about us. *Philia* is the brotherly love we feel for people we know and interact with. *Agape* is our own personal love affair with all humankind, including all the people we come into contact with and those we've never met.

The Art of Giving and Receiving Love

Eventually, as *Eros* love grows, it will lead you to *Philia* and *Agape* love. *Eros* begins to lose some of its selfishness as you begin to recognize and care for the needs of your beloved. You truly want to be there for the one you love. You learn to honor the needs and concerns of another and stop putting your own needs and wants first. You learn to give and not just take.

Some people are good at giving love, and yet they can't receive it. Others are good at taking love, but can't give love in return. To truly love means to give and receive love in equal measure. In your own life, are you a "Giver?" Are you always giving without expecting anything in return? How do you respond when someone gives you a gift or a compliment? If you have trouble accepting good things, then you need to work on your self-esteem and self-worth issues. In PART TWO of this book, you'll work on learning to love and respect yourself. Know that if we can't accept love, then our mates will continually feel hurt, rejected, and frustrated since they can't seem to please us, no matter how hard they try. Or we could also find ourselves constantly drawing people into our lives who are "Takers."

From the day "Takers" were born they were fed the formula, "Take all and give nothing." Could you be a "Taker?" Do you ignore the needs of your mate? Do your needs always have to come first? Do you buy yourself expensive gifts, yet resent having to buy gifts for others? Do you take your mate for granted? Do you expect to be waited on hand and foot? If so, you need to learn how to give love. People who constantly take and never give are *Energy Vampires*. Their mates feel drained and exhausted, for no one is there to recharge their batteries.

A great, romantic love affair includes all three ways of loving: *Philia,* or loving each other like best friends from the heart and mind; *Eros,* or loving each other with the body and soul via Sacred Sexuality; and *Agape,* or the unselfish, unconditional giving and receiving of love.

The greatest gift is to love and be loved in return.

Some Final Thoughts on Agape Love

Agape love is exemplified in the following New Testament passage: "But I tell you who hear: love your enemies, do good to those who hate you, bless those who curse you, and pray for those who mistreat you. To him who strikes you on the cheek, offer also the other; and from him who takes your cloak, don't withhold your coat also" (Luke 6: 27-32, WEB version).

God hopes a great love will bring us to the sacred knowledge that there is "nothing above, save God; nothing below, save humankind."

The word "save" has many meanings. To truly understand the above expression, you must understand all the meanings of the word "save." "Save" can mean to help or to rescue from harm. It can also mean to keep safe or to safeguard. It further means to deliver from sin. "Save" can also mean "with the exception of"; so, therefore, you can substitute the words "except" or "but" for "save."

LOVEWORK ASSIGNMENT

"Nothing above, save God; nothing below, save humankind."

Read the passage above over and over again, until you understand all the meanings of the word "save." Then meditate on these sacred words. Think of them as a mantra. Say this mantra often.

This mantra can help you attain the Tenth Rung on *The Ladder of Love, Agape* love and Cosmic Consciousness, as well as the Eleventh Rung, *Unio Mystica* or *The Mystical Union with God,* which we'll explore in STEP 10.

Recommended Reading

To gain a deeper understanding of *Agape,* a good book to read is *Agape Love* by John Marks Templeton. His exhaustive study of the world's major religions reveals the truth that the concept of *Agape* love is universal to all.

You can also read traditional religious texts, since they all contain many passages about *Agape* love. For instance, try reading The New Testament, *The Dhammapada, The Torah, The Koran,* or *The Upanishads* to see how many examples of *Agape* love you can discover. Write down these passages and read them often!

LOVEWORK ASSIGNMENT

Reflect upon the times in your life when you have experienced *Agape* love, either by giving love and assistance without expecting something in return, or when others have performed unselfish acts of love and assistance for you. Reflect upon how you felt at those times. Write down some of your thoughts.

My Reflections on *Agape* Love

Agape Love Graces the World with Miracles

Cosmic Consciousness or Universal Consciousness

Agape love will lead us to Cosmic Consciousness. Cosmic Consciousness is our collective sense of affection and affinity for, and oneness with, all of God's creations. This cosmic connection is a spiritual and intellectual illumination in which we gain an inner knowingness that life is eternal, only love is real, and everything in the cosmos has a spirit.

Cosmic Consciousness is not something you find outside of yourself, some kind of Holy Grail you seek. It already exists within each of us, buried in the deepest recesses of our collective unconscious. Know that the divine light of this illuminating state of being burns within you. You're under karmic obligation to discover it.

The key to opening the portals to this highest level of consciousness is our own personal experience of Enlightenment, in which we have the Biblical moment on the mountaintop when transfiguration occurs, and we see the entire universe through our spiritual third eye. Suddenly, the once unfathomable mysteries of the cosmos become clear to us.

When we achieve this heightened state of awareness, the immortals begin channeling vast volumes of information and knowledge to us, and our emotional, psychological, spiritual, and intellectual growth evolves in quantum leaps.

The divine gift of *Twinsoulship* or any *Mirror Soul* relationship carries with it the remembrance of Cosmic Consciousness. Just as *Sacred Duad* and *Serene Sacred Duad* relationships are rare occurrences at this stage of human evolution, so is this peak higher consciousness experience a rarity. However, as we advance further into the Age of Aquarius, and as people begin to do their inner spiritual work, the human race will rapidly embrace the concept of universal consciousness. The great gift this higher consciousness brings is the promise of a blissful universe filled with peace, joy, love, and harmony.

To learn more about this peak experience, read *Cosmic Consciousness,* by Dr. Richard Maurice Bucke. This book, published in 1901, predates the psychological work of both Freud and Jung. This revolutionary book, which was light years ahead of its time, proves that eternal truths are just that – everlasting and timeless. When reading this book, however, you must keep in mind the era in which it was written (as we had to do earlier in our study of Plato). Keeping the timeframe of when he lived in mind, you won't be offended by some of the word choices he uses; the fact that he basically believes that Cosmic Consciousness is province of the male gender; or by some of his observations and conclusions, which could be construed as racist and politically incorrect.

Dr. Bucke describes the experience of Cosmic Consciousness as a deep awareness that the entire cosmos is a vibrant, living presence. This higher consciousness reveals the human soul to be immortal, and the universe divinely ordered for the collective good of all. Most important is the revelation that the founding principle of the universe was none other than – love.

Dr. Bucke further asserts that every new faculty of higher power we, as a human race, acquired had to be attained first by one individual. This is a phenomenal awareness for you to come to, so let me say it again. Every new faculty of higher power we, as a human race, acquired had to be attained first by **one individual.** That solitary individual then revealed to the world another human skill which all human beings could attain, although in reality, it would take thousands of years for the entire race to acquire that same skill.

Dr. Bucke felt that this rare form of higher consciousness had been experienced by only a small number of people who walked the earth. Among these rare individuals were Buddha, Jesus, Mohammed, Dante, William Blake, Francis Bacon, and Walt Whitman. In his book, Dr. Bucke describes the cosmic awakening each of these men experienced. Reading this section of his book leaves you with an elevated feeling that you have just walked in the footprints of these immortals.

Despite its shortcomings, this extraordinary book remains a classic work of mysticism. (Read more about mysticism in STEP 10.)

To further your understanding of Cosmic Consciousness, read any of Eckhart Tolle's books. He is a contemporary spiritual teacher who is working hard to usher in this new higher consciousness.

Agape and Cosmic Consciousness in Action

To learn how to put *Agape* into action, read and learn about Mother Teresa, Albert Schweitzer, and Mahatma Gandhi. There are countless books, articles, documentaries, and films about the lives of these three outstanding humanitarians. I've included a brief biography of each of these extraordinary beings, but I highly recommend that you do some in-depth exploration of these three people who truly represent the concepts of *Agape* and Cosmic Consciousness.

Mother Teresa of Calcutta

Mother Teresa (August 26, 1910 - September 5, 1997) was a Catholic nun who founded the Missionaries of Charity in Calcutta, India. There she tended to the needs of the orphaned, the destitute, and the dying.

In 1979, when Mother Teresa was awarded the Nobel Peace Prize, she asked not to have a banquet in her honor, which was the usual protocol for laureates; instead, she requested that the money set aside for the banquet be given to the poor in Calcutta.

Upon receiving the award, Mother Teresa was asked what each of us could do to promote world peace. She answered, "Go home and love your family."

The book *Come Be My Light: The Private Writings of the Saint of Calcutta* reveals the inner turmoil and the long, dark night of the soul that Mother Teresa experienced over the course of her life. In reading this book, we can all take comfort in knowing that we can have a crisis of faith, and we can have negative thoughts, but our words and deeds speak the real truth as we answer our divine calling, even when to do so fills us with angst.

Albert Schweitzer

Albert Schweitzer, M.D., O.M. (January 14, 1875 - September 4, 1965) also received the Nobel Peace Prize. This prize was awarded to him for his philosophy of "reverence for life," which he put into practice by becoming a medical missionary and founding and maintaining a hospital in Africa.

Dr. Schweitzer's views on life and love were based on the acknowledgement that we must cultivate a will to live, and we must honor that same will to live as it manifests throughout the universe.

He further believed that each of us must find and maintain an intimate spiritual relationship with all of God's creations.

Mahatma Gandhi, "The Missing Laureate"

Mahatma Gandhi, "*the Great-souled*" (October 2, 1869 - January 30, 1948), was a major spiritual and political leader of India and of the Indian independence movement.

He advocated nonviolent civil disobedience as a way to effect change. He tirelessly campaigned for an end to poverty, for the liberation of women, and for a comradeship among all people regardless of religious, cultural, racial, or ethnic differences.

The fact that he was nominated for a Nobel Peace Prize five times, including just a few days before his assassination in January 1948, and yet never received one, has come back to haunt the reputation of the Norwegian Nobel Committee and cast a shadow over the Nobel Prize itself.

The obvious omission of this legendary man, who espoused the philosophy of peaceful resistance, bespeaks loudly the *Errors in Thinking* inherent in the members of the Norwegian Nobel Committee. Time and time again, they succumbed to the fear of the political backlash that would occur if they gave the award to this controversial figure.

But, we can all take comfort knowing that accolades and worldly goods meant nothing to this Enlightened man anyway. He did what he did for the good it would accomplish and not for the recognition it could bring him.

Recommended Reading

The Best Gift is Love: Meditations by M. Teresa, compiled and edited by Sean-Patrick Lovett

Blessed Mother Teresa: Her Journey to Your Heart, by T.T. Mundakel

Out of My Life and Thought: An Autobiography, by Albert Schweitzer

Gandhi: His Life and Message for the World, by Louis Fischer

LOVEWORK ASSIGNMENT

Over the next few days, reflect upon your life, family, community, and career to see how you can be a missionary of *Agape* in your everyday life. For instance: Could you start a fundraiser for a worthy cause; volunteer your skills and services to help the aged, the infirm, or children in need; give your time or money to a food bank; get involved with a project to clean up the environment; or check in on an elderly neighbor?

God doesn't ask that you go off to some remote area of the world to offer your services to humanity; He asks that you do what you can, right where you are.

What Can I Do to Help Make My World a Better Place?

I Am Becoming Love in Action

Taking the Next STEP

There is only one Rung left to explore on *The Ladder of Love.* In STEP 10, we'll take a great leap of faith together as we discuss the greatest love of all – our personal love affair with God.

Each STEP you've taken thus far has prepared your heart, soul, mind, and body for the higher love that is your birthright.

Take a moment to sit with God right now. Say a prayer – any prayer. Make one up or simply tell God what's in your heart. Then ask God to grant you a higher love. Then close your eyes and meditate for a few minutes.

Remember that prayer is your way of talking to God, and meditation allows you to hear God's response.

Each STEP you complete leads you closer to the love you desire. Take a moment to give thanks for lessons learned.

STEP 10 - YOUR INTIMATE RELA-TIONSHIP WITH GOD

"I rest in God today, and let Him work in me and through me, while I rest in Him in quiet and in perfect certainty."
(*A Course in Miracles,* Lesson 120)

ELEVENTH RUNG LOVE

The Greatest Love of All

Unio Mystica - The Mystical Union with God

God is Love

The following passage from the New Testament, "Don't judge, and you won't be judged. Don't condemn, and you won't be condemned." (Luke 6:37, WEB version), helps us to understand the kind of unconditional love God has for us.

In the next New Testament passage, we can further see how God loves us: "Beloved, let us love one another, for love is of God; and everyone who loves is born of God, and knows God. He who doesn't love doesn't know God, for God is love." (1 John 4: 7-9, WEB version).

A great love will bring you first to *Agape,* with its deep love for all humankind, then to Cosmic Consciousness, and ultimately to the great desire to have an intimate relationship with your Maker.

Having a personal relationship with the Creator can be a difficult thing to envision, if you have a distorted image of God. Do you have a dogmatic view of God that has been hammered into your head from when you were a child going to Sunday school? Do you fear the wrath of God, remembering the vengeful God of the Old Testament who unleashed His fury in the form of plagues and floods? Do you fear having a personal relationship with God because you view Him as a chastising parental figure? Or perhaps you feel unworthy to talk directly to God, and so you allow a priest, a rabbi, or some other "holy person" to do the talking for you. If you feel any of the above sentiments, then it's time you and God got reacquainted.

God is love. That's the plain and simple truth. God is love. Know that every step you take toward love is a step toward God, and that every step you take along the path of fear is a step away from God.

God's Great Love for You

The more you open your heart to *Agape* love, the more you'll come to see how God loves you.

If you're judgmental and harsh, then you'll continue to see God in the same light. As you become more compassionate, tolerant, and merciful, watch how your vision of God changes.

Remember that *Agape* love also refers to the kind of love God feels for us. God's love is steadfast, merciful, patient, tolerant, nonjudgmental, kind, enduring, generous, willingly given, neverending, forgiving, understanding, just, gentle, and compassionate.

God is Calling. Why Aren't You Answering?

When we have a dogmatic view of God, we tend to have this once-a-week church or temple thing going on. This weekly nod to God is oftentimes done out of guilt and a superstitious belief that if we don't go, God will punish us, and if we do go, God will reward us. It's the fear of God that keeps us bound to our weekly Sabbath ritual, with little thought given to God between these token visits.

The Eleventh Rung on *The Ladder of Love* invites you to have a different kind of relationship with God – a one-on-one, day-to-day, loving one. Weekly religious services are great, but God likes to hear from you often, spontaneously and joyfully, without a sense of obligation or duty. As you become more intimately acquainted with the unconditional love God offers, you'll see and welcome The Divine One in every moment of your day.

Unio Mystica

Unio Mystica is the experience of an intimate relationship with God in which you don't need an intermediary in the form of an "ordained holy person" to speak for you. Rather, you speak directly to God whenever and wherever you wish. You begin to have a divine love affair with God, and this deep intimacy and heartfelt closeness becomes your guiding light.

When we attain this exalted height on *The Ladder of Love,* the *Unio Mystica,* the search is over; we have come home. While we're still on earth, we witness the eternal truth that we were never separated from God in the first place, for God is within us. We know in our heart of hearts that this separation was but an illusion.

Reaching this Enlightened Rung of Love doesn't mean you stop being yourself. Nor does it mean you have no personal likes and dislikes. It just means that you become the true *you* that you were meant to be. You become the benevolent master of your destiny. You're no longer the puppet of pop culture and Madison Avenue.

Unio Mystica ultimately fills us with deep, heartfelt joy, peace, love, compassion, and serenity.

Sometimes people come to have an intimate relationship with God (*Unio Mystica*) after they've been given a *Soul Mate* relationship. Through the brilliant light and immense power of this higher love, they heal their issues and come to a deep place within that radiates peace, joy, and gratitude. In this inner state of bliss, they find God. Still others may first obtain a great love of humanity (*Agape* love), or have a great love affair with God, and then be given a *Soul Mate* to further their spiritual growth.

Just remember, we're all capable of having an intimate relationship with God, regardless of what path takes us there.

Mystics

The word "mystic" denotes different things to different people. Some people think it has something to do with the occult, cult-like New Age religions, or ancient mystery sects, while still others think mystics are heretics.

But mystics are simply Enlightened people, from any time or any place, who seek to commune with God through direct experience, trusting their own insights, visions, transcendent experiences and perceptions in an effort to return to oneness with God and with the universe (Cosmic Consciousness).

Kabbalah is a mystical movement within Judaism. Islamic mysticism is known as Sufism. One kind of mysticism in the Christian religion is Gnosticism.

Traditionally, mystics have sought, through the study of religious texts, meditation, contemplation, transcendental experiences, prayer, or a life of asceticism and sacrifice, to have a deep, personal communion with the Divine. In the past, many of these esoteric methods of seeking God were shrouded in mystery because organized religions forbade them, and furthermore it was believed that a person could attain this knowledge only through secret teachings.

Putting it in the simplest terms, the goal of mysticism is to have a sacred union with God in this life.

The Way of the Mystic
Mystics:

- Honor the divine source within.
- See the world through their spiritual eye (third eye).
- Know they are eternal spiritual beings housed in a temporal body.
- Hunger for true knowledge.
- Do not pursue the past or lose themselves in the future.
- Live in the here and now.
- Live in a state of joy and gratitude.
- Commune regularly with those who have passed on, with angels, Ascended Masters, spirit guides, saints, and God.
- Know that everything has a spirit and pay homage to that spirit.
- Search tirelessly for truth.
- Need solitude.
- Seek deep and meaningful communion with others.
- See God in everything, in everyone, and everywhere.
- Continually worship God with all they do, bear witness to, and say.
- Offer their whole life to God as a prayer.
- Are awake, aware, and Enlightened beings.
- Practice loving-kindness.
- Cultivate universal compassion.
- Seek not to judge, for they are tolerant and patient.

- Recognize laughter as a holy sound.
- Believe it's all good.
- Are ever mindful of their thoughts, feelings, and deeds.
- Are people of their word.
- Closely observe the world around them.
- Love unconditionally.
- Are wise beings.
- Bring healing and peace wherever they go.
- Know that love dispels hate.
- Live free from fear, for they possess courage.
- Are not attached to the material possessions of the world, but are grateful for what they have.
- Are free from craving.
- Are beacons of light and joy wherever they go.
- Bring the message of God to all they meet.
- Are peaceful and serene, for they know the oneness of all things, having achieved Enlightenment and Cosmic Consciousness.
- Surrender to the will of God.
- Painstakingly seek to know the secrets of eternity.
- Passionately answer their sacred calling by honoring the *Yang Factor*. (Read more about the *Yang Factor* in STEP 11.)

You as a Modern-Day Mystic

From the above list of mystical traits, you can see that to walk in the footsteps of a mystic means we have some pretty big sandals to fill! But God isn't asking you to be Moses or Muhammed; God is asking you to be you – the real you, the eternal you.

In this new millennium, know that it's not only possible, but greatly encouraged, that all of us seek a personal and intimate relationship with God. "Ask and you shall receive." It's really that simple.

For the first time in history, we're asked to be "mystics" and "monks" in our everyday lives. This doesn't mean that God wants you to go off and live in some remote hermitage. Quite the contrary, God asks that wherever you choose to live, whatever profession you practice, you become a beacon of light and help raise the vibration and consciousness of everyone you meet.

There is a Buddhist expression, "Before Enlightenment there is chopping wood and carrying water. After Enlightenment there is chopping wood and carrying water." In other words, everything changes deep within us, while everything on the surface may still remain the same. If things should, however, change drastically on the surface, it's because all that is untrue must fade away, making way for that which is real and permanent.

In the dawn of this New Age, God is asking you to master both the material world and the spiritual world. This is the first time in the history of humanity that God is revealing to each and every one of us that we're all gurus and Anointed Ones. God wants you to talk the talk, walk the walk, and take your spiritual show on the road. God doesn't need you to go off and live on a mountaintop. God needs you, right here and now, to make your life an everyday ministry.

God realizes the enormity of this task. It's much easier to be a spiritual being when you're safely tucked away in a monastery where everyone you deal with on a day-to-day basis is on a spiritual path. It's infinitely easier to stay calm and peaceful when you don't have to worry about scratching a living out of the earth or putting food on the table for you and your family. It's not easy to stay serene as you try to raise your children in a fast-paced world, juggle a career, and try to have quality time for your love life. Undeniably, it's much harder to master the spiritual world when you're knee-deep in the muck and mire of daily living. But remember, everything is possible with God. In due time, you'll learn to be in this world, but not of it.

In this life or in another, you'll come to the place of nirvana, of inner peace. Suffering will cease to be when you crave nothing. You'll come to know that it's all good, and obstacles and problems won't be seen as bad or negative. Rather, they'll be seen in a positive light – as opportunities to learn and grow.

There's no denying that you'll still encounter difficulties, no matter how "Enlightened" you become. You'll still freeze to death out in the cold without proper clothing and starve to death without food. This proves that while we inhabit the earth plane, we must never forget that our immortal soul is temporarily housed in an all-too-mortal body.

But as you grow in spirit, you'll learn to face fearlessly whatever you must, knowing you have the tools with which to cope. You'll learn serenity – changing what you can, accepting what you can't change, and having the wisdom to know the difference.

Don't worry about possessing all the previously mentioned traits of a mystic. It's something to work toward and strive for. God loves you unconditionally. God is patient. God waits.

No one can tell you what kind of relationship you should have with God. Each of us has to find that out for ourselves. Just know that in learning about love, you're learning about yourself and about God.

To learn more about mysticism and Gnosticism, a good starting point would be to read works by and about William Blake, Carl Jung, Baruch Spinoza, Arthur Schopenhauer, Madame Blavatsky, W.B. Yeats, Walt Whitman, Dante, and Henry David Thoreau.

To learn about Sufism, you could start by reading the poetry of Rumi or Hafez.

To learn about Jewish mysticism, you could start by reading the works of Martin Buber or by studying Kabbalah.

How Can I Have an Intimate Relationship with God?

- In order to have an intimate relationship with God, you have to know who you are. This takes a great deal of soul searching. The second part of this book, DEMYSTIFYING LOVE, will help you get to know yourself intimately. When we know ourselves intimately, we can know God intimately as well.
- A good starting point for anyone who wants to have a more personal relationship with God would be to find your calling or to do some meaningful or creative work.
- Praying and asking God for help is another good way.
- Meditation or practicing the art of being in silence by stopping all the mindless chitchat

is another way of being intimate with God. In silence we can wait and listen for God's answers.

♦ Working on making all your relationships "soulful" ones is another good way.

♦ Learning all you can about the nature of love is another path.

♦ Doing your inner homework by going to therapy, a twelve-step program, spiritual retreats, lectures, or workshops can lead to a deeper relationship with God. Attending church or temple if you're so inclined certainly helps, but if the dogma of your religion hampers your spiritual growth, then you must honestly deal with whether your experience with organized religion is helping or hindering you on your path toward God.

♦ Getting more in touch with nature can do it for some people.

♦ Doing some charity work helps others.

♦ Reading religious texts or spiritual books helps others to connect with God.

♦ Spending some time around children or pets can open your heart to God.

♦ Chanting can be another way to feel close to God.

♦ Listening to music can open your heart and soul to love and to God.

♦ Doing Yoga, dancing, singing, and playing an instrument can help tap into the God Source. The Sufis did the dance of the Whirling Dervish to feel at one with God.

♦ Try different things and see where they take you.

Recommended Reading

How to Know God, by Deepak Chopra

Your Sacred Self, by Wayne W. Dyer

Metaphysical Meditations, by Paramahansa Yogananda

Love Burning in the Soul: The Story of the Christian Mystics from Saint Paul to Thomas Merton, by James Harpur

The Essential Rumi, translated by Coleman Barks

The Prophet, by Kahlil Gibran

The Essential Kabbalah: The Heart of Jewish Mysticism, by Daniel C. Matt

Spend some time in the library, bookstore, or browsing the Web to find other books that will open your heart to God.

LOVEWORK ASSIGNMENT

Take some time to reflect upon your current relationship with God. Are you happy with that relationship? How could you improve your relationship? Write down any words, phrases, or thoughts that characterize your feelings about God. From time to time review this list. Add to or delete from this list as you continue reading this book and your vision of love and God change.

My Relationship with God

I Vow to Have a More Personal Relationship with God

Before we go to PART TWO – DEMYSTIFYING LOVE, let's take one more, quick look at the Rungs on *The Ladder of Love.*

A Brief Overview of the Rungs on *The Ladder of Love*

Cellmates

- ◆ First Rung – Brutal, Conditional Love

- ◆ Second Rung – Still Brutal, Conditional Love

- ◆ Third Rung – Interchangeable Conditional Love

Razor's Edge Mates

- ◆ Fourth Rung – "The Old Ball and Chain" Conditional Love

- ◆ Fifth Rung – Old Archetype Marriage – Conditional Love

Soul Mates

- ◆ Sixth Rung – New Archetype Marriage – Unconditional Love

- ◆ Seventh Rung – Seventh Heaven Love – Unconditional Love

- ◆ Eighth Rung – *Twin Souls* – Unconditional Love

♦ Ninth Rung – *Mirror Souls* – Unconditional Love

Cosmic Love

♦ Tenth Rung – *Agape* and Cosmic Consciousness (Love of all God's creations) – Unconditional Love

♦ Eleventh Rung – *Unio Mystica* – Unconditional Love

A Quick Review of PART I

You've reached the halfway point in your journey toward a higher love. This is an important milestone for you and should be recognized as such.

Before proceeding to PART II, I highly recommend that you go back over PART I to be sure you understand the concepts and terminology given there. You really need a thorough understanding of the material we've covered thus far before attempting the next part.

The Teacher archetype in me can't resist giving you a Love Test to help you review the material we've covered in PART I.

First see how many questions you can answer without using the book. Then, feel free to use the book to find the answers. Doing this test will help you see how much you've learned thus far, and which areas you still need to review before proceeding.

The Love Test

1) The opposite of love is _____.
2) What word means there are no coincidences?
   _____
3) What is the new astrological age that we're entering into called? _____
4) What astrological age are we leaving? _____
5) What do we call the kind of love that is contingent upon behavior, either ours or someone else's? _____
6) What do we call the kind of love that is a divine gift, freely given, with no strings attached?
   _____
7) Our romantic mates are meant to be with us forever. True or False?
8) We have to hate someone to leave them. True or False?
9) Love is a compromise. True or False?
10) Love is conditional. True or False?
11) Love is going to rescue us. True or False?
12) When two people love each other in a romantic way, it means they own each other. True or False?
13) We're capable of loving another even if we hate ourselves. True or False?
14) Please list the SEVEN TENETS OF MANIFEST DESTINY:

    I.
    II.
    III.
    IV.
    V.

VI.

VII.

15) What do we call a romantic relationship that shows some characteristics of a *Cellmate* relationship and some characteristics of a *Soul Mate* relationship? _____

16) *Soul Mates* bring out the best in us. True or False?

17) What do we call recurring personality types, stereotypical in nature, that are common to a culture, a people, and, to a large extent, all human beings, and whose images are housed in our collective unconscious? _____

18) In our relationships, it's healthy to play out the roles of rescuer, victim, and persecutor. True or False?

19) You should aspire to have a First Rung Love relationship. True or False?

20) What Rung on *The Ladder of Love* is all about ego, power, and trying to impress the world with our trophy mate – who, by the way, is easily exchanged for a new, better model? _____

21) We want to perpetuate the old archetype of marriage in our relationships. True or False?

22) What do you call the Goddess energy of your soul or higher consciousness which is stored in the base of your spine? _____

23) What word do we use to describe the spiritual awakening that allows us to see the world through the tolerant, compassionate, and nonjudgmental eyes of God? _____

24) What do we call the divinely guided, pre-birth contracts we make with our *Soul Mates*? _____

25) What do we call the untimely ending of a *Soul Mate* relationship? _____

26) What Rung on *The Ladder of Love* represents the new archetype of marriage? _____

27) At this stage of human consciousness, *Twin Soul* relationships almost always end in "Happily Ever After." True or False?

28) What do we call the lessons we have incarnated on earth to learn? _____

29) *Twin Soul* relationships can only take place between people of the opposite sexes. True or False?

30) *Twin Souls* usually meet in their very first incarnation. True or False?

31) *Agape* is the Greek word for "brotherly love." True or False?

32) We have only one *Mirror Soul.* True or False?

33) What do we call the relationship that is composed of the **Sacred Duad** known as *Twin Souls* and one *Mirror Soul?* _____

34) There are three Karmic Principles that govern relationships. True or False?

35) *Cellmate* and *Soul Mate* **Celestial Contracts** tend to run in six-year cycles. True or False?

36) What do we call the kind of love that's unconditional for all humanity and for all of God's creations? _____

37) *Eros* is another word for "brotherly love." True or False?

38) What do we call the mystical union with God?
_____

39) The goal of mysticism is to have a sacred union with God in this life. True or False?

40) Mystics are people whom we would never meet in our everyday life because they have to live in a monastery or off on a mountaintop. True or False?

Once you have finished the Love Test, you've earned your wings to fly into PART II. (Answers to the Love Test are at the end of this STEP.)

Moving On to PART II

In PART II, we'll be demystifying love by studying in detail the Eight Golden Rules of Love.

Take a moment to read the brief overview of these rules to familiarize yourself with them before proceeding to PART II.

A Quick Look at The Eight Golden Rules of Love

The First Golden Rule of Love – Know Thyself

The Second Golden Rule of Love – Love Thyself

The Third Golden Rule of Love – Learn to believe in the Sacred Law of Synchronicity, which states: The meeting of two people which leads to love is never accidental.

The Fourth Golden Rule of Love – Perfect love asks that we love our *Soul Mate* with our entire heart, soul, mind, and body.

The Fifth Golden Rule of Love – True love calls for us to surrender our entire heart, soul, mind, and body to its power.

The Sixth Golden Rule of Love – True love asks that we commit to our *Soul Mate* with our entire heart, soul, mind, and body.

The Seventh Golden Rule of Love – Heal Thyself

The Eighth Golden Rule of Love – If two people meet and then separate, know there were powerful lessons to be learned in their communion, and still more powerful ones to be learned in their separation.

Congratulations – You've made it to the halfway mark. Have faith. A great love is awaiting you.

According to the ancient science of numerology, the number 10 is a karmic number (representing accrued good karma), and signifies completion and rebirth.

Know that the completion of these first 10 STEPS marks the halfway point in your journey toward a higher love.

Rejoice in the knowledge that your diligent efforts are being applauded by the universe.

You've already accrued a great deal of good karma, and in the remaining 9 STEPS, we'll work hard to clear away the *Errors in Thinking* and behaving that keep you from obtaining a higher love.

Answers to the Love Test

1) Fear

2) Synchronicity

3) The Age of Aquarius

4) The Age of Pisces

5) Conditional love

6) Unconditional love

7) False

8) False

9) False

10) False

11) False

12) False

13) False

14) I. Ask and you shall receive. II. Practice the art of positive conversation. III. Honor the Laws of Karma. IV. Cultivate Clear Vision. V. The Good Faith Performing of Labors of Love. VI. Patiently Wait for a Higher Love to Manifest, for it is Your Destiny. VII. Every Morning when You Wake Up and Every Evening Before You Go to Sleep, Say the Higher Love Prayer.

15) Razor's Edge Relationship or *Razor's Edge Mates*

16) True

17) Archetypes

18) False

19) False

20) Third Rung – Interchangeable Conditional Love

21) False

22) Kundalini Energy

23) Enlightenment

24) Celestial Contracts

25) A *Sacred Betrayal*

26) Sixth Rung – New Archetype Marriage – Unconditional Love

27) False

28) Karmic lessons

29) True

30) False

31) False

32) False

33) A *Sacred Trinity*

34) False: There are Five Karmic Principles That Govern Relationships.

35) False: *Celestial Contracts* tend to run in five-year cycles.

36) Agape

37) False: *Philia* is brotherly love.

38) Unio Mystica

39) True

40) False

The End of Part I

PART II

DEMYSTIFYING LOVE

STEP 11 – UNDERSTANDING THE FIRST GOLDEN RULE OF LOVE

"The shadowy figures from the past are precisely what you must escape."
(A Course in Miracles, Chapter 13)

The First Golden Rule of Love – Know Thyself

In order to truly know yourself, you must look deep within and bring forth all that is hidden. Needless to say, this can be a frightening experience at times. Please trust that all the divine guidance you need to make your inner journey easier will be provided. You are not alone. I am right there beside you, and your angels, spirit guides, deceased loved ones, and God all walk with you as well.

Unmasking the Shadow Self

Understand that from this day forward, you're going to see your life in a whole new light by bringing forth the shadows and the darkness. You'll come to see that you have the innate ability to learn from the past, let it go, and choose again.

Know that what you keep hidden will destroy you. Expect what you bring forth to heal you.

In confronting the shadow, fear inevitably will arise. When fear arises, we instinctively run. Visualize fear as a huge attack dog. When a dog is charging at you and you run, it will continue charging after you. If, however, you override your initial impulse to run and stand still, the dog will instinctively retreat. The same truth holds for fear – don't run, don't hide, don't distract, stay still. In the stillness, answers will come.

You'll soon learn to ride the tsunami of panic. Fear will no longer drag you down or drag you out to sea. The terrifying feeling that you're drowning in fear will soon pass.

The human body is biologically constructed in such a way that panic can only last for so long. Panic, by its very nature, is an extremely physically, emotionally, psychologically, and spiritually exhausting force, and we soon find ourselves collapsing under the weight of it.

Patience, fortitude, and courage are powerful allies to conjure up when the panic button goes off. In the end – the truth shall set you free.

In this STEP, you're going to work on bringing forth the hidden parts of yourself. Fasten your seatbelt and hold tight. Before long you'll learn the secret of who you really are. Digging deep within is the only way to become the true, authentic self you were meant to be. *A false self will surely find a false love. A true self will surely find a true love.*

Remember – An authentic self will find an authentic love.

In this STEP, we have limited time to cover the topic of the shadow self. I strongly suggest you read one or all of the following books to further enhance your understanding of this fascinating topic: *Owning Your Own Shadow Self,* by Robert A. Johnson; *Tarot and the Journey of the Hero,* by Hajo Banzhaf; *Guilt is the Teacher, Love is the Lesson,* by Joan Borysenko, Ph.D.; and Debbie Ford's *The Secret of the Shadow* and *The Dark Side of the Light Chasers.*

The poet Robert Bly metaphorically compared our shadow to a big bag we drag behind us.

The Shadow and the Persona

The shadow self is the part of us that we keep hidden. Our persona is the part of ourselves that we reveal to the world. The shadow self is revealed behind closed doors, when we're intoxicated, or when a life-altering experience rips off our mask. Sometimes we're blessed with a dear companion who allows us, even briefly, to reveal the shadow, and for a moment the weight of the world seems lifted from our shoulders. Our persona consists of the mask or masks we wear when we're out in public.

To come face to face with the shadow, we must first give up our distractions and our addictions.

Our distractions and addictions keep us in a state of deep denial. When we have a habit so big that we can't control it, know the shadowy side of ourselves is rearing its ugly head and saying, "Pay attention to me."

Twelve-step programs are brilliant in their understanding that our higher self or spiritual self needs to be known if we're to overcome our addictions. Although addictions have their roots in obsessive-compulsive tendencies, peer pressure, genetics, and a host of other factors, one aspect of our being that continually feeds addictions is a **shame-based identity.** Our desperate need to hide our feelings of shame not only from the world, but from ourselves, keeps us enslaved to our addictive behaviors. In essence, our addictions serve as an outlet for all the bottled-up thoughts and emotions we work so hard to keep under check while masquerading around in our persona. Our addictions help us to distract, deny, and run from our true feelings.

Healthy Shame and Pernicious Shame

There is healthy shame that we *learn* as a child. This shame teaches us that certain parts of our bodies are private, and we soon learn not to go running naked in the streets. This healthy shame is nature's way of protecting children from sexual predators.

Human beings also possess *innate* shame, which is housed in the collective unconscious as a protective survival tool for the species. This healthy shame helps us to develop a conscience, so we can live in the civilized world. Without healthy shame we'd all become antisocial, sociopathic, or even psychopathic. Healthy shame teaches us boundaries of socially acceptable behavior, and allows us to become part of the tribe known as the human race.

Pernicious shame is *unhealthy shame* that is learned. Traditionally in our culture, we were told not to air our "dirty laundry" in public. However, in recent years, television talk shows have allowed people to publicly vent a great deal of this pernicious shame. Whether we like these shows or not, they do serve a cathartic purpose, hence the popularity of this kind of "let it all hang out as we duke it out" type of reality talk show. These shows, as obnoxious and lower-chakra-mentality as they are, serve a purpose by bringing forth the shadowy side of human behavior.

Learning More About Pernicious Shame

Pernicious shame is unhealthy, learned shame that makes us feel there's something fundamentally wrong with us, and as a result we become shame-based people. It's as if the core of our being is rotten, and no matter what we do, or how hard we try, we can't escape the truth of our inherent unworthiness. We then create a new self (false as it may be), hoping that no one will ever see the real evil that lurks within us.

The creation of the false self forces us to live in a state of nervous agitation, knowing that someday, somehow, someone will discover the truth about us – that deep down inside we're damaged goods, unworthy and undeserving. No matter how competent, gifted, or talented we may be in reality, we'll always feel like an impostor, and we can't escape the uneasy feeling that it's only a matter of time before the jig will be up. (We develop what's known as an "impostor complex.")

What Causes Us to Become a Shame-Based Person?

People who have been sexually, physically, or psychologically abused; exploited; unwanted; raised by alcoholic or drug-addicted parents; abandoned; neglected; raised in poverty in a world surrounded by material wealth; or raised by parents of a different ethnic, cultural, or religious background than that of the norm; are prone to develop pernicious shame.

Reconnecting with spirit and remembering our true self is the only cure for shame-based behavior with its myriad addictions. Our addicted behaviors can take many forms, including alcohol and drug abuse, workaholism, overeating, anorexia and/ or excessive worry about fitness and health, compulsive shopping or gambling, impulse shoplifting, and religious fanaticism, to name just a few. If we don't heal the core issue of pernicious shame, we'll just go around and around this wheel of addictions, trading in one addiction for another, falsely believing we're cured.

When we go from an addiction like alcoholism, which is always viewed as negative behavior, to a more socially acceptable addiction, such as being a workaholic, we can delude ourselves and the rest of the world into believing that we're healed. We're not healed. We've just spun the wheel of addiction and landed on a somewhat safer space. A healed being instinctively knows when something is becoming excessive and seeks to bring balance back into life.

How Can I Distinguish My True Self from My False Self?

1. Our true self knows how to love unconditionally.
2. Our false self only knows how to love conditionally.
3. Our false self is highly judgmental of others.

4. Our false self is intolerant and highly envious of someone who appears to be living an authentic life.

5. Our false self seeks inauthentic power. Inauthentic power is the power that can be taken away from us, such as our material possessions, our looks, and our status. (Read Gary Zukav's insightful book *The Seat of the Soul* to learn more about inauthentic and authentic power.)

6. Our true self is natural, spontaneous, easygoing, and happy, and lives in a state of gratitude.

7. Our false self must always appear to be in control, even when the addictions we try so zealously to hide are raging way out of control.

8. Our false self is controlling of others, miserable, and constantly whining and complaining.

9. Our false self is filled with victim consciousness.

10. Our true self has learned to take responsibility for our actions.

11. Our false self prays to God for what it wants, and is angry at God when those prayers appear to go unanswered.

12. Our true self prays often for the sake of prayer, and when we do ask for something we know to preface our requests with, "Thy will be done."

13. Our true self knows why we're here on this planet and has a good sense of what lessons need to be learned, and what we're expected to give back to the world.

14. Our true self knows that in this life we can take what we want, but we must be willing to pay for it.
15. Our false self thinks life owes us something. Our false self believes that life is a free ride, and feels justified in taking what it wants without feeling the least bit responsible for paying for it.
16. Our false self is manipulative and self-serving.
17. Our false self views the world as a black-and-white place.
18. Our true self understands that the world is composed of a rainbow of colors.

The Birth of the Shadow Self

The shadow self is born as soon as we begin to recognize what the world around us views as good or bad. We hear things like, "That's a good girl," or "You're being a bad boy." These types of admonitions start when we're about six months old, as we begin exploring the world on our own. When we began to crawl, Mommy told us just how far we could go and what we should and should not put in our mouths. In general, she let us know what she thought was good or bad for us. At this stage in development, we had no experiences of our own with which to weigh the pros and cons of what we were being told.

Young children don't realize that many of the restrictions placed upon them are for their own protection. Depending upon our own personal karma, and the strength of our will, we either comply and accept what we're being told, thus earning the reputation of being "good" children, or we simply don't listen, do what we feel like, and thus become labeled as "bad" children. Through these thousands and thousands of interactions with our primary caretakers, we begin to formulate the concepts of what's good and acceptable, and what's bad and unacceptable. This is how we become indoctrinated in the ways of the family and its traditions, and of society and its rules and regulations.

Since we learn at a very young age that our primary caretakers don't like us very much when we're behaving in ways they deem unacceptable, we come to fear first their rejection, then their abandonment of us, if we don't comply. Most of us became indoctrinated in the ways of conditional love long before we were even potty trained. We learned to curtail our individual desires because we wanted to remain part of the group, and this is not entirely a bad thing, since humans, by their nature and needs, are pack animals that truly can't survive if they're abandoned or banished to go off and live all alone.

In a nutshell, we control our impulses, both the good and the bad ones, because of the collective unconscious fear or primal fear known as the *fear of abandonment*. We so fear abandonment that we learn to abandon those parts of ourselves that the world around us deems unacceptable.

Thus, our shadow self or false self is a byproduct of conditional love. In other words, conditional love *conditions* us to behave in ways that are deemed socially acceptable. When we're young and dependent, we want to be good and not anger our caretakers too much, for we desperately fear losing their love. In actuality, this is a survival fear, for we know full well we couldn't last long in this world without them. The need to please our caretaker is nature's way of protecting us from danger before we're old and wise enough to know how to keep ourselves from harm's way. The problem with this thinking is that when we grow up we still have this childlike need to please those who love us, no matter what the cost to us personally may be.

Keep in mind that what is considered good in one culture might be considered bad in another, so our shadow self is very much a product of "tribal traditions" that are part of our particular family and society.

For example, in our patriarchal culture, the "boys will be boys" way of thinking allows boys a far greater range of acceptable behaviors than girls, particularly as far as aggression is concerned. For a woman in our western culture, aggression may be part of her shadow self, the self she keeps hidden, while aggression for a man in our culture may be a part of his persona, or the part he reveals to the world. Furthermore, the level of aggression that is acceptable can vary greatly even within a particular culture, depending upon the family and/or the community in which one lives.

For instance, if you were born into a family that was part of an organized crime syndicate, violent outbursts and expressions would be acceptable ways to interact and behave. If you were later abandoned by your mob family and adopted by a family of Quakers, you can bet your bottom dollar that your violence and aggression would soon be stashed away in your shadow bag for fear that your newfound pacifist family and community might reject or abandon you if you continued to act out your old ways of behaving. As children are growing up, they're instinctively and acutely aware of the particular value system surrounding them.

If we're so blessed as to be born into a family and/or a society whose basic philosophies and needs suit our own, we won't have to abandon huge chunks of our true selves.

Of course, abandoning certain parts of ourselves can be a positive thing as far as our antisocial behaviors are concerned, but it can also be a negative thing if we learn to suppress our innate talents and gifts.

For example, if we're destined to become an artist, and we're born into a family of artists who don't try to suppress our artistic inclinations, but, in fact, nurture them, our artistic nature will flourish out in the open. However, if we're artistic by nature, and we're born into a family that views art as a waste of time, we'll repress our artistic inclinations, and they'll be banished into our shadow bag. With any luck at all, we'll return at some later date to retrieve this long-lost buried treasure.

In truth, people can be more afraid of the good stuff that's buried in their shadow bags than the bad stuff. The buried bad stuff keeps us in check, thus ensuring our place in the "tribe," whereas our good stuff has the potential to raise us above the everyday tribal mentality. Our inner buried treasure holds the key to the **big answer** as to why we're here and why we were born in the first place. People instinctively fear following their unique calling, for it might mean leaving the old world behind in order to embrace the new world that is waiting for them. This sends them crashing head-on into their primal fears of abandonment and rejection. Over the course of our many incarnations, we've all come to have a deep inner knowing that prophets are never recognized in their own country, and we've come to fear the symbolic crucifixion that our friends, families, and communities might subject us to.

But you can take comfort in knowing that if you've been born into a family or culture that doesn't resonate with the same inner truths you hold to be self-evident, this is part of God's divine plan and part of your own *Celestial Contract* to ensure that you'll be forced to leave behind a false world in order to embrace a new world created from your own higher consciousness.

God hopes the world you were forced to leave behind will one day recognize and be illuminated by your light, but at this stage of human consciousness, many times our light will not be seen by those we most wished would see it.

For this reason, answering your sacred calling may mean mustering up the courage to stand alone, risking banishment or self-imposed exile, armed and comforted by the powerful inner knowing that you've embarked on the mythological hero's journey in search of your true self. Remember that courage is not something only the fearless possess. Courage is acknowledging that you're afraid, but making a choice to go forth and do what you must do, despite the fear. Courage is the virtue God bestows upon us to help us answer our divine calling and seek a higher love, despite the high price we might have to pay for doing so.

LOVEWORK ASSIGNMENT

Write down the areas in your life that could use some more self-exploration. What areas of your life are still shrouded in darkness? What are you still hiding from? Where do you practice deep denial? Which part of your life would you least like to see plastered on the cover of a tabloid?

The Hidden Aspects of Myself I Would Least Like
Anyone to See

I Feel Safe to Open up My Secret Shadow Bags.
I No Longer Feel a Need to Sweep Those Aspects
of Myself Under the Carpet

"The Devil Made Me Do It!"

The shadow self has the power to make us behave in ways that leave us feeling out of control and confused. Since the shadow lurks in the subconscious mind (read more about the subconscious in STEP 15), we seem to have no conscious idea why we're doing what we're doing, and why we can't stop doing it even when we want to. This uncontrollable behavior can manifest as a one-time impulsive act we commit without a clue as to why, or it could be a compulsive act we keep repeating, such as binge eating or maxing out our credit cards. Before we can embrace our shadow self, we have to examine these out of control behaviors very closely. They hold the key to the parts of ourselves that we don't own up to.

The shadow self houses all that we've managed to suppress – in other words, all that we've buried deep within ourselves hoping that no one, not even our own true self, will ever uncover them. But uncover them we must. That which we keep hidden will destroy us, since we'll continue to be guided by a dark force that we don't understand and can't control.

View the shadow self as our personal inner hell, complete with our own live-in devil. When our inner demon acts up, our life can become a seemingly unending horror movie.

See and learn to embrace the shadow self as a dark angel. The angels of light speak to us in loving ways. When we don't listen, the universe sends us dark angels who may manifest as anxiety, depression, and obsessions and compulsions. The menacing voices of these dark angels can't be ignored.

Understanding Our *Yin Factor* and Our *Yang Factor*

Human behavior is driven by two opposing forces: the power of fear and the power of love. Our collective unconscious or transpersonal fears of abandonment and rejection are the powerful tools the ego uses to keep us locked in our fear-based patterns of thinking and behaving.

The all-powerful fear of abandonment is our *Yin Factor,* since it's the feminine part of our being that houses the fears of abandonment and rejection. If we're shame-based in our identity, then our fear of abandonment is all the more controlling, because we never want to revisit those painful childhood days when we were so emotionally and/or physically neglected that we felt helpless and utterly alone in the world.

To make matters worse, we all possess the transpersonal fear of not doing what we incarnated on this earth to do in the first place. This fear of not answering our sacred calling is our *Yang Factor,* since it's the masculine part of our being that knows we have work on earth that must be accomplished.

If our fear of abandonment, *Yin Factor,* is greater than the fear of failure to answer our divine calling, *Yang Factor,* we'll give up our dreams and goals rather than risk our sense of safety and security.

On the other hand, if our fear of not answering our divine calling, *Yang Factor,* is greater than our fear of abandonment, *Yin Factor,* we might walk away from even a great love, if we feel it will interfere with our life's goal.

People with a strong *Yang Factor* are easy to
recognize by their excessive drive, single-minded-
ness, and tireless efforts to reach their goals.

People with a strong *Yin Factor* are equally easy
to recognize because of their excessive dependency
and neediness issues. But be forewarned: Never underestimate the strength of weakness. People with
big abandonment issues can be highly manipulative
and cutthroat in their efforts to hold on to someone
or something they don't want to lose.

A Real Life Example of the Way the *Yang Factor* and the *Yin Factor* Affected a Relationship

If you were to examine closely the *Twin Soul*
relationship of the actress Jeanette MacDonald and
the actor Nelson Eddy, you'd see how the fear of
abandonment and the fear of not answering the sacred calling eventually led to a lifetime of sorrow and
suffering for these two star-crossed lovers.

Their angst-filled relationship also reveals the
inherent obstacles to *Twinsoulship* that human beings
at this stage of human consciousness often face. The
separate karma each of these lovers accrued over
many separate incarnations proved to be too large an
obstacle to overcome, although their romance, which
had more negative twists and turns than a cheap romance novel, spanned a thirty-year period.

Jeanette's and Nelson's heated love affair began during the 1930s, when actors and actresses were
essentially owned by the studios. The movie industry
was truly a place where the Master/Slave archetype

was played out with the studio heads as "Masters" and the movie stars playing the roles of "Slaves," albeit glamorous ones.

Although Jeanette loved Nelson passionately, she succumbed to the demands made on her by MGM studios to leave him, lest her career suffer. Jeanette's *Yang Factor* was great, and at first her need to have her career outweighed her *Yin Factor*. In the end, however, it became clear that she had underestimated and greatly denied her *Yin Factor*, since her sense of abandonment led to a nervous breakdown and eventually to the ruination of her career.

On the other hand, Nelson had a greater *Yin Factor* than *Yang Factor*. He tried to convince Jeanette that their innate talent would see them through, and they should take their chances in saying to hell with MGM studios. Unfortunately, he was unable to convince Jeanette to totally commit to him mind, heart, body, and soul.

Eventually, the two of them married other people, but even that couldn't keep them apart. Their true love and true selves were then relocated to the shadow as they engaged in an illicit affair. Their "for show only" marriages became their personae or false selves.

Now that you know more about *Twin Souls*, why do you think God brought Jeanette and Nelson together? What was their contribution to society supposed to be?

For one thing, they were supposed to stand up to the pressures of Hollywood and the tyranny of the studios and say, "Our private life is our private life," thereby putting an end to the Master/Slave archetype that kept movie stars chained to a persona that falsely proclaimed an exciting, glamorous,

freewheeling lifestyle, and a dark shadow that revealed the true story – a life of oppression, suffering,
and sorrow. Had Jeanette allowed their relationship
to see the light of day, it would have paved the way
for other actors and actresses to have private lives of
their own choosing while maintaining a very public
career.

Of course, over time Hollywood did change
because other stars did stand up and say, "Enough
is enough," but Jeanette and Nelson were meant to
help accelerate this process, and so, ultimately, they
failed to fulfill one of their lives' purposes.

For more information about these passionate
star-crossed lovers, read *Soul Mates and Twin Flames*,
by Elizabeth Clare Prophet, and *Farewell to Dreams*, by
Sharon Rich and Diane Goodrich.

The Shadow – The Two Big Bags We Drag Behind Us

Visualize the shadow as two big bags we drag
around behind us. To the left of us we drag **a big,
red toxic waste bag** in which we store all the negative
things about ourselves that we're trying to hide. This
is **our red, pernicious shame bag** that houses all the
toxic waste of our being. To the right of us, we drag
a white shadow bag called **our magical buried treasure bag,** in which we've stuffed all the positive attributes about ourselves that we wish to keep hidden.
We spend enormous energy trying to keep these red
and white shadow bags tightly sealed.

What we show the world is our persona, but a
persona that is dragging, not too far behind it, two
heavy shadow bags.

Some people, such as the town drunk, wear their shadow selves on their sleeves. This open display of toxicity can make us uncomfortable, but we can feel equally uncomfortable being around "perfect people" who never let down their guards (personae).

Our Magical Buried Treasure Bag

What is stashed away in your magical buried treasure bag? What tricks have you got up your sleeves? Opening up this particular Pandora's Box can be both fascinating and frightful.

In Greek mythology, there are two versions of what was found in Pandora's Box. One version correlates with our red, pernicious shame bag. When Pandora opens up the box, evil escapes. The other version correlates with our magical buried treasure bag. When Pandora opens this box, blessings come out, and only hope remains inside.

So, think of your magical buried treasure bag as being filled with blessings which are just waiting for you to accept. Hope never leaves this bag, so these blessings are always there for you. What is hope? Hope is the undying feeling that what we wanted and wished for can be had, and that things will turn out for the best despite everything.

Now is the time to open your magical buried treasure bag and see what's waiting in there for you to discover. Let your creativity resurface. The time has come for you to start making some of those long-ago dreams come true. Take one baby step at a time. Begin anywhere. Vow to learn how to paint, sew, cook, garden, write, dance, play a musical instrument, or rediscover an old skill you discarded long ago. In doing so, you might put yourself in the right place at the right time to meet your *Soul Mate.*

LOVEWORK ASSIGNMENT

Try to bring to mind the specific times, places, people, or things in your life that have made you feel ashamed. Were you ashamed of the clothes you wore, or the house you grew up in? Were you of a different religion or ethnic background than most of your peers? Perhaps your parents were alcoholics, drug addicts, or gamblers, and you felt ashamed of them. Write your feelings down.

Some Times in my Life When I Felt Ashamed

I Vow to Bring Forth All that is Hidden Deep Within Me. I Ask God to Show Me the Way to Do This

Why We Have to Stop Being Afraid of Our Own Shadow

If we continually avoid confrontation with the darker side of ourselves, we'll also try to avoid seeing the darker side of anyone else. The problem with this tunnel vision is that it sets us up to be victimized time and time again, since we never see what's coming, and we never know what hit us. We have a *blind spot*, and we can never see how people continually take advantage of us. At the root of this night blindness is our fear of confrontation and our inability to stand up for our rights. We have to come to see that the real reason we avoid confrontation is because we fear that people won't like us, and therefore, they'll leave us. This is the "peace at any price" that many of us maintain, in order to avoid abandonment.

We have to learn in life when to be the peacemaker and when to be the warrior. We can only know when, why, and how to discern the difference, when we know ourselves, particularly the self that lies beneath the surface.

LOVEWORK ASSIGNMENT

Write down a time in your life when you didn't speak your mind. What were the consequences? What were you afraid of? For example, were you afraid of losing your job, or perhaps even your mate? Were you afraid of being perceived as a bad person? Were you afraid of hurting someone's feelings?

A Time in My Life When I Didn't Speak My Mind

I Vow to Speak my Mind With Great Honesty, Tempered by Kindness, Regardless of the Outcome

How Do We Begin to Cast Light on the Shadow Self, so We Can Open Up this Double-Edged Pandora's Box and See What's Housed Inside?

The first thing you need to do is begin closely observing your own behavior. Watch the way you voice an opinion. What makes you get really vocal? What do you profess to hate in people? Remember, we only hate that which is part of ourselves. If you find yourself gossiping about other people's sexual escapades, or speaking openly about your neighbors' ostentatious ways, you have to ask yourself, "Why should I care about what these people are doing? How do their lifestyle choices affect my life?" If you were to think about it, most of the things other people do affect your life very little. Their behavior mirrors something about yourself that you despise, and reveals to you some hidden desire or wish of your own to engage in those same kinds of activities. You clearly recognize something in these people that you refuse to see within yourself, since you're too afraid to unzip your red, pernicious shame bag.

Every time you judge other people's behavior, be aware that you're revealing more about yourself than you are about them. If you want to know what lurks beneath your shadow, pay close attention to your self-righteous, judgmental behavior.

Also pay close attention to those people you envy. The person you envy reveals the kind of person you might wish to be and might even be capable of being, if you weren't so afraid of what's stashed in your magical buried treasure bag.

To Exorcise the Shadow Demons, We Need to Tell Someone We Trust About the Things We Keep Hidden

This need to tell someone about the things we keep hidden is the basis of all talk therapies. Once we let the cat out of the shadow bag – it has no power over us.

So, if you've never told anyone about the time someone molested you or how you closet eat or whatever clandestine activities you engage in, find someone you can trust and start talking.

LOVEWORK ASSIGNMENT

Draw a stick figure of yourself which represents your persona, that part of yourself that you feel safe revealing to the world. Then draw two big bags that your stick arms are dragging behind you. One bag represents your magical buried treasure bag, and the other represents your red, pernicious shame bag. Inside the red, pernicious shame bag write down the so called "bad stuff" that you're hiding from the world, such as your laziness, your gambling problem, your alcoholic mother, your greed, or whatever qualities you feel ashamed of. Then, in your magical buried treasure bag, write down all the "good stuff" about yourself that you keep hidden, such as your desire to go back to school, or your desire to be more spiritual. Can you see how difficult it is to be your true self when you wear the mask of your persona and then drag all that excess baggage behind you?

A Drawing of Me (Persona), Myself (Red, Pernicious Shame Bag), and I (Magical Buried Treasure Bag)

Ask God to Help You Bring Forth All That Is Hidden

Summing Things Up

The shadow self is built on the rocky foundation of conditional love, which is really a manifestation of fear. Our true self is built on the solid foundation of unconditional love. The shadow self is the part of us that desperately tries to control the external world. It tries to control the way people see us, and the way we see ourselves. Unexamined, it becomes the out of control engine that runs our life, an inner dictator, a monster.

Congratulate yourself on your noble efforts to know yourself.

In STEP 12, we'll be examining in detail The Second Golden Rule of Love – Love Thyself.

STEP 12 – UNDERSTANDING THE SECOND GOLDEN RULE OF LOVE

"And as you let yourself be healed, you see all those around you, or who cross your mind, or whom you touch or those who seem to have no contact with you, healed along with you."
(*A Course in Miracles*, Lesson 137)

The Second Golden Rule of Love – Love Thyself

To Know Me Is to Love Me

"Love thy neighbor as thyself." This is a scary concept if you're the kind of person who's your own worst enemy, beating yourself up for every transgression, error, or mistake. Many of us are much harder on ourselves than we'd ever dream of being to anyone else.

If the above description fits you, and you operate out of that place of deep-seated feelings of **inferiority,** you need to learn to *"Love thyself as thy neighbor."*

Thomas A. Harris, M.D., the author of the book *I'm OK – You're OK,* calls the self-deprecating attitude described above the **"You're OK, but I'm not OK" mindset.**

On the opposite spectrum of human behavior, we have the type of people who are highly critical of others, yet fail to see their own shortcomings.

Heaven help us if these people happen to be our mates, parents, children, siblings, teachers, or bosses, because they continually make our lives miserable with their impossible-to-meet demands. This hypercritical behavior also stems from a place of self-hatred, only it doesn't manifest itself in an inferiority complex. Rather, it manifests as a **superiority complex – the "I'm OK, but you're not OK"** mindset.

These overly critical people love playing the psychological game known as **"Blemish,"** where they can see *your* every flaw and blemish a mile away, and yet they see none of their *own* flaws, even if they possess those exact same flaws and then some. These people tend to make us feel that no matter how perfect we try to be, in their eyes, we're never good enough, and we know we can never please them, no matter how hard we try.

Other people come from the place that nobody's OK, not me, and certainly not you! **"I'm not OK, and you and the rest of the whole stinking world aren't OK, either."** These people always proclaim, "The sky is falling." They see doom and gloom everywhere. These people are filled with anger, and at times their rage can grow so out of control that they become a danger to themselves and others. These are the kind of people who commit suicide, but only after they've gunned down a slew of innocent victims first.

We all need to come to the healthy psychological place that states, **"I'm OK, and you're OK, too."** *We know we're not perfect – no human being is – but we're perfectly human, and that's good enough for us.*

For more information about Transactional Analysis and the mind games people play, I highly suggest you read *I'm OK – You're OK*. It's a practical, easy-to-read, and doable approach to understanding human behavior. Another great book to read to further your understanding of the psychology of human relationships is *Games People Play,* by Eric Berne, M.D.

LOVEWORK ASSIGNMENT

Pick five people from your life, from either the past or the present, with whom you've had a close relationship. Write down their names.

Next to each name, write down whether you think that person functions from the healed place of "I'm OK – you're OK" or one of the three dysfunctional places of "You're OK, but I'm not OK"; "I'm OK, but you're not OK"; or "I'm not OK and you aren't, either."

Which of the above four mindsets fits you? Does your mindset change from person to person, place to place, or day-to-day; or is it pretty much a fixed position? From now on, your mantra is: "I'm OK – you're OK."

Who's OK, Anyway?

"I'm OK – You're OK"

The Mindsets of *Soul Mates* and *Cellmates*

1. True *Soul Mates* love each other unconditionally, which fosters a sense of self-worth, self-love, and self-esteem ("I'm OK – you're OK").

2. *Cellmates* love each other conditionally, which tears down an already shaky sense of self, fosters continued self-hatred, and damages self-esteem further ("I'm OK – you're not OK"; "You're OK – I'm not OK"; or "I'm not OK – you're not OK").

3. We enter into a *Soul Mate* relationship from a place of self-love. However, if we are unhealed, our self-loathing (fear-based emotion) will overcome us, and may undermine our relationship because we become incapable of receiving love ("I'm not OK – you're OK").

4. We enter into *Cellmate* relationships from a place of self-loathing. One or both *Cellmates* are willing to sacrifice all, including self, just to keep the relationship going. If one *Cellmate* begins to awaken to self-love, the other *Cellmate* will inevitably feel threatened. At this point, the stagnant *Cellmate* will do anything and everything to keep the growing *Cellmate* disempowered. The stagnant *Cellmate* usually won't respond positively to the other *Cellmate's* pleas for him/her to grow and evolve as well. This causes a metaphorical earthquake in the relationship, and both *Cellmates* will have to decide whether to stay or go. The stagnant *Cellmate* resents that the growing *Cellmate* has come to know that he/she is "OK". Sadly, at this stage

in human consciousness, it's extremely common for the threatened *Cellmate* to continue to chisel away at his/her partner's self-esteem, eventually undermining any hopes of healing the relationship.

If we're going to love ourselves, we have to first like ourselves. Liking ourselves comes naturally when we stop practicing the Five Deadly Sins Committed in the Name of Conditional Love.

Understanding the Five Deadly Sins Committed in the Name of Conditional Love (Selfishness, Narcissism, Greed, Envy, and Jealousy)

Selfishness, narcissism, greed, envy, and jealousy – do you possess any of these fatal-to-love traits?

The Five Deadly Sins Committed in the Name of Conditional Love can ruin any relationship with their toxic power. These pernicious feelings don't come from a place of self-love, even though we might think they do; in actuality, they come from a place of self-hatred.

Selfishness

When we're **selfish**, we become overly concerned with our own needs and desires, oftentimes at the expense of others. This self-absorption, however, isn't coming from a place of love, but from the deep inner feeling that we're unworthy of love. Since we feel unlovable, we think that no one else is ever going to love and care for us. We start feeling that we'd better learn to take all and give nothing, lest we be left out in the cold.

Selfishness can, therefore, be seen as a self-protective mechanism meant to ensure our physical, emotional, and psychological survival. Selfish feelings stem from an *Error in Thinking* brought on by our continual exposure to conditional love. We come to feel that the world isn't an abundant place, and we must scratch and claw our way to the top. It's a dog-eat-dog mentality.

Selfishness has its strangulating roots in our primal fears of abandonment and rejection. I've done Tarot readings for clients who honestly feel that they're not selfish, but who think that they've been stuck with selfish mates. Oddly, however, when we talk about how it's time for them to move on from this relationship, I meet up with strong resistance to this idea. They all say some variation of this: "I bet if I leave him, it's just my luck that he'll meet some new woman, and she'll benefit from what he learned because I walked out the door. How fair is that? I do all the hard work, and she reaps all the benefits." These people get caught up in the negative energy of **envying** their mates' potential future partners. These kinds of covertly selfish and envious people rarely leave the relationship no matter how bad it gets, because they keep thinking that they might miss out on something. I have to try and get them to see that this covertly selfish view is part of their shadow self, and that their mates' outwardly selfish behavior is a mirror of their own repressed feelings of selfishness. These people have to learn how to bless their selfish mates and let them go. Let the chips fall where they may. Pray your mate learns from these errors, and, yes, pray for the new partner that she/he will be the recipient of all these hard-learned lessons.

       Selfishness can also come in the guise of spirituality. I've come to call this **spiritual egotism.** Spiritual egotists use their so-called spirituality as a means of manipulating the world in an effort to obtain their own selfish needs and desires. They think becoming spiritual will free them from the slings and arrows of life. They wield their spirituality like a sword, believing it will protect them from life's woes. This is just another fear-based *Error in Thinking*. True spirituality simply provides us with the inner and outer resources, strength, and courage to face the inevitable adversities of life. You can take comfort in knowing that as you continually listen to your inner guidance, grow in spirituality, and learn your karmic lessons, you won't have to face the same hurdles, obstacles, or problems ever again, but this doesn't mean life will always be a bed of roses.

Narcissism

       Narcissistic people are highly self-absorbed and self-centered. They're fixated at an infantile mindset in which they truly believe the whole world revolves around them. No one hurts as much as they do. They're never at fault for anything that happens in their lives. They view themselves as helpless victims.

They demand total attention when they talk, and yet never hear a word anyone else has to say. They project all their flaws and faults onto others, and refuse to take responsibility for their own actions.

A person who is outwardly *selfless* almost to a fault can be **narcissistic** all the same. These people practice the psychological defense mechanism known as **reaction formation,** in which a repressed emotion that can be perceived as negative, such as greediness, can manifest itself in the exact opposite behavior – extreme generosity. (Read more about psychological defense mechanisms in STEP 15.) The outwardly selfless behavior is the persona or the mask the person wears to hide the shadow, which is highly narcissistic. It may take us a long time before we see the narcissist behind the so-called selfless mask.

For example, mothers who appear to be self-sacrificing almost to the point of martyrdom can actually be highly narcissistic people. They want their children to do well and be successful so that they'll come out looking like the all-time best mother. These mothers are also adept at manipulating their children by instilling a deep sense of guilt in them should they not do what Mommy wants or what Mommy perceives to be best for them.

Envy

Envy is the venomous desire to have what someone else has, be it material goods, status, talents, or life situation. We don't congratulate these people for their good fortune or hard work. Instead, we curse them, ourselves, and an unjust God.

Oddly enough, we tend *not* to envy people who are way out of our league. We may not envy Donald Trump's wealth and fame because that's not the life we'd wish for anyway, but we can be viciously envious of our neighbor who has just gotten a brand-new, expensive car while we're still driving an old, beat-up jalopy. We may not be envious of our daughter's youth, but we may well envy our sister's face lift.

We usually envy what other people have when these things are seemingly within our reach, but we just haven't been able to procure them for ourselves. **We don't usually envy celebrities, politicians, or the rich and famous** (unless, of course, we feel that we possess as much talent, brains, and know-how as they do, and yet no one else seems to recognize our gifts). **Rather, we tend to admire those people who are out of our league,** and take vicarious pleasure in watching from afar their exploits, pursuits, and day-to-day affairs. However, our envy of celebrities can sometimes manifest itself in our harsh judgment of them, and in the self-righteous satisfaction we get from reading juicy gossip about them in the tabloids.

Greed

Greed is an insatiable craving. No amount of money, material goods, fame, power, sex, or beauty is ever enough. Greed comes from a deep place of fear.

Greed is a useless attempt to fill the holes in our heart caused by deep-seated feelings of inferiority. We keep saying, "If only I had this or that, then I would be happy." So, God gives us what we wished for, but in record time, the thrill is gone, and we discover that the hole inside us has not diminished at all. Rather, it has become a bottomless pit. Once again, we get back on the greed treadmill, seeking still another person, place, or thing to fill the ever-gaping hole within.

Greedy people will go from one relationship to the next, believing the grass is always greener on the other side.

Remember, God will provide us with everything for our needs, but not necessarily for our greeds!

Greedy people are usually envious people. They envy what others have, and love it when others envy them.

To understand more about these deadly sins, read *The Secret of Staying in Love,* by John Powell. This little book is full of giant insights!

LOVEWORK ASSIGNMENT

Which of the above four mentioned sins are you most guilty of committing? Which are you least guilty of committing?

Keep in mind that some of these sins we wear on our sleeves for all to see. These are the easier sins to stop committing, since they're so out there.

The sins we keep hidden, stashed away in our red, pernicious shadow bag, are the ones we need to watch out for. Could you be a secret narcissist? Are you a closet envier?

Over the course of the next week, be highly conscious of times when you're guilty of committing any of the deadly sins.

Every time you **act in a narcissistic, selfish, greedy, or envious way** this week, take a moment to briefly write down what you did. Pay attention to what you thought and felt, as well.

What is this list of deadly sins revealing to you?

The Deadly Sins I've Committed This Week
(Not just those sins obvious to everyone, but the
closet ones I've stashed in my red, pernicious
shame bag as well.)

I'm Seeing My Behavior with New Eyes

The final deadly sin – Jealousy – has so many ramifications and is such a complicated emotion that it demands an entire STEP of its own.

Be sure you understand the first four deadly sins before proceeding, since jealousy encompasses all of these deadly sins and a whole lot more!

In loving yourself, you pave the way for a higher love. A Soul Mate relationship demands that we give and receive love in equal measures.

Congratulate yourself on your noble efforts to love yourself.

STEP 13 – TAMING JEALOUSY AND BUILDING HEALTHY BOUNDARIES

"Trusting in your brothers is essential to establishing and holding up your faith in your ability to transcend doubt and lack of sure conviction in yourself."
(*A Course in Miracles*, Lesson 181)

Everything You've Ever Wanted to Know About Jealousy

In the simplest terms, jealousy is the fear of loss. When you're jealous, you fear someone or something will take someone or something from you.

Jealousy is perhaps the most pernicious of the Five Deadly Sins Committed in the Name of Conditional Love, since it's a complex emotion which encapsulates within it the first four deadly sins – envy, selfishness, narcissism, and greed.

Jealousy comes from a place of envy, since we fear that someone we love will find someone else more desirable.

The ravenous demon known as jealousy epitomizes selfishness when we keep our mates chained like prisoners and clip their wings in an effort to keep them by our side.

There is also a high degree of narcissism involved with jealousy, since we're only concerned with our own needs and wants and often can't see how our controlling, irrational behaviors are driving others crazy.

Jealousy is also a **greedy** emotion because it demands all of our mates' affection and attention. Jealous people can't bear when their mates show affection for others, and pathologically jealous people even resent the attention their mates give to their children or other family members.

Jealousy isn't about love. Jealousy is all about fear.

In this STEP, we're going to take a rather long detour on the jealousy highway, since very few people seem to be free of this toxic emotion. Freud was probably right in his estimation that those people who claim to be free of feelings of jealousy are severely repressed. So repressed, in fact, that they have no idea what they're really thinking or feeling.

As we've already come to see, sometimes it's very difficult to distinguish love from fear. For instance, even if you're the one who left a relationship, it's still quite possible that you'll experience pangs of jealousy when you discover that your ex-mate has found someone new – in other words, that you've been replaced. Does this mean that you still love your ex? <u>NO</u>! **Remember, jealousy isn't about love. It's about fear.** This feeling of jealousy stems from the immature mindset of, "I want my cake, and I want to eat it, too." We no longer want our mates, but just in case we might ever change our minds, we want them to be waiting in the wings.

Jealousy is a big issue, and some of you might need more help, insight, and guidance than I can provide here. If this is the case, I highly recommend that you read Nancy Friday's book, *Jealousy*, or seek professional help if your jealousy issues are interfering with your daily life.

Jealousy Made Me Do It!

Jealousy belongs to our shadow self, our dark side; however, since very few people seem to be free of this emotion, we tend to feel okay about wearing our jealousy on our sleeve.

At this stage of human consciousness, most people have not yet mastered the jealousy demon because this powerful emotion is deeply ingrained in our collective unconscious. Remember that our collective unconscious houses images and visions which are inborn in varying degrees to all human beings. In other words, we don't need to learn these things through life experiences. **When we experience jealousy, we're really dealing with how human beings have, as a whole and historically, dealt with loss or even just the perceived threat of loss.**

Although jealousy is a part of our collective unconscious, our own subconscious mind and energy body will house more or less jealousy depending upon our own personal karma. (Read more about the subconscious and your energy body in STEP 15.) If you're a particularly jealous person, overcoming jealousy and its underlying fear of loss, abandonment, and rejection are some of the karmic lessons you've incarnated on this planet to learn and overcome. Start now!

Certainly there's no denying that the way our infantile needs were handled in this lifetime greatly affects our ability to cope with loss. If we were neglected, we may develop a low frustration tolerance for even the slightest threat to our financial, emotional, or psychological well-being. Consequently, our jealousy is easily provoked, while other people, who have had more nurturing during these crucial early years, might need a real threat to arouse such feelings.

But you can't blame everything on Mommy and Daddy, either. The "parental myth," that perpetuates the idea that our parents are responsible for all our failures, neuroses, and shortcomings, is another grave *Error in Thinking* that is very prevalent in our society today. Just as we're born with certain physical traits, we're also born with certain God-given psychological traits that help us to master the karmic lessons we're here on earth to learn.

Our own accrued karma over our many incarnations also has a profound impact on the level of jealousy we may be experiencing. Some of us have never overcome our jealous feelings in any lifetime no matter how nurtured, loved, and pampered we were. Therefore, in this lifetime we might be highly jealous regardless of the level of nurturing we received as children. Others of us, while still in spirit, might have chosen or agreed to have parents who would neglect and abandon us so we could confront our fears of abandonment and rejection, and eventually overcome jealousy within this lifetime.

Jealousy as a Projection of the Shadow Self

As you've already learned, jealousy is part of our shadow self, and anything that belongs to our shadow self has a projected part to it.

This means we tend to accuse our mates or project onto them what we fear we might do or desire. We're essentially projecting our own lustful thoughts or our own desire for infidelity onto our partner. Anytime you feel jealous, it's necessary to examine your own red, pernicious shame bag to see if you might be guilty of this behavior.

The Many Faces of Jealousy

As we've already discussed, jealousy is a complex web of emotions incorporating envy, greed, selfishness, and narcissism.

As if all those compounded emotions weren't enough, jealousy further reveals our collective unconscious fears (transpersonal fears), including the fear of abandonment, fear of rejection, fear that we won't be able to survive, fear of betrayal, and fear of losing face; as well as our own personal fears, including the fear of our own repressed feelings and desires.

Unhealed anger issues and bottled-up rage can also be manifestations of jealousy. Jealousy can incite two people, with tons of repressed anger, to fight viciously, permitting them to play out their pent-up feelings of rage. The nuclear explosion that takes place behind closed doors might well be the only thing that allows these two rage-filled people to function normally in the outside world.

Now add to this volatile mixture of bottled-up rage, deadly sins, and killer fears – both personal and transpersonal – the element of paranoia, the need for revenge, feelings of powerlessness, feelings of inferiority, and fear of losing control, and you have a better idea of why feelings of jealousy pack such a devastating punch.

The truly hard part in coming to terms with jealousy is trying to figure out what our jealousy is revealing about ourselves. Suffice it to say, jealousy is within us, both superficially and to the very depths of our being.

The Message in the Bottled-Up Emotion Called Jealousy

External events and people bring forth only what's already there.

If you're to understand what your feelings of jealousy are trying to reveal, you have to start by giving up victim consciousness, and stop blaming your mate for making you feel jealous. No one has the power to make us feel anything. Learn to acknowledge that the jealousy you're feeling is coming from a place of insecurity, and what's going on in the outside world is just reflecting what's really going on deep inside.

When our mates do something that pushes our jealousy buttons, we have to examine to what degree there is a realistic threat to the relationship. For instance, if your husband has an infatuation with the long-dead Marilyn Monroe, does that fascination really pose a threat to your marriage? Is your relationship a very low level of love, such as a Rung One, Two or Three *Cellmate* relationship? Then, let's face it: It would take only a huff or a puff to blow it away anyway, so everyone and everything realistically could pose a threat to your relationship. But think about it, is this really the level of love you want in your life anyway?

On the other hand, if you're blessed with a *Soul Mate* relationship and find yourself having irrational feelings of jealousy, could your own insecurities and feelings of unworthiness be at the core of your jealous feelings? Take responsibility for the unhealed issues inside yourself that are so desperately trying to surface.

Conditional love, which gets turned on and off again depending upon circumstances, has programmed us to acquire the false belief or *Error in Thinking* which basically boils down to this: I am loved so long as I do what you wish; therefore, my self-worth does not originate from within me. My self-esteem is not an endless, self-generating fountain that bubbles from within. Rather, my self-esteem flounders or flourishes depending upon the outside force that is feeding it. This convoluted logic leads to the conclusion that I have to jealously guard over my mate because if, God forbid, he/she should leave, then I will shrivel up and die.

LOVEWORK ASSIGNMENT

Reflect upon your current relationship or any past relationship, either a platonic or romantic one, to see if you've ever felt jealous or acted in a jealous manner. What unhealed issues was this feeling of jealousy asking you to examine closely?

What Unhealed Issues Are My Jealous Feelings Trying to Reveal to Me?

I Vow to Work on Healing the Issues that Are Being Revealed to Me Through Jealousy

No matter how jealous we might feel, it's never okay to violate our mates' boundaries by spying on them. We must heal our boundary issues if we're going to have healthy and happy relationships.

What Are Boundary Issues?

Boundary issues are dependency issues. Healthy boundaries allow us to remain a separate being, a unique individual, within the context of a relationship.

Boundaries allow us to have the healthy mindset that I'm "me" first of all, and you're, first and foremost, "you," coming together separately to form "we." Our separate identities allow us to answer our individual calling (*Yang Factor*) as to why we're here on this planet in the first place.

If we don't have healthy boundaries, we become **enmeshed** with another person. **Enmeshment** is the psychological entanglement and bondage we experience when we don't have a clear idea of where "I" end and "you" begin.

When we're enmeshed with another person, it can feel like intimacy, but it's not. Enmeshment is a violation of basic human rights of the highest and most destructive order.

In an enmeshed relationship, we're not permitted to have interests, opinions, or desires that aren't in agreement with our mates'.

People who have been raised by intolerant, judgmental, and opinionated parents have learned to keep their true feelings and ideas to themselves (locked away in their shadow bags). Consequently, they easily fall prey to partners who will reinforce this way of thinking.

When people tell us what to think and feel, know that this is an invasion of our boundaries.

People who were physically, sexually, emotionally, or psychologically abused as children can often have trouble setting boundaries later on in life. They unwittingly allow people to violate their boundaries simply because they don't even know they have any boundaries or the right to say, "No."

If you find that people tend to invade your boundaries, you need to learn to set limits. You need to learn how and when to say, "No."

Our Inner Circles

In setting healthy boundaries, it can be helpful to visualize our interpersonal boundaries as three circles: our First Inner Circle, our Second Inner Circle, and our Third Inner Circle. We allow our family members, close friends, and romantic partners – in other words, those people we have an intimate, soulful relationship with – into our First Inner Circle.

If our boundaries have been violated when we were children by physical, sexual, psychological, or emotional abuse, we tend to either not allow anyone into our First Inner Circle, or to let everyone into our First Inner Circle without discretion. Promiscuity is a boundary issue. It's indiscriminately allowing people into your First Inner Circle.

If you have trouble letting anyone into your First Inner Circle, then your karmic lesson is to learn to trust.

If you tend to let everyone into your First Inner Circle, you'll soon find yourself drained of energy and resources. Only a limited number of people belong in your First Inner Circle, not everyone you meet. Your karmic lesson is to learn discernment.

Less intimate relationships with acquaintances, neighbors, or coworkers are relegated to the Second or Third Inner Circle.

When you meet a person, you must decide how intimate you want to be with this person. If you decide a particular coworker belongs in your Third Inner Circle, but he/she wants to be in your First Inner Circle, you'll have to learn to set boundaries, or you'll soon have an Energy Vampire loose in your midst.

Boundary Issues Are Power Struggles and a Playing Out of the Collective Unconscious Master/Slave Archetype

In any one relationship, the Master/Slave archetype can shift between partners depending upon the issues. For instance, as far as money goes, he may be in control of the purse strings, but when it comes to how and when they have sex, she may be the dominant one.

Remember that these power struggles are unhealthy psychological games people play with each other. In a healthy relationship, **both partners are equal.**

When we invade our partners' boundaries it becomes an enactment of the Master/Slave archetype. We feel that we own our partners, and therefore we have a right to monitor their behavior.

When you seek information about your partner through spying, understand that you're violating your partner's boundaries. If you feel that this is the only way you can find out what your partner is doing, know that your relationship has descended to the lowest Rungs on *The Ladder of Love*. When you spy on your partner, you're enacting the role of "Master," believing that you own your partner, and therefore you have the right to check up on him/her.

When you enact this Master/Slave archetype, you and your mate become chained together, enmeshed and enslaved by a complex web of lies, deceit, guilt, and blame. Regardless of whether your partner is guilty as charged or not, the spying behavior is totally unacceptable. You're under karmic obligation to reveal your suspicions to your mate, allowing him/her the opportunity to either dispel your fears or confirm them. If you still feel your mate is not coming clean with his/her indiscretions, and therefore you feel you must begin spying, know that the relationship is in dire trouble regardless of what your espionage reveals, since the sense of trust no longer exists between the two of you.

How Do We Know When We're Overstepping Boundaries?

1. **Spying on a person is never okay.** If you feel you must do this, then know that your relationship is in serious trouble. Even if you discover that your partner is completely on

the up and up, by spying, you have committed a violation of the highest magnitude upon your partner.

2. **We overstep boundaries when we tell people what to do based upon what we perceive to be best for us, knowing full well that it's not in their best interest.** For instance, we tell our partners to stay stuck in a job that they hate because we fear what will happen to us if they should leave the job. (This is our own personal agenda without regard for our partners' happiness, fulfillment, and divine calling; therefore, we have totally disregarded their *Yang Factor.*)

3. **We overstep boundaries when we tell other people how to spend *their* money.** For instance, your mate might love to *buy* books, but you personally feel buying books is a waste of time when you can *borrow* them for free from the library. Of course, couples must discuss the *big* money issues, but the *small* money issues should be left to the discretion of each partner. **No one can tell another person what is valuable.**

4. **We overstep boundaries when we try to control people's behavior by controlling the purse strings.** We enslave them when we withhold money or bribe a person with money to get them to do what we want. It's wrong to use money or sex as a weapon or a reward. This is a reinforcement of the oldest archetype in the book – that of the "Prostitute." Women used to be the ones who enacted the Prostitute archetype the most, but as women have begun

to bring home the bacon, men are falling victim to this ancient archetype as well.

5. **We overstep boundaries when we expect, coerce, or force our mates (with veiled or overt threats of punishment by banishment or abandonment) to think, act, or do things exactly the way we tell them to.**

6. **We overstep boundaries when we speak in an abusive manner.**

7. **We overstep boundaries when we feel we own people because they're somehow involved with us. No one ever owns anyone.**

8. **We overstep boundaries when we interfere with free will. It's not up to us to determine the actions and outcome of someone else's life.**

(For more information about the all-important topic of boundaries, please read *Boundaries,* by Anne Katherine, M.A.)

The Ladder of Jealousy

To help us better understand our jealous tendencies, we're going to place them on the rungs of a ladder, in much the same way as we did with love.

Rung One is the highest level of jealousy and is placed at the top of the ladder. Rung Seven represents the lowest level of jealousy and is placed at the bottom of the ladder.

Rung One Jealousy

If I Can't Have You ... Nobody Can.

First Rung jealous people are jealous way out of proportion to reality. This is delusional jealousy.

People with **First-Degree Jealousy or pathological jealousy issues** become violently angry if anyone so much as looks at their mates. God forbid their mates even talk to another person for what is perceived to be too long.

Everyone and everything in the world is seen as a threat. First Rung jealousy types often try to isolate their mates from everyone, even from friends and family. They view their significant other as chattel. Since they truly believe they own their mates, they are convinced that they have the right to control everyone their mates see, talk to, or come in contact with.

First-Degree jealous types have no respect for boundaries and have no problem with violating their mates' basic human rights. They will open their mates' mail, rummage through their mates' belongings, check their mates' emails, monitor their mates' phone calls, constantly check up on their mates' whereabouts, keep their mates under close surveillance, and basically keep them under house arrest or held hostage. This is another enactment of the still all-too-prevalent Master/Slave archetype, and explains to some extent why someone would stay in such a dysfunctional relationship, as he/she plays out the role of the "Slave" to a jealous "Master."

People stay with abusive mates for many other reasons as well, which basically all boil down to some manifestation of fear.

A fear of abandonment can keep abused people from walking away because they know that, no matter what, their abusive mates will never leave them.

Oftentimes, there is additional fear brought on by veiled and not-so-veiled threats of violent consequences for themselves or the people they love should they try to "escape." A pathologically jealous person feels that, "If I can't have you, nobody else can, either."

Furthermore, First Rung jealous people have real potential to lash out at anyone they feel might be responsible for the breakup. And if there should happen to be a romantic rival, all hell will break loose. A jealous person has to "save face." They can't stand to look like they've been cuckolded. Their narcissism will not allow them to appear publicly humiliated.

The very real potential for violence is the chief characteristic of pathological jealousy. If you couple a First-Degree *Cellmate* love affair with First Rung jealousy issues, you can bet that violence will follow wherever these two *Cellmates* go.

Sometimes a person may stay with a pathologically jealous mate, if that mate has at some point in time served in the role of protector or "rescuer." For instance, if a woman marries to escape sexual abuse from her father, she may fear that without a husband to protect her (albeit an abusive one in his own right), she'll fall prey to her father's unwanted sexual advances once again. We have to come to understand that the role of rescuer as played out here is part of the Transactional Analysis dysfunctional triangle we learned about in STEP 3. The jealous mate "rescues" the damsel in distress, "the victim," from the sexually abusive father who is playing the role of the "persecutor." As soon as the damsel in distress goes with her so-called rescuer, she becomes re-victimized as he begins to persecute her with his jealous tirades.

In order to step outside of this dysfunctional triangle, we have to come to understand that no one can rescue us but ourselves. We have to step out of victim consciousness and take responsibility for our own well-being. Refuse to play the game of "victim/rescuer/persecutor."

Other people stay with such possessive mates because they have tremendous personal and transpersonal fears of abandonment, and have come to feel that they couldn't survive emotionally on their own. Couple this with the fear that they might not be able to survive economically on their own, and it's easy to see how the weight of these combined fears can cause some people to become psychologically paralyzed to the point at which they become incapable of leaving. Fueling these primal and paralyzing fears is a battered sense of self-esteem. In their heart of hearts, these deeply wounded human beings have come to believe that they're worthless, and therefore, no one else will ever love them. They fear leaving their abusive mates, lest they be destined to live and die all alone.

Adding to these psychologically paralyzing fears is the very real possibility that if they do muster up the courage and resources to leave, their jealous mates will hunt them down and harm them or even kill them. At this point it would be necessary to seek outside assistance, including having the abusive mates arrested should their menacing behavior continue.

The entire relationship of Rung One jealousy is based on fear. The one thing these codependent mates have in common is their overwhelming fear of abandonment. However, after a certain amount of time, a person under the paws of a jealous tyrant can learn that being alone is preferable to an enslaved life. Ultimately, overcoming the primal fear of abandonment will be the great karmic lesson learned here.

Rung One jealousy types are highly narcissistic, selfish, greedy, and envious as well. In other words, they're guilty of committing all Five Sins in the Name of Conditional Love on an everyday basis.

Rung Two Jealousy

Under House Arrest

Rung Two types are still very jealous people, but not quite as delusional or pathological as those on Rung One. They too don't recognize boundaries and will spy on their mates, check up on them, etc. **They can also become quite violent when threatened, but it does take a somewhat more concrete threat to arouse them.**

Even rational, otherwise normal people can at times find themselves experiencing this level of jealousy. For example, perhaps you were never a particularly jealous person before; but, after having been involved in a serious relationship in which your mate actually cheated on you, you discover that in any subsequent relationships, you can't stop yourself from behaving in an over-the-top jealous fashion. Unless you heal the trauma of that past relationship, you'll continue to remain fixated at this oppressive level of jealousy. The rational part of your being trusts your new mate, but the traumatized part of you is raging out of control. No amount of reassurance from your current mate can or does make you feel secure. The only way to end this jealousy nightmare is to recognize and acknowledge that the jealousy is within you. Stop punishing everyone else for the crimes of the past. Forgive, bless, and then let go of your ex-mate. If you don't forgive your ex, you and your current mate are still victims of the past. If you don't know how to forgive your ex, just say, "I forgive you," over and over again. Pray to God to help you learn to forgive. You don't even have to believe what you're saying; the process works miracles in spite of your outward resistance. For instance, even if you don't really believe that lifting weights will build muscles, but you lift them anyway, you'll develop muscles all the same. So start flexing your forgiveness muscle and watch it get stronger. Eventually, God will see to your intention and remove the pain. Soon you'll find yourself forgiving your ex-mate. Remember: to forgive is divine. It's unfair to expect your current mate to keep paying for the sins of another.

Additionally, as we evolve and grow spiritually, we'll come to an enlightened viewpoint of life. We will know that "it's all good." We'll move away from victim consciousness and come to see that no one does anything to us that we need to forgive. We take responsibility for our own karma and come to see every experience as a necessary stepping stone on the way to healing and toward the enlightened path. Some of you reading the above sentiments might be in violent disagreement with me on this point. So be it. In due time, in this lifetime or any other, you will come to see the world through the eyes of God and come to understand divine justice and retribution. Eventually, you'll stop judging what's right and wrong and what's good or bad based upon whether the experience brought you pain or pleasure, fortune or misfortune. Start coming to terms with the concept that every experience we've ever had, and every experience we will ever have, serves a greater good. Either we or someone else needed to learn something, and it's our responsibility to step back and view each experience objectively to see what karmic lessons we needed to learn or to teach.

The art of forgiveness means that we have to give up our need for revenge. For many people at this stage of human consciousness, the thought of not seeking vengeance is unfathomable. Examine your heart. Are you the kind of person who wants to see someone who has betrayed or hurt you suffer and suffer, but good? Would you feel right about the situation only upon seeing your nemesis brought to his/her knees? Remember, it's not for us to judge nor to punish. Let go and let God. Leave things in the just and fair hands of karma and go in peace.

Rung Three Jealousy

Probationary Love

Rung Three jealousy types are slower to boil than the volatile Rung One and Rung Two types, but once provoked, they can be just as unrelenting with their manipulative behavior as those on the first two Rungs.

Rung One, Two, and Three types can be quite threatened by their mates' interest in a celebrity or a well-known personality, even though, in reality, there is no way their mates could run off and be with this person. However, their mates' interest in another member of the human race serves as a red flag signaling the fact that the world doesn't begin and end with them. Once again, we're dealing with self-esteem issues, and with another manifestation of envy. When we envy other people because we believe they possess attributes that we don't, such as good looks, money, talent, or status, we come to feel others are more worthy than we are. This leads us to wonder why, then, should our mates settle for us? The fear that our mates might start looking for someone better sets off the jealousy demon.

Rung Three jealousy types, like those on Rungs One and Two, cope with the ending of a relationship by seeking vengeance on their ex-mates and anyone assisting their ex-mates in the great escape – particularly if the one doing the assisting happens to be a new romantic interest. Rung Three jealousy types will seek revenge, not by killing their mates, but by undermining their success, slashing their tires, or posting a really nasty message about them on a web site.

Rung Three jealousy types tend to try and replace their ex-mates in record time. They desperately need to "save face" and end the anxiety brought on by abandonment and rejection.

Another characteristic of Rungs One, Two, and Three jealousy types is the inability to ever learn anything or heal anything because they never allow themselves to do the real inner homework and suffering that inevitably is required when a relationship ends. Instead, they spend all their time tracking the whereabouts of their ex-mates, plotting and planning revenge, talking nonstop about their ex-mates to anyone willing to listen, frantically searching the Internet or classifieds for a replacement (after all, they view their mates as property, so it should be as easy as shopping to replace what they've lost, or what they perceive to have been stolen from them), roaming the bars, or bothering their friends and family to set them up on a date, so they won't have to confront any of their real issues.

Rungs Four and Five Jealousy

"Good Old Ball and Chain" Jealousy

"Normal Jealousy"

I've grouped these two Rungs together because they're essentially your average, everyday, garden variety jealousy, just a matter of a degree here or there that might separate these two Rungs.

Basically, this is the level of jealousy that everyone accepts as "normal" behavior. Although it may take a considerable event to arouse jealousy in these two Rungs, with Rung Five being even slower to boil than Rung Four, when they do get jealous, it can still feel very intense.

A Rung Five jealous person will seem normal to most people, since most people feel jealousy is normal. A Rung Four jealous person can still sometimes come across as a little over-the-top to other people, particularly if his/her mate isn't all that desirable to begin with. For instance, imagine Marie Barone on the sitcom *Everybody Loves Raymond* vigilantly guarding over her less than desirable husband, Frank. The rest of the neighborhood would think she's nuts, wondering who else would even want to be with the likes of her husband anyway.

Rung Five jealousy types usually take with a grain of salt or a sense of humor their mates' interest in, or even infatuation with, celebrities, models, or some other public personality who could never pose a real threat to the relationship. A Rung Four type, however, can still get all hot and bothered if the infatuation goes too far.

Violent behavior and craziness can still manifest even in these more "normal" Rungs of jealousy if there seems to be any concrete threat to the relationship. At this point, Rungs Four and Five jealousy types can rapidly find themselves behaving like a Rung Three, Two, or One jealousy type, especially when under the influence of alcohol or drugs.

But for the most part, this is the kind of jealousy that plays itself out in our heads. We may still obsess about our mates' whereabouts and sometimes even spy on them by checking their emails or cell phones. Perhaps we seek constant reassurance from them, but we don't usually do anything considered by others to be too over-the-top.

To come to grips with this "normal" level of jealousy, we have to come to recognize that the problem is within our own minds. Your own ego is the enemy and the saboteur of your relationship(s).

Note: There will be times in life when we're suspicious of our mates' behavior. This can be our gut feeling or our power of **clairsentience** that is guiding us to see that something is rotten in Denmark. This gut feeling is our intuition coming from our higher consciousness to open our eyes to see the writing on the wall. This is a healthy reaction, since it's not coming from that place of fear that characterizes jealousy, but from self-love. In this day and age of incurable venereal diseases such as HIV/AIDS, to know if your mate is having sexual relationships with another person can be a matter of life or death. But in our discussion of jealousy, we're not talking here about a mate who **is** doing something behind your back. We're talking about the kind of mate who **isn't** doing anything to hurt you, and yet you still watch over him/her like a rabid pit bull ready to attack at any time.

When we're consumed by irrational jealousy we may find ourselves overeating, drinking to excess, or taking tranquilizers or recreational drugs in order to silence or at least placate the jealous demon within. Unfortunately, these behaviors tend to exacerbate the problem.

What distinguishes Rung Four or Rung Five jealousy types from the first three Rungs is that these people have a certain level of awareness that sometimes their jealousy can be over-the-top. Rungs Four and Five jealousy types are aware (to varying degrees) of the toll their irrational fears are taking on them, their mates, their friends (who are forced to listen to their jealous tirades ad nauseam), and their relationships. Yet they just can't seem to stop themselves.

Rung Five types are more capable of putting a cap on their behavior when it starts going off the charts than Rung Four jealousy types. In due time, Rung Four jealousy types can find their mates getting fed up with living under a microscope, having all their privacy invaded, and having to account for every minute of the day. Eventually these mates might leave, not because they don't love their mates, but because they've come to not **like** them. They begin to feel that they can't make any new friends, take a job that their mates might feel somehow threatened by, or do anything without the approval of their mates.

This everyday, garden variety jealousy can serve a positive purpose if we choose to see it as a signal to pay more attention to our mates and to not take each other for granted. View this type of jealousy as a dark angel saying, "You're neglecting each other, and leaving each other vulnerable to the kind word, listening ear, or passionate embrace of another. Choose to be the one speaking the kind words to your mate. Be the one who is attentively listening. Be the one who is doing the passionate embracing. Truly be there for your mate, in mind, heart, body, and soul, and watch him/her do the same in return." (Read more about loving with the heart, soul, mind, and body in STEP 15.)

In order to heal our jealousy issues, we have to deal with our own inner issues and learn the necessary karmic lessons that are being revealed to us. Perhaps we need to learn that we can stand on our own two feet no matter what. Maybe we need to learn how to set healthy boundaries, and what is acceptable and unacceptable behavior. We could need to learn to trust people or to trust our own judgment. Maybe we need to work on our self-worth issues.

What we really need to do is examine our shadow selves. Is it possible that we might, under certain circumstances or situations, be the one capable of betraying our mates?

We also have to come to terms with the deadly sin known as **envy.** When we envy other people's looks, fame, fortune, status, or other blessings, this reinforces our feelings of inferiority. We start to feel that other people are more worthy than we are, so why should our mates settle for us? This kind of thinking can only serve to make you feel more and more insecure about your place in your mate's life.

Come to see envy as a good thing, a dark angel revealing the positive steps we need to take to be more like those people we envy. For instance, if you envy someone's true spirituality, then work on your own spirituality. Use that envy as a catalyst for self-growth.

When we're given a *Soul Mate*, we're expected to learn that we're as irreplaceable to our mates as they are to us. Therefore, if you've been blessed with a *Soul Mate* but are still plagued by jealousy, start telling yourself, "My *Soul Mate* loves me. Only love matters. Only love is real. All else is an illusion." If all else is an illusion, why let an illusion torture you?

Remember, love on the lower end of *The Ladder of Love* is the kind of love that's interchangeable. Being jealous isn't going to keep a *Cellmate* with you; in fact, it'll usually make them run away faster. Try working on your jealousy issues while you're still in a *Cellmate* relationship. Stop blaming your *Cellmate* for your jealousy issues. When you heal yourself and come to terms with your own feelings of jealousy, you may be surprised by just how quickly you leave a *Cellmate* relationship in which you or your mate could easily be replaced in record time. Before long, the universe will applaud your courage, and bless you with a true *Soul Mate* relationship in which you and your *Soul Mate* are the only two people on earth either one of you would ever choose to be in an intimate relationship with.

Heal thyself!

Rung Six

If You Truly Love Someone, Let Him/Her Go...

A Rung Six type is a mildly jealous person. Only an honest-to-goodness threatening event could arouse these feelings. Even in the midst of a true betrayal, this person remains rational and quite stoic about his/her jealous feelings.

Rung Six people would never choose to try to keep their mates against their wills, or to try and manipulate their partners to remain with them by utilizing guilt or fear tactics. They would never seek revenge or act in a menacing or threatening manner.

Rung Seven

Enlightened Being

Finally, a Rung Seven type would be the kind of person who displays no jealous tendencies at all. At this stage of human consciousness, this is indeed a very rare being walking this earth. Rung Seven types are probably *Bodhisattvas*.

According to Buddhist teachings, *Bodhisattvas* are no longer bound to the wheel of *samsara*. What this means is that they've learned all of their karmic lessons and no longer have to return to the earth plane. Rather, they freely choose to return in order to expand the consciousness of human beings and to ease their suffering.

A *Bodhisattva* is a living example of unconditional love; therefore, they're free from the Five Deadly Sins Committed in the Name of Conditional Love.

Or Could It Just Be that I'm Too Repressed to Even Know What I Feel?

Of course, a person who claims to be jealousy-free could simply be lying, or they could also be Freud's totally repressed human being!

Those people who claim to never feel jealousy may actually be in such a deep state of denial of their jealous feelings that they're completely unaware of what is really going on deep within.

Still other people who claim to be jealousy-free might have dealt with this all-too-powerful and painful emotion by giving themselves the *illusion* that they're not jealous. They've done this by settling for an extremely low level of love in which losing the person they're involved with is of so little consequence that it wouldn't arouse any great emotional response anyway.

For most of us walking the earth plane right now, to achieve a Rung Seven level of jealousy would take exhaustive inner and outer work, but it's certainly a worthy goal to aspire to. Please don't punish yourself if you're unable to achieve this goal. Work toward it without worry or fear of outcome. Godspeed!

LOVEWORK ASSIGNMENT

How jealous would you say you are? Place your jealous feelings on the Jealousy Ladder.

Review the main love relationships of your life. Have you gotten more or less jealous as time has gone on? If you've never had a love relationship, think of how jealous you were when a friend of yours got a new friend or lover, and place those feelings on the Jealousy Ladder.

Note if, in some relationships, with certain people, or after certain life events, your jealous feelings seemed to move up or down the ladder. What does this reveal to you?

Just How Jealous Am I?

I Vow To Understand My Jealous Feelings

Dealing with Loss

Know that when we feel jealous, we're dealing with a powerful inner experience deeply ingrained in our collective unconscious, plus we're re-experiencing all the losses we've ever encountered during our lifetime.

If we haven't dealt with our past losses, but have suppressed, repressed, denied (read more about these defense mechanisms in STEP 15), distracted from, or anesthetized them, we're in for a real whammy when our jealous demon rears its ugly head, since all of our unhealed issues will come avalanching at us.

Coming to Terms with Our Dependency Issues

Perhaps the most important task in overcoming jealousy is to work on our dependency issues.

1. We must come to believe – with every fiber of our being – that inside us, we possess everything we need to survive.
2. If you're economically dependent on someone, and you feel a tremendous sense of jealousy, these painful feelings do make sense at some level. You know that you couldn't maintain your current lifestyle without this person. You might need to go out and work to reassure yourself that you could, in fact, survive without your mate. Although you might not be able to afford the grandiose lifestyle you

have with your mate, you might be surprised to discover that your wants are really fewer than you'd imagined. Just making some outward changes can go far in reducing our fears, and consequently reducing our jealous feelings.

3. We have to look long and hard to discover what our jealous feelings are telling us. If you haven't come to terms with your midlife crisis (yes, we all must go through this painful rite of passage), then you'll be threatened by every young face you see. If we're economically dependent upon our mates, then we'll feel doubly jealous and insecure. We'll come to fear that we might be replaced by a younger model. If you find that you're envious of younger people, and that they've become a source of many of your jealous and envious feelings, it's time to sit still and examine your feelings about aging. A midlife crisis is really a spiritual crisis in which we're meant to learn that we're much more than just our physical body. If you've totally identified your sense of self with your physical body, then of course, aging would be seen as a loss – a loss of your looks and the power your physical being generates. Learn to see your body as the vehicle that houses your immortal soul. Come to see that your mind is meant to grow wiser with time, and that the human heart is a perennial child. We all know there's a mind/body connection. We must free ourselves of the *Error in Thinking* that age is an unconquerable enemy, and there's nothing we can do about it. We can then begin to take responsibility for

our own laziness and bad habits that are making us age in dog years, and start making the lifestyle choices and changes that can keep us looking and feeling healthier, stronger, and better than ever.

What Effect Does Our Jealous Behavior Have on Us and Those We Love?

1. It can make us do a lot of crazy, irrational things that leave us feeling that we're totally out of control.
2. It can make us leave people just because we fear they might be thinking about leaving us (thus saving face and avoiding our fears of abandonment and rejection).
3. It can make us spy on our partners in ways that would put the F.B.I. to shame.
4. It can make us scream and act violently with our mates.
5. Since we can't bear to have our mates out of our sight, we must know where they are at all times. We demand they comply with our need to have every single minute of their day accounted for. If we call them on their cell phones, they'd better pick up, if they know what's good for them. This attitude can make our mates become nervous wrecks and fosters a lot of resentment.
6. If our mates should go out with their friends, family, or coworkers without us, they'd better not have a good time. (They quickly learn to

tell us what we want to hear, regardless of the truth.)

7. We try to control our mates' behavior by making them feel guilty or by withholding sex or money.

8. We become increasingly suspicious of everyone and seek to isolate or remove our mates from any people, places, or things that make our jealousy worse.

9. We begin to lose tremendous amounts of energy as the jealousy demon begins to drain our being.

10. We stop doing even the things we want to do, if it means we won't be able to keep an eye on our mates.

11. It can literally drive us or them to drink.

12. We begin to have trouble concentrating because our mind is constantly worrying about our mates' whereabouts and doings.

13. We might even cheat on our mates just to get even with them *for making us feel so jealous.*

14. As we continue to fall prey to our jealous feelings, we become more and more insecure. Consequently, our already lousy self-esteem takes a beating, and begins feeding the jealousy demon even more.

15. We begin to suffocate our mates and ourselves in the process.

16. Ultimately, what we fear is what we get. Eventually, we or they will not be able to tolerate a life controlled by and revolving around jealousy.

17. Jealousy can make us turn our backs on love altogether.

18. It can make us settle for a very low level of love. This way we don't have to care if our mates stay or go.

How Does Jealousy Make Us Feel?

1. It makes us feel unworthy.
2. It makes us feel ugly.
3. It makes us feel stupid.
4. It makes us feel humiliated.
5. It makes us feel out of control.
6. It makes us feel angry.
7. It makes us feel irrational.
8. It makes us feel hateful.
9. It makes us feel betrayed.
10. It makes us feel abandoned.
11. It makes us feel rejected and unwanted.
12. It makes us feel panicky and anxious.
13. It makes us feel vengeful.
14. It makes us feel disempowered.
15. It makes us feel depressed.
16. It makes us feel sick.
17. It makes us feel helpless.
18. It makes us feel like we did when we were a kid and somebody "flat left us."
19. It makes us feel like life is hell on earth.
20. It makes us feel like stalking our mates.
21. It makes us feel like we just have to get out of that relationship, so it will all just go away. (Yeah, right!)
22. It makes us feel cornered and threatened.
23. It makes us feel like spying on our mates, and it makes us feel that it's all right to do so.

24. It makes us feel like interrogating everybody.

25. It makes us feel like talking about these jealous feelings to anyone who will listen.

26. It makes us feel like doing all kinds of crazy things in hopes that the awful jealous feelings will go away.

27. It makes us feel like distracting by overeating, drinking, gambling, shopping, whatever, any addiction will do.

28. It makes us feel violent.

29. It makes us feel like fantasizing, planning, scheming, and plotting our next move.

30. It makes us feel like a kid when we came to realize that Mommy really did love our sibling(s) more than us.

31. It makes us feel rage.

32. It makes us feel.

The real question is – what are you going to do about all these feelings, and what are they trying to reveal to you?

The Ancient Roots of Jealousy

Most people walking the earth right now have never known love without jealousy.

Jealousy is part of our collective unconscious and is deeply rooted in our human evolutionary past, when survival of the fittest actually meant holding on to our mates. For a woman, holding on to that healthy, strong man, who could actually bring home the buffalo, was paramount to her very existence and that of her offspring. As for men, holding on to a strong, healthy woman, who could bear strong, healthy children to eventually help with the work-load, was equally important.

Know that we are and always will be a part of the animal kingdom. The everyday struggle for food and shelter is a burden that all animals, including the human animal, have to contend with. For this reason, human consciousness has been slow to evolve upward from stone-age thinking and worrying about day-to-day survival. Even in this modern day and age, most humans, if they feel any threat to their way of life or survival, will become extremely stressed out, often to the point of irrationality.

Perhaps jealousy was, in the past, such a nec-essary component of survival that over the millen-niums, only those human beings who possessed the greatest amounts of those feelings lived to tell. Since we are direct descendants of these ancient humans, jealousy, as a vital survival tool, has been carved deep-ly into our collective unconscious. As part of natural evolution, we must free ourselves from the shackling vestiges of jealousy.

In this millennium, as we move more and more into the Age of Aquarius mindset, which views mar-riage as a sacred union, and not as an economic unit, the universe is asking us to stop jealously guarding over our mates as if our very survival depended upon them. Since the latter half of the twentieth century, women have taken quantum leaps in their ability to support themselves, and, if need be, their children as well. This economic independence of women is part of God's divine plan to help human consciousness evolve toward an understanding that jealousy is an emotion that we, as higher-order human beings, are ready to let go of.

Differences in How Men and Women as a Whole Respond to Jealousy

1. Women tend to experience jealousy more intensely than men since, in the history of humankind, not only did a woman's survival on this earth depend upon keeping her man, but her maternal instincts told her that the very survival of her children depended upon it as well.

2. Although men as a group tend to be able to keep their jealousy demon under control better than women as a collective whole, when jealousy does get the better of a man, he can react much more violently than a woman. This can be a triggering of the collective unconscious belief deeply rooted in men that women are their property. Consequently, someone who tries to take their property is stealing and should be punished for such an obvious crime.

3. Women tend to get hit more on the physical level, wondering if her rival is "prettier, younger, thinner, or sexier than me?"

4. Men's pride tends to come into play. They don't usually care about what their rival looks like. They demand to know, "Can he provide better for you than I can?"

Can Jealousy Serve Any Good Purpose?

Jealousy can definitely help us heal our issues if we allow it to. It can also serve to keep us on our toes, so that we don't take our partners for granted.

When we feel we have a rival, we become more attentive to our mates' needs. We might actually try to change some of our behaviors that are driving our mates crazy. We might start taking better care of ourselves, as well. We might start dieting or going to the gym, so that we might appear more attractive to our mates. So, try and use whatever jealousy may remain in your heart for the greater good.

Summing Things Up

As you can see from our discussion of jealousy, human beings are highly complex creatures. We have our own personal fears as well as transpersonal fears, and a mind that is capable of higher consciousness thinking and the lowest possible thoughts as well. Add to this, a body with many conflicting needs and desires; a heart that can open to encompass the entire universe, and yet is quite capable of shutting out the whole world; and an indomitable spirit with a host of needs and desires of its own. Mix all this together with the past, the present, and the future, and it's no wonder that half the time we feel we don't know who we really are or what we really want. Just know you're not the only one who feels this way. At one time or another, we all feel this confusion and chaos.

Take comfort in knowing that by reading this book and doing the ***LOVEWORK ASSIGNMENTS*** with care, you're steadily moving toward a place within, a place that is not so much a new place to us, but a remembered place – that divine place of peace, love, and joy which is every person's birthright. When we're at peace with ourselves, we're laying the foundation for building loving and healthy relationships with others.

Where We Go from Here

In STEP 14, you'll learn to believe in the Sacred Law of Synchronicity, which states: The meeting of two people which leads to love is never accidental.

As I stated in the Introduction, this is the Golden Rule that will have the "Moral Majority" ready to tar and feather me. So be it.

Congratulate yourself on your earnest efforts to build healthy boundaries and overcome jealousy.

You're another STEP closer to attaining the love you desire.

STEP 14 – UNDERSTANDING THE THIRD GOLDEN RULE OF LOVE

Believing in the Sacred Law of Synchronicity

"Everything that comes from love is a miracle."
(*A Course in Miracles*, Chapter 1)

<u>The Third Golden Rule of Love</u> – Learning to believe in the Sacred Law of Synchronicity, which states: The meeting of two people which leads to love is never accidental.

If true love should appear to arrive at a wrong or inopportune time, we must ask ourselves, "Why, God? Why this? Why now?"

If the universe hands you a situation that seems utterly impossible and wrong, and yet – you just can't seem to walk away from it, then this warrants your asking God point-blank, "Why did you bring this experience to me in the first place, and what do you want me to do with it?"

In life, it's the piece that just doesn't fit, the thorn in your side, or the cross on your back that can show you which aspects of your life need more reflection and the most healing.

For instance, you may find yourself saying, "My life would be perfect *if only* I hadn't had my daughter. She gives me so much grief that she's driving me crazy."

The illusion of your so-called "perfect life – if only" scenario is a lie. Your daughter or whomever or whatever is your Achilles' heel is there to strip away your mask of denial that allows you to pretend your life was so hunky-dory in the first place.

If that daughter of yours is making your life impossible because she makes you feel out of control, then it's the illusion that you're ever in total control that needs blasting through.

In life we're expected to be careful, to practice healthy habits, and then let go and let God. Even if we're cautious and careful to a fault, there's no guarantee that the drunk driver on the other side of the highway isn't going to suddenly careen in front of us. Even if you exercise, don't smoke, never eat red meat, and do everything the doctor orders, all these healthy doings don't necessarily guarantee you'll never have a heart attack or come down with a disease. We have to get over the illusion that we can control everything. We have to stop playing God.

Giving us a situation or a person we can't "control" is one way the universe reveals to us that we're control freaks. Eventually we'll come to realize that no one can control another person's behavior, and there are many situations in life that are just beyond our control. Never forget – it's a freewill universe. For the most part, the average human being can't even control his/her own behavior, so how is it that we've come to have the false belief that we can control someone else's?

We're asked to guide our children, to love them unconditionally, and to set good examples for them to follow. Children do as we do much more than they do as we say. For example, if you drink like a fish, but tell your children to stay away from booze, they'll tend to do what you do and not what you say. So, if you truly wish for your children to break the family tradition of alcoholism, then you must first show them the way by conquering your own drinking problem. With any luck at all and by the Grace of God, our words and deeds will eventually ring loud and true in our children's hearts, minds, bodies, and souls. Trust that as you heal your own issues, you will find a way to communicate more effectively with your children, even the out of control ones.

Also, keep in mind that at this stage of human consciousness, many of us are raising children who have accrued heavy karma from their many other lifetimes. If this is the case, there may come a point in our childrearing experience when we have to let go of the Martyr archetype. We're then expected to stop carrying our children's crosses and allow them to carry their own, even if it means leaving them to fall where they may. As much as we might wish to, we can't learn our children's life lessons for them; they have to learn them for themselves. For many of us, this is the hardest karmic lesson of all.

Every time you're forced to confront the "if only this or if only that" scenario, start getting your higher consciousness radar going to find out what God is trying to reveal to you.

For example, if you have a boss who makes you feel like everything you do is wrong, and you keep thinking how perfect your life would be if you just had another boss, try analyzing the situation from the Transactional Analysis, "I'm OK – You're OK" way of looking at things.

Your boss only feels OK when he makes others feel like they're not OK. If your boss wants to go on living that false belief, that's his choice, isn't it?

What you're asked to do is examine those aspects of yourself that are so unhealed that your boss can even make you feel that you're not OK in the first place. You have to examine why, as a grown-up, you can still be made to feel like a bad little child. Who does this impossible-to-please boss remind you of – your mother or perhaps your father? Do you have unresolved parental issues? Do you need to be working on your self-worth and self-love issues, so that you can stop plugging into your boss's manipulative nonsense? If you were to just quit that job without working on your own issues, you'd find yourself revisiting this same kind of situation time and time again, until you finally faced what has to be faced.

If, however, you stayed put in that job until you healed your own issues, you would eventually get to the point where you'd be content to simply do your job to the best of your abilities and let the chips fall where they may.

"Let the chips fall where they may?" you scream. "What if I get fired when I stop jumping through hoops to please my boss?" If you get fired, and you are honestly doing your best, then know that God doesn't want you to be there anymore. You learned what you needed to learn. Now God will provide a better and more suitable job for you, one in which you don't have to put up with a tyrant breathing down your neck all day long. (View this firing as one of God's blessings in disguise.)

Now that you have a better idea of how the piece in your life that doesn't fit serves your higher good by revealing your unhealed issues, let's see how love being brought to two people at a seemingly inopportune time is another example of this concept in action.

Love is Always on Time

Now, seriously, do you think that for even one minute, God doesn't know exactly what time it is down here on earth? It's absurd to think that God would miscalculate the timing of anything, particularly such an earth-shattering event as falling in love.

Remember – To God, Only Love Matters.

People in long-term committed relationships or marriages who find themselves involved in a love affair must do a great deal of soul searching to find out what this experience is trying to reveal to them. They need to ask themselves, "Why, God? Why this? Why now?" Then they need to pay close attention to what will be revealed to them. All the while, they must keep in mind that true love always comes from God.

The So-Called Injured Party

If we happen to be the "injured party," the person left waiting in the wings to see what our mate will do, then we're asked to look past the jealous feelings (reread STEP 13, if necessary) and try to see the situation through the eyes of the soul and higher consciousness. Why did our mate seek comfort or solace in the arms of another in the first place? We need to ask ourselves honestly if we, too, hunger for more than the relationship is providing. Have we been taking each other for granted for far too long? Has the relationship been more dead than alive for a long time? Have we been ignoring the warning signs that the relationship was in trouble? Were we practicing deep denial, hoping things would just get better on their own without putting any real effort into the relationship? Have we been taking advantage of our mate? Have we been staying in this relationship out of fear, long after the love was gone? Was the relationship the right one from the beginning, or did we settle for a low level of love in the first place?

We can use our mate's infidelity as a wake-up call – not blaming him/her or ourselves for the situation, but looking at it as a moment of truth. If you honestly want your relationship to last, then fight for it. If you realize the affair is just a symptom of the larger disease of a terminally ill relationship, then perhaps it's time to end the marriage in a karmically correct fashion, and get on with your life.

If we continually whine and complain and play helpless victim to a philandering mate, we cease to take advantage of the opportunity for real growth, honesty, and truth that this situation affords.

We have to stop with the "my life would be perfect if only my mate weren't having an affair" scenario. This is the time for truth telling and not for telling tall tales. Was your relationship truly perfect before this? Can you allow this experience to point you in the direction of a higher love, by either healing your marriage or ending it and moving on?

Where there is a higher love, there's always God saying, "Be truthful. Be true to your heart. Be true to yourself. Be true to your Soul Mate. Listen to your heart. Your heart never lies."

The Wanderer

If you're in a troubled marriage or a loveless one and have fallen in love with someone else, this is God's way of asking you to examine every aspect of your life and yourself. God wants you to microscopically examine all of your *Errors in Thinking* and change your life one way or another. Most of us don't like change; in fact, we prefer the devil we know to the devil we don't. No one said it was going to be easy.

Initially, this means taking the harder path and not the path of least resistance. Yes, you might have to cause an earthquake in ending your marriage – but for the rest of your life, you'll be on the path of love and truth. Ultimately, this becomes the easier path to travel on in our journey through life.

If, however, you choose the path that initially seems easier – keeping the peace by staying in an unfulfilling marriage – in the long run, your broken heart and wounded spirit will torture and torment you all the rest of your days.

Eventually, all the truth you didn't follow and the watered-down version of love you revealed to the world will come back to haunt you. Perhaps it'll come back decades later when you see your own child reliving your unhappy marriage. Maybe you won't see the error of your ways until after you leave this earth and receive your life review. At that point, you might be quite shocked to see the happy life God intended for you – if only you had had the courage to embrace real love when it was offered. You'll be in agony as you see the long-term ramifications of your bad choice to stay in a loveless marriage (how unhappy your children turned out to be; how miserable you made your spouse, etc.), and realize, all too late, that your self-sacrifice was in vain.

LOVEWORK ASSIGNMENT

Know that a higher love is always a great gift from God. Therefore, it always comes in the exact right package, delivered to exactly the right people, at the exact right place, and at the exact right time.

Read the above passage over ten times, and then reflect upon its true meaning and deep truth. Feel these words. Trust these words. Believe in these words. Learn to honor this Sacred Law of Synchronicity.

If You're Unhappily Married and Currently Having an Affair with Someone You Truly Love, Know that You Have Three Choices:

1) **You can choose to go on having your affair in private and living your public life.** Know that living such a deceptive life is compromising your sense of integrity, truth, and honor. Whenever we compromise these core values, it costs us biologically. In other words, in the long run it will have a detrimental effect on our health. If we carry on with the affair long enough, we'll end up with some kind of chronic illness that never seems to get better no matter what medicine, herbs, or external treatments we endure. The cure is living a truthful life. Are you willing to sacrifice your health and your lover's health?

2) **You can simply end the affair.** Before doing this, you'll have to know your motives and your intentions. Are you leaving the affair because you're afraid of what others, particularly your family members, would say if they found out? Are you afraid of what others would say if you divorced your spouse to embrace your newfound love? If these are the kinds of reasons you're ending the affair over, know that you have chosen to care more about what other people think than what you feel. Perhaps you're afraid that you won't be able to survive economically should your spouse find out and decide to leave you. (To stay in the marriage for economic reasons, and economic reasons only, is to be guilty of living out the Prostitute archetype. God sees clear to your intentions and knows full well that you're not acting nobly out of love or respect for your marriage or your mate, but you're simply watching out

for your wallet!) If you're ending the affair because you lack the courage to make the changes or sacrifices that would be necessary in order to bring this love affair into the light of day, then at least acknowledge that in ending the affair this way, you're choosing a life dictated by fear over a life directed by love.

3) **You can follow your heart and in doing so – choose love.** You'd most definitely have to end your unhappy marriage in a karmically correct manner, and then begin living a life based on love and truth. In being honest, you're honoring the path of greater good for both yourself and your spouse, who deserves to be with someone who truly loves and cares for him/her as well.

Never forget that a higher love always comes from God.

God Sees Clear to Our Intentions

God sees clear to our intentions and knows full well when we're acting out of love or fear. God honors what we do for love, for that is right thinking. What we do out of fear is viewed as an *Error in Thinking*. God will continue to give us experiences that are meant to awaken us from a nightmarish life based on fear, so that we can come into the light and live an authentic life based on love and truth.

Remember: To God, only love matters. If you're staying in a loveless marriage for the sake of the children, know that you're choosing to teach your children that love doesn't matter. Is this truly what you wish for your children to learn? At best, you're teaching them to settle for a low Rung of love, and if you and your mate are constantly fighting, bickering, and battling with each other, then you're teaching your children how to wage war.

In staying married for the sake of the children, you must honestly ask yourself, "Am I truly acting out of love for them, or do I fear losing their love should I choose to terminate the marriage?" Take the time to examine your real motives.

Bear in mind that your children will relive your marriage with their future mates. (We all relive our parents' marriage, especially if it had been a bad one, somewhere along the line. We do this so that we can see for ourselves how easy it is to make the same mistakes they did. At this point, we stop seeing our parents through the eyes of a judgmental child, and we learn to forgive them for the crime of being all too human.)

Do you want your children to settle for a watered-down version of love? Imagine your grown child coming to you one day and saying, "I'm no longer in love with my spouse. What should I do?" Would you honestly ask that beloved child of yours to sacrifice his/her life? Follow the advice you would give to your own child.

If you're staying in this unhappy marriage because you're afraid of what everyone will have to say, then you're sacrificing your own happiness for the sake of others and choosing a life based on martyrdom.

Jesus hung from the cross to symbolize that He was to be the only martyr, not you. Sacrificing our true self is never a noble deed or something to aspire to. If you're going to be martyred, let it be because you acted out of love and told the truth, not because you were too afraid to defy the status quo, or too frightened to make the necessary changes that would lead to a life of love, peace, and joy.

If you're staying in a loveless marriage for economic reasons, then you're little better than a prostitute. (Harsh, yes, but nonetheless true.) This is just another re-enactment of the ancient Prostitute archetype. In this new millennium, God asks us to stop selling our soul for material goods. Love will find a way if we allow it to.

If you're staying in an unhappy relationship out of feelings of guilt, then you need to be reminded that guilt is an attribute of fear and not of love. To help alleviate your guilt, you must examine your motives and intentions for leaving the relationship. If your intention is to serve the greater good, then your guilt is unfounded, and you'll need to leave the relationship despite the guilt. Unearned guilt will eventually disappear.

People who are loyal to a fault, and old souls usually are, will feel guilty leaving even an abusive relationship. We have to learn to be loyal to those people who deserve our loyalty in the first place. Ultimately, we must be loyal to our true self – "To thine own self be true." If you're honoring the inner dictates of your heart, soul, and higher consciousness, then you'll find comfort in knowing that you have been loyal to your true self and to your mate as well by leaving a relationship that no longer serves anyone's higher good.

All of us have a foolproof compass to guide us in our journey through life, and that compass is our heart. The heart never lies. When you follow your heart, you're ultimately doing what is best for not only yourself, but for the world.

In following the dictates of your heart, you're walking the path of love, leading the way for others to follow.

LOVEWORK ASSIGNMENT

If you're currently involved in a relationship, but are trying to decide whether you should continue to stay in that relationship or leave it, please take some time to write down the reasons why you're currently choosing to stay.

Be brutally honest with yourself. For example, "I'm staying in my marriage because I'm afraid that I can't make it on my own financially." Place this under the category of "Staying out of fear." Another example would be, "I'm staying in this marriage because I'm afraid of what my parents, children, friends, etc. might say or do." Once again, place this response under the category of "Staying out of fear." Or if you respond, "I'm staying in this relationship because I care more about what other people think than what I feel," then once again, place this in the fear category.

But if you write, "I'm staying in this relationship because I enjoy being with my mate, in spite of the fact that we fight a lot," place this response under the category of "Staying for love." (Vow to work on healing the issues between the two of you, so that you can learn to live in peace and harmony.)

Add up the two columns. Are there more fear-based responses than love-based ones? If so, know that you're staying in this relationship because you're still listening to the voice of fear over the voice of love.

If you're not facing the choice of whether to stay in a relationship or to leave it, then think of someone you know who is going through this situation. List the reasons you think he/she is staying in the relationship. Break those reasons into the categories of "Staying for love" and "Staying out of fear." From your observations, do you think this relationship is based on love or fear? What would you advise this person to do, if he/she should ask you?

The Reasons Why I'm Staying in My Current Relationship
(Or the Reasons Why You Think Someone Else Is Staying in a Relationship)

<u>"Staying out of fear"</u>   <u>"Staying for love"</u>

To God, Only Love Matters

GRANT ME A HIGHER LOVE

Thomas Moore's amazing book *Soul Mates* is an in-depth study of relationships and the way our souls act and interact when we're in love. Chapter Nine, "Endings," discusses in great detail the way in which we must learn to honor the beginnings of relationships and the endings as well, for there are powerful lessons to be learned in both experiences. I sincerely hope you'll take the time to read this book, especially if you are debating the pros and cons of leaving a relationship.

Summing Things Up

This STEP asked that we honor the Sacred Law of Synchronicity, knowing that where there is a higher love, there's always the hand of God.

If you're currently wrestling with the heart-wrenching decision of whether to stay in your current relationship or leave, go back to STEP 2 and reread the section "Romantic Love and Our Top *Seven Errors in Thinking.*"

Then jump ahead to STEP 19, to learn more about paying homage to the ending of a relationship.

After that, spend some time in quiet meditation and reflection. Pray and ask God to show you the way.

Continue reading this book and doing your **LOVEWORK ASSIGNMENTS,** and trust that you'll be divinely guided toward whatever path will lead you to a higher love.

Taking the Next STEP

STEP 15 will teach you the Art of Loving with your entire heart, soul, mind, and body. It's a rather lengthy STEP, and so you might want to take one or two days to study each of the subdivisions of the STEP. For instance, start with LOVING FROM THE HEART. Take as much time as you need to really ruminate on and assimilate the knowledge given in that section before moving on to LOVING FROM THE SOUL.

Congratulate yourself on your efforts to see clear to your intentions, so that you may know the truth of any given situation. Living a life based on truth will lead you to a true love.

STEP 15 – UNDERSTANDING THE FOURTH GOLDEN RULE OF LOVE

The Art of Loving with Your Entire Heart, Soul, Mind, and Body

"Fear arises from lack of love. The only remedy for lack of love is perfect love."
(*A Course in Miracles*, Chapter 2)

The Fourth Golden Rule of Love – **Perfect love asks that we love our *Soul Mate* with our entire heart, soul, mind, and body.**

LOVING FROM THE HEART

Love radiates from the heart. Since the heart is pure energy, it follows the scientific Law of the Conservation of Energy that states: Energy can neither be created nor destroyed. The energy known as love always was and always will be.

Know that the loving energy you give and receive is everlasting.

The Way of the Heart

♦ God dwells in our hearts.
♦ Know that the heart has logic of its own.

- Understand that the heart has a will of its own.
- Our heart is our compass. Learn to follow it.
- The heart never lies. People do.
- The heart is all-knowing.
- The heart is pure kindness.
- The heart demands love, commands love, desires love, needs love, thrives on love, and dies without love.
- The heart remembers, yet harbors no grievances.
- The heart manufactures loving energy without limit.
- The heart is big enough to embrace the entire universe.
- The heart expands with every loving act and gesture we give or receive.
- The heart houses all the wisdom of heaven and earth.
- Listen to your heart.
- The heart is the most powerful muscle in your body. To strengthen it, use it.
- When you radiate love from your heart center, you light up a room. Others catch your light and your good vibrations.
- Vow to radiate love to all.
- The heart loves unconditionally. It knows no other way.
- The heart is filled with love, peace, and joy.
- The heart is bliss.
- The heart holds the key to your life.
- The heart knows the answer.
- The heart always finds a way.
- The heart is filled with hope, faith, and trust.
- The heart is a perennial child.

- ◆ The heart is patient.
- ◆ The heart waits.

Most of us have learned to put walls, barbed wire, guard dogs, surveillance equipment and the like around our hearts. Ask God to help you dismantle the fortress surrounding your heart.

When the heart speaks, it uses words like "us" and "we," as opposed to "I" and "me." If you're currently involved in a relationship, listen carefully the next time the two of you talk. Are either of you saying, "Me, myself, and I" most of the time? *What does this tell you?*

Learning to Open the Heart

1. We learn to open our hearts by giving generously of ourselves without thinking, *What's in it for me?*
2. We open our hearts when we're kind, tolerant, and forgiving regardless of the outcome. Remember, the heart houses no grievances and keeps no tallies.
3. We open our hearts when we listen, really listen, to others with compassionate, tolerant, and nonjudgmental ears.
4. We learn to open our hearts when we come to understand the healing power of love. In a given situation, if you find yourself unsure of what words to speak, silently pray and ask your guides and angels to assist you. In a moment,

the right words will flow, and the floodgates of your heart will burst open.

5. Nothing opens our hearts as quickly as a healthy dose of humor. Humor has proven healing effects on the body, and when we share a good laugh with others, we immediately experience a heartfelt connection to them.

6. Ask your angels and spirit guides to assist you in the opening of the heart. These discarnate beings are the support system that surrounds you with unconditional love. They're eagerly waiting for you to ask them for help, so they may assist you. (Again, I state: It's a freewill universe. You must ask for assistance before it can be given. There are exceptions to every rule, as we all know, and in a life-or-death situation assistance may come, even if there was no time for you to ask for help. In these life-and-death situations your angels and guides know if it's your true heart's desire to live, and so they are not truly interfering with free will when they assist you, even if you were in no position to ask for help.)

7. As your heart begins to open, you'll notice a shift in the way others begin to relate to you. Anyone who comes into contact with you will sense the unconditional love emanating from your being and will respond in like form.

Remember: If you want love – be love!

LOVEWORK ASSIGNMENT

Reflect upon the most significant interpersonal relationship in your life right now, or choose someone from the past (living or deceased) who meant the world to you. Now take the time to write a love letter to this person.

Be sure to write this letter from your heart, telling this beloved person exactly how you feel about him/her and how much this person will always mean to you.

If the person you've chosen to write to is deceased, take comfort in knowing that he/she is still capable of receiving your heartfelt words, since love is the energy force that allows telepathy to take place between souls.

If the person you've written this letter to is still living, it's your choice as to whether you wish to show it to him/her, but once again, the power of telepathy will transmit the loving energy to this person regardless of whether or not you actually give it to him/her.

A Love Letter from My Heart

Would This Person Be Surprised by the Things You
Have Written? Are You Surprised as Well?

LOVING FROM THE SOUL

In reading this book, you're already coming to a profound understanding of what loving from the soul is all about. Loving another from the soul allows you to form a bond that no one can put asunder.

People will do anything, no matter how absurd, in order to avoid facing their own souls. (Carl Jung)

Things You Need to Know About the Soul

1. Your soul is composed of pure light and, like the heart, knows only how to love unconditionally.
2. In loving from the soul you must learn how to blend your spirit with another's. The alchemy or the blending of two souls brings forth feelings of safety, trust, joy, peace, and unconditional love.
3. You know you've blended your spirit with another's when you feel peaceful and happy after that encounter, and you long to experience that kind of intense interaction again.
4. When you love from the soul, you have an inner knowing that this deep bond can thrive and grow only if you surrender and commit to it with your entire heart, mind, soul, and body. (STEP 16 deals with The Fifth Golden Rule of Love, in which we must learn to

surrender to love; and STEP 17 explains in detail The Sixth Golden Rule of Love, which calls for us to commit to love.)

5. When you love from the soul, you're never bored. You feel totally alive and energized because you're vibrating with a very high frequency of light that is of God and higher consciousness.

6. **No experience, no matter how brutal or earth-shattering, affects your essential spirit.** Although our heart, mind, and body may carry the memories of our personal traumas, our soul remains untouched. At times our soul may dissociate from our physical body for a while to protect itself. (For instance, during episodes of sexual abuse or when we're witnessing any horrific event.) During these traumatic times – and, often, long afterwards, while we're experiencing severe Posttraumatic Stress Disorder – our soul will hover above us. As we heal our inner issues, we call back our spirit, and it returns to us unmarred and unscarred. **For this reason, no matter what kind of trauma life has dealt you, your soul still knows how to give and receive perfect love.**

7. The soul's brilliant light and energy has tremendous transformational powers. Allow those powers to heal, change, and surround you and everyone you come in contact with.

8. If you've been negligent of your physical being, as you expand in soul love, your soul will teach you how to love, care for, and respect your body as a holy temple. If, on the other hand, you have been neglecting spirit in your quest for physical perfection, know that it's

time to pay attention to the needs of the spirit as well.

9. Learn to care for and think about your soul on an everyday basis.

10. The soul flourishes amidst beauty. For this reason, the soul loves nature, music, literature, dance, and any art form. Surround yourself with these aspects of life. Your soul will soar.

11. When you love from a place of soul, you're nonjudgmental, kind, tolerant, forgiving, and highly enthusiastic.

12. Loving from the soul allows you to see the higher purpose in your relationship. What does God expect to come forth from this union – inner healing, children, art, humanitarian works, or some other service? Why did God so bless you with this union? What are you and your *Soul Mate* asked to learn, create, or give back to the universe?

13. When you love from the soul, you can communicate telepathically with each other.

14. When you love from your soul, you want others to become all they were meant to be, and they in turn wish the same for you.

15. Soul love never dies. Soul love is eternal, and the ability to commune telepathically reaches clear to heaven. Those people we love at the level of soul may leave us in a physical sense, but their spirit never abandons us. As you learn to commune with those loved ones who have crossed over, and as you learn to see the signs and hear the messages they send, you'll grow in soulfulness.

16. When you love from the soul, your entire being is filled with love, peace, and joy.

17. When you love from the soul, you're in touch with God-consciousness and Cosmic Consciousness as well.

All of humanity benefits from soul love as it shines like a beacon of light for all to see and emulate.

Knowing When We've Lost Touch with Our Soul

We know we've lost touch with our soul when we begin to obsess about little things and unimportant matters. This is the way the ego sabotages the soul. Without spirit, we become more and more neurotic, and we begin to feel that we have to control everything. In other words, we begin to play God. On the flip side, when we're in touch with spirit, we learn to let go and let God be in the driver's seat.

When we don't listen to our soul, we become depressed. Our soul whispers to us all the time, but when we don't listen to it, it has no choice but to scream at us. This screaming comes in the form of anxiety and depression.

Depression is a feeling of loss, real or imaginary, accompanied by a sense of hopelessness and anger that's been turned inward.

God knows we can't ignore anxiety and depression for long. These life-draining experiences force us to reflect upon our life. We begin to ask, "What's bothering me? What's really wrong with my life? What am I missing or longing for? What can I do about it? How can I fix it? Who or what am I really angry at?"

Many of us spend our entire life in a state of low-grade depression. This depression has been with us so long that we cease to recognize it for what it is. Only when this depression gets out of check do we seek help.

At times we appear to be fooling ourselves and everyone around us because we don't appear depressed at all – we appear angry. When we can no longer bear to keep the anger turned inward, we begin lashing out at anyone and everyone, most often at those nearest and dearest to us. We can't be angry and depressed at the same time, so our anger is like a volcano of depression that finally erupts. The problem with these angry outbursts is that they're not healing us one bit. They're just making those closest to us run away in fear, lie to us, or tiptoe around us.

We have to look long and hard at our lives to see what might have triggered this low-grade depression. We have to examine our entire life, and go back in time and retrace our every step. Did someone we love pass away? Did we move away from a beloved neighborhood? Did our parents get divorced?

We have to stop blaming ourselves for things that weren't our fault in the first place. Children, by their very nature, are egotistical and narcissistic and think the world revolves around them. This magical thinking can have dire consequences if, for instance, a parent dies and the child believes, *If only I hadn't been so bad, my beloved parent wouldn't have died and left me.* The child begins to be plagued by nameless guilt and anxiety, and this scenario plants the seeds for a chronic state of low-grade depression to take root and grow.

Children can also feel guilty about their parents' divorce, blaming themselves for being bad or causing problems, particularly if their parents fought about the proper way to raise them. This neverending guilt further contributes to the development of low-grade depression.

To end this vicious cycle of depression, we need to stop seeing the world through the eyes of a wounded child, and start looking at our life circumstances with grown-up eyes.

Next, we have to figure out who we're really mad at. Are we mad at ourselves, our mates, perhaps our parents? When we've been depressed for years or even decades, it becomes hard to imagine what would be in our heads without this sense of depression and loss. **Peace** – without depression there would be peace within, and as a direct consequence, there would be peace surrounding us.

Unfortunately, in our fast-paced modern world we tend to look for the easy answer in the form of a quick-fix pill or an instant solution. In the midst of our worst symptoms, antidepressants can help us, but over the long haul we have to do our own inner homework and find out what our soul is really trying to tell us.

If you're currently feeling depressed, look at your depression as a dark angel telling you, "This is not the life you were meant to live." Take some time to reflect upon your life and what you had imagined it would be like by now. Over the next few days, imagine what your ideal life would be like. Visualize this ideal life over and over again. Ask God, your angels, and your spirit guides for help in making this idealized dream life become a reality. Start taking one baby step at a time toward that life.

For instance, if in your ideal life you'd be healthier, take one small step in that direction each day. Try drinking more water or eating more fruits and vegetables. Go for a walk. As you make these small changes, you'll harness the power of the universe, and watch miracles start to happen.

We know we're neglecting our spirit when we have behaviors we can't control. This is the soul speaking. Our souls are like out of control teenagers, who think they're immortal, and therefore there is no stopping them or reasoning with them.

When your soul asserts itself, it overrides your mind. You can't will away these behaviors because your soul is saying, "Pay attention to me!" So you find you can't stop eating, drinking, shopping, gambling, or whatever. See these over-the-top behaviors as a warning sign telling you that your soul needs nurturing.

Remember – psychology means the study of the soul.

Your soul is saying, "I'm in here. I'm the real you." I can't say this enough to you: The real you is not your body. Your body is the sacred temple that houses your immortal soul. If you're abusing your body through drugs, alcohol, lack of exercise, or neglect, you need to continually remind yourself that your body is a holy temple and strive to treat it as such. Look at these abusive behaviors as a signal from your soul that something is terribly wrong.

Keep in mind that when we become more and more negative in our thinking and in our actions, we've lost touch with our soul. The natural state of our spirit is one of love, peace, and joy.

When we just can't shake the feeling that there has to be more to life than just this, our spirit is trying to tell us that we've lost our way. When life seems pointless, empty, meaningless, and hopeless, we know we're lacking in soulfulness.

As we try to get back in touch with our soul, we may find that many things we thought needed changing in our lives are really okay to begin with. Trust that those aspects of your life that need changing will change. Those aspects of your life that were right and true to begin with – will remain the same.

For more information on loving from the soul, read *Soul Love,* by Sanaya Roman, and *Loving from Your Soul,* by Shepherd Hoodwin.

LOVEWORK ASSIGNMENT

Reflect upon all of your relationships, both romantic and platonic, past and present, to see if you've ever truly loved someone with your soul. Write down your reflections.

Have I Ever Really Loved Someone Unconditionally from My Soul?

I Vow to Bring the Element of Soul into Every Relationship

LOVING WITH THE MIND

The mind is the most complex element of our being.

We're never going to be able to fully love another person if we can't keep our moods in check because we're continually tormented by our own thoughts and obsessions. Learning how the mind works is an important step in becoming the master of your thoughts.

The mind is composed of our conscious or outer mind and our subconscious or inner mind. Our outer mind houses the thoughts and behaviors that we're aware of. Our inner mind houses our collective unconscious, fuels our impulse desires, and represses those thoughts and feelings that we find too threatening. Our inner mind also serves as the seat of our higher consciousness or God-mind and provides the raw material for our dreams. Additionally, our inner mind controls our autonomic body functions, such as breathing and the circulation of our blood.

Dr. Sigmund Freud gave these different levels of consciousness names: **the id, the ego, and the superego.** In Transactional Analysis the different levels of consciousness are called **the Child, the Adult, and the Parent.**

The Id or the Child

The id is the unconscious part of our self that wants what it wants when it wants it. The id is ruled by the <u>pleasure principle.</u> In hot pursuit of its desire, the id demands instant gratification. Our addictive, obsessive, and compulsive behaviors are id driven.

In Transactional Analysis, this impulse-oriented part of our nature is called **the Child and consists of three distinct parts: the Natural Child, the Spoiled Child, and the Wounded Child.**

The Natural Child is spontaneous, delightful, and fun. It's the carefree part of our mind that prompts us, on an impulse, to play hooky from work and go fishing. This kind of occasional playful indulgence takes the drudgery out of everyday life. On the other hand, too much spontaneity and too much throwing caution to the wind could cost us our jobs and so much more, so we learn, as we mature, not to go too far or too wild with our whims.

The other side of this enchanting, id-oriented child is **the Spoiled Child,** who screams, "I want … I need… Give me… me… me… me! No, I won't do that… I'll never grow up… I'll never go to school." **The id** might know what it wants, but since it is a perennial child, it has no idea how to go about getting what it wants and has no clue as to the high price one must pay to indulge in these wanton desires. Remember: **The id** is part of our unconscious mind and not rooted in reality. If we were to let this part of us go unchecked for too long, sheer chaos and outright insanity would ensue.

Of course, we're all too familiar with **the Wounded Child,** that part of us that whines continually about what a lousy childhood we had.

The Ego or the Adult

The ego is the conscious part of our mind, and is ruled by the <u>reality principle</u>. The ego helps to keep the id's need for instant gratification in check, even if it means pulling out every defense mechanism in the book to make this happen. The healthy use of these defense mechanisms keeps our id in check so we don't go out raping, plundering, and pillaging the world. But their excessive use can become a pathological way of controlling and rearranging reality.

Some of the More Common Defense Mechanisms the Ego Employs Are:

1. **Rationalization** – conjuring up excuses or justifications for your actions.
2. **Suppression** – stopping the anxiety-producing thought or feeling in its tracks, so that you don't act upon it.
3. **Repression** – banishing desires, thoughts, memories, and impulses from our conscious mind by burying them deep in our unconscious.
4. **Projection** – ascribing your own unacknowledged feelings, thoughts, or actions to another person.

5. **Denial** – pretending something doesn't exist by refusing to see or acknowledge its very existence (hiding our head in the sand or sweeping the issue under the rug).
6. **Intellectualization** – avoiding the emotional implications of a problem by performing an intellectual analysis of it.
7. **Displacement** – transferring an emotion from its original source to another person, place, or situation. For instance, instead of yelling back at your boss, you come home and kick the dog.
8. **Sublimation** – redirecting our psychic energy, particularly our libido or sexual energy, from a negative outlet to a more socially acceptable achievement, such as the creation of art or the playing of sports.
9. **Reaction Formation** – repressing an emotion so deeply that it manifests itself in the exact opposite behavior.

Dismantling Our Defense Mechanisms

In Transactional Analysis, the ego is called **the Adult. The Adult** listens to the hurts of **the Wounded Child** and keeps the impulses of **the Spoiled Child** in check, while allowing for the spontaneity and innocence of **the Natural Child.**

The ego state or **the Adult** helps us to understand and process our childhood experiences and allows us to heal our issues and think for ourselves.

Defense mechanisms can be seen as a gift from God, given to children to protect them from the harsh realities of life. As grown-ups, we're asked to stop overusing these defense mechanisms and face what we must face – head on.

If we're going to eradicate our *Errors in Thinking*, then we have to acknowledge the defense mechanisms we use most often to keep our distorted vision of reality in check.

For example, do you go into denial when you're told something you don't want to hear, pretending you never even heard it? Other people practice denial by saying things such as, "No, don't tell me," "I don't want to hear it," or "Only tell me good things."

Do you do things you know in your heart to be wrong, and then come up with a series of complex rationalizations as to why they really weren't that bad after all?

As a way of displacing your anger, do you come home from work and nag and yell at your mate rather than deal with your abusive coworkers or boss?

For the next few weeks, pay attention to the way you cope with reality. Are you always twisting it, turning it, and manipulating it? Do you tend to sweep everything under the carpet and hope it will all go away? If you usually go into a state of denial, force yourself to confront the issue. If you usually dump all your stuff on your mate or children, stop yourself in your tracks. Whatever defense mechanism you usually utilize, just stop doing it. Then observe what happens next. Do you find yourself instantaneously switching to your second-string defense mechanisms?

For example, instead of "displacing" your stuff onto your mate when you come home from work, perhaps you now try to "rationalize" that your coworkers and boss are just idiots, so it doesn't matter what they think. If you stop yourself from rationalizing, do you suddenly find yourself practicing "deep denial" by simply sweeping the whole thing under the carpet?

See your defense mechanisms as chameleons. Learn to watch out for and identify their constantly changing colors. Instead of trading one defense mechanism for another, try to talk openly about your fears, disappointments, and hurts. Letting down your ego defenses is the first step toward attaining lasting intimacy with another human being. When we stop being defensive, we stop playing games and allow real communication to take place.

The Superego or the Parent

The superego or the Parent, as it's called in Transactional Analysis, is the part of our mind that houses our conscience. This is the part of us that has internalized the values of our parents and the world around us.

The main weapon the superego uses to control our impulses is guilt. Our superego further controls us by rewarding us with a feeling of well-being after we have said or done the "right thing."

A portion of the superego belongs to our unconscious mind. These are the values and *Errors in Thinking* that we've acquired before the age of five, when the world around us told us what was right or wrong (tribal thinking). At this point in our lives, we were still too young to ascertain right from wrong for ourselves.

The other part of the superego belongs to our conscious mind. As we grow into self-understanding, we come to question the tribal value system into which we were born, and we begin to formulate our own deep inner sense of what is morally correct.

In Transactional Analysis, the Parent is divided in two halves, **the Pig Parent** and **the Nurturing Parent.**

The Pig Parent speaks in critical and harsh words such as, "You should do this," or "You shouldn't do that!" Our **Pig Parent** runs through our mind like a tape recording that plays over and over again all the demands, commands, and harsh words ever spoken to us before the age of five. This state of consciousness corresponds to the Old Testament patriarchal God, Jehovah, who loves us conditionally and has us trembling with "weeping and gnashing of teeth." **The Pig Parent** is the unrelenting, dogmatic, judgmental voice inside that castigates us for every indiscretion, real or imaginary, and warns us of the dire consequences of ignoring its advice.

On the other hand, **the Nurturing Parent** inside of us speaks in unconditionally loving terms, and is wise in its advice and infinitely forgiving of our shortcomings. It's the protector of life, and through its life-sustaining, gentle voice it teaches us how to live a healthy and productive life. It's the unconditionally loving voice of Jesus in the New Testament.

Who's Really in the Driver's Seat of Your Life?

Let's envision what your mind goes through as it weighs out every life choice. For example, let's see what happens inside your mind when you go shopping for a car.

You walk into the car dealership as an **Adult** with your **Pig Parent** and **Nurturing Parent** at your side, and your **Spoiled Child, Natural Child,** and **Wounded Child** tagging along as well.

Your **Spoiled Child** wants the most expensive and impractical car in the lot. Your **Natural Child** wants the fastest, most fun car in the lot. Your **Wounded Child** wants a better car than any of your siblings have.

Meanwhile, your **Pig Parent** thinks you *should* still drive your old car since there really isn't anything wrong with it.

Still, your **Nurturing Parent** thinks that you have been working hard all year and really do deserve to have a new car, within budgetary limits, but make sure it's the safest one ever made.

With any luck at all your **Adult** will take charge and walk over to the cars that are well within the budget, and are not only practical and safe, but are still nice to look at, with a couple of neat gadgets to make driving a little easier, more pleasurable, and fun, too, paying homage to both the wants of **the Natural Child,** and the protective needs of **the Nurturing Parent.**

Which voice or voices do you listen to when buying a car? This answer reveals who's really in the driver's seat of your life. Are your actions and decisions being dictated by a demanding **Spoiled Child** or a castigating **Pig Parent?** Or is your **Adult,** who acknowledges the needs and wants of both your **Natural Child** and your **Nurturing Parent,** fully in command?

LOVEWORK ASSIGNMENT

Think about a life change you would like to make, but don't. Why not? Is it because **the Pig Parent** in you tells you that you'll fail? Is it because **the Spoiled Child** in you won't do the necessary work to make this change possible?

Write down what these observations reveal about you. Do you need to work on developing a more **Nurturing Parent** inside of you? Do you have to learn to stop listening to the judgmental **Pig Parent** that lurks within? Do you have to tell the spoiled brat in you that it's time to grow up? Do you need to get reacquainted with the inner child who would eagerly and spontaneously accept and rejoice in a life change? These are the parts of yourself you need to know and own, so that you can become the master of your destiny.

Write down some concrete steps you can take to make this life change happen.

Making Change Happen

I am Ready to Change my Life

Time for Self-Analysis

Take some additional time today to reflect upon your primary relationships. From what part of your consciousness do you relate to these people most of the time? Are you mainly the stern parent flying off the handle at every little thing? Do you know when, where, and how to respond in a nurturing fashion? Are you mainly in your rational **Adult** state, sizing up each situation realistically and then responding appropriately? Are you a spoiled brat demanding constant attention and expecting everyone to cater to your every need? What does this self-analysis reveal to you? What aspects of yourself do you like? Which don't you like?

Now that you're aware of the different aspects of your mind, from which part of your being do you wish to operate? Start doing it. Stop yourself midstream when you find yourself falling into your old patterns. If you hear the harsh voice of your **Pig Parent**, acknowledge it and let it go. Allow the kind and gentle voice of your **Nurturing Parent** to take over. Eventually, the screaming voice of **the Pig Parent** will grow silent, and the caressing voice of **the Nurturing Parent** will sing its lullabies louder. When you find yourself telling others what they should do, back off and ask them what they would like to do. **As you embrace the loving Adult, the loving Parent, and the loving Child within, this natural state of being will become your everyday way of interacting with yourself and the rest of the world.** If we all reacted in this kind, tolerant, joyful way, what a wonderful world it would be. Go for it!

Dreams – The Gateway to Our Subconscious Mind

In reading this book and doing your *LOVE-WORK ASSIGNMENTS,* you've been working hard to access your **subconscious mind,** giving you a better idea of the issues you still need to heal and the unfulfilled dreams you still need to satisfy.

Our subconscious mind is always "on duty," even when we're sleeping, since it's responsible for keeping our automatic body functions running smoothly at all times and for providing the content of our dreams. Since our subconscious mind authors our dreams, understanding them can be the fastest route to knowing ourselves better. This is particularly true since our dreams can reveal what's hidden in our shadow bags. For instance, you might not be in touch with all the anger you have buried deep inside, so in your waking life you may appear easygoing and forgiving; however, your violent and vengeful dreams tell another story as they reveal all the rage you've locked deep within. By respecting the insightfulness of your dreams, you can see how you really feel, and begin taking positive steps to remedy the situation.

Any recurring dreams merit a close examination of their content. These dreams will stop occurring only when we've addressed the repressed emotion or rectified the issue at hand. For example, if you keep dreaming about being trapped in a cave with no way out, you would need to ask yourself, "What aspects of my waking life leave me feeling trapped with no way out?" This dream could be reflecting a dead-end job, a stifling marriage, or a claustrophobic living arrangement.

In terms of dream analysis, you often know best what your dreams are trying to say. When you interpret a dream correctly, it'll be as if a bulb went off in your head, shedding light on a particular life situation.

To interpret dreams, you'll need to first recognize those images that are coming from your personal subconscious and have become a part of your personal dream repertoire. For instance, if you had a beloved tuxedo cat that was hit by a car and killed, a black and white cat appearing in your dreams would more than likely represent an image from your personal dream repertoire. Therefore, it would mean something entirely different to you than if a black and white cat showed up in my dreams, since my association to that image doesn't carry an emotional charge.

Second, you'll need to recognize the archetypal images that are part of the transpersonal dream landscape of most or all human beings living within your particular culture. Besides providing the backdrop for many of our dreams, these primordial images often furnish the landscapes for fairytales and movies. Some archetypal images we frequently encounter are: a dark forest, a deep pool of water, rainbows, caves and tunnels, winding roads, narrow passageways, the sun, the moon, waterfalls, a steep staircase, a desert, mountains, and hidden valleys. Just seeing these images sets the mood of the dream, just as they provide the tone of a movie when we see them on the big screen.

Archetypal characters can show up in our dreams as well, serving as a kind of subconscious shortcut to shed light on a particular situation in our life. We all know instinctively that seeing a "Wicked Witch" or a "Devil" in our dreams can't portend good things. If we examine these dreams closely they might be warning us to watch our backs with a particular situation or person.

Learning to recognize our personal dream symbols and understand the transpersonal archetypal images becomes easier the more we analyze our dreams. Owning a few dream dictionaries or encyclopedias can help. *The Encyclopedia of Dreams,* by Rosemary Ellen Guiley, is a good place to start.

If you want to remember your dreams, you have to make a conscious effort to do so. Each night, before falling asleep, tell yourself that you want to remember your dreams. Keep a pen and paper or a tape recorder next to your bed. As soon as you wake up, write down all that you can remember about your dreams, or relate the details into the tape recorder.

Dreams and Their Purposes

1. Dreaming helps us remember, process, and come to terms with our repressed feelings, memories, and personal traumas.
2. Dreams help us to acknowledge and access our repressed desires.
3. Through the subconscious drive known as **wish fulfillment,** dreams can help us satisfy these repressed desires in a safe way.
4. Dreams can bring us messages from God or from those who have crossed over. Therefore,

dreams can help us gain greater access not only to our higher consciousness, but to Cosmic Consciousness as well.

5. Dreams can help us access the collective unconscious. Our dreams are rich with archetypal images, symbols, and visions that reveal our greatest primal fears. Understanding the archetypal images that govern our thinking and behavior can also help us better understand ourself, our life's mission, and our life choices.

6. As we come to understand dream symbolism, our ability to create and understand art, literature, music, and mythology will greatly expand and evolve.

7. The universal symbols (archetypal images) found in dreams are the language of the soul. Angels, spirit guides, and those who have passed on use many of these symbols to communicate to us with. Many Tarot card decks, such as the Ryder-Waite deck, use these universal dream symbols to convey messages and to provide guidance.

8. Some dreams incorporate past life memories. If you have recurring dreams about a particular place or era, such as ancient Egypt or Nazi Germany, it would be wise to pay attention to what these dreams are revealing to you.

9. Dreams can often contain images we've recently seen on television or experienced during the day, and these images may or may not have much meaning. In other words, sometimes a cigar is just a cigar and not a phallic symbol!

10. Dreams can remind us of things we need to do, or people we need to call.

11. Dreams help us process any learning that may have taken place during the day. This is why, after a good night's sleep, we may come to the solution of some complex problem or have a profound insight.

12. Dreams often deal with our major conscious emotional problems and traumas. Sometimes these dreams represent our desire to come to terms with these troubles.

13. Some dreams can be revelatory. These dreams can expose something we need to know in order to solve a problem or handle a life situation more effectively. Through revelatory dreams, our unconscious mind is able to give us information we failed to notice in our waking life. Through this process, suddenly something we hadn't realized is made perfectly clear to us.

14. Some dreams can foretell the future, either on a personal level, dealing with our own life circumstances, or on a grand scale, predicting a natural or manmade disaster.

15. Sometimes our dreams incorporate noises from the outside world. We incorporate these external events into our dreams in order to go on sleeping. For instance, we hear thunder going on outside, and we dream about watching fireworks, so we don't actually wake up. Or we hear the doorbell ring, and we dream that someone is calling us on the phone.

16. Sometimes our dreams are a way of giving closure to a situation. If we didn't get to say

goodbye to someone or tell him/her everything we needed to say, we can find ourselves
doing so in our dreams.

17. Sometimes we have lucid dreams. These
are particularly vivid dreams in which we're
aware that we're dreaming, and therefore,
we can take an active part in them and control not only the content, but the outcome
as well. This is quite different from most of
our dreams, which seem to be coming from
a place beyond our control, where we can't
seem to stop them even if we're scared to
death. At times, our dreams can be so terrifying that we wake up scared to the bones,
and then we fall back to sleep, only to find
ourselves dreaming the same nightmare all
over again. The next time you wake up because a dream frightens you, try practicing a
lucid dreaming technique that involves staying awake for a few minutes, during which
time you tell yourself where the dream
should go. When you fall back to sleep, you
may be surprised to see that the dream actually went the way you wanted it to. In lucid
dreaming, we begin to rewrite our dreams
and take them where we want them to go.
Lucid dreaming is a psychologically empow-
ering experience because it helps us realize
that we can access and influence our subconscious mind, and that we're not just puppets
being manipulated by unseen forces beyond
our comprehension or control. This experience further empowers us because we begin
to feel that if we can influence and change
the world that goes on while we're sleeping,

we can certainly influence and change our waking life.

18. We also have out-of-body experience dreams in which our astral body or energy body separates from our physical body and travels to other places throughout the world, joins others in the dream world, or visits other spirit realms. (Read more about our energy bodies in the next section, "LOVING WITH THE BODY.") These out-of-body dreams allow us to meet with our spirit guides, angels, or God to receive guidance or some training that will help us in our life's journey. This type of dream can also enable us to visit someone we miss who is far away. *Twin Souls* are famous for their ability to meet each other in their dreams or to project astrally to each other. (Read more about astral projection in the next section, "LOVING WITH THE BODY.")

19. Nightmares can happen when we're physically ill, particularly if we have a fever. Sometimes we may have nightmares after a remembered tragic event. Many people remember dreaming about the collapse of the World Trade Center long after the tragic event known as 9/11 took place. If we have repressed memories of trauma, such as being sexually abused, these memories can begin to resurface in dreams or nightmares. Any kind of recurring dream, particularly a nightmare, merits taking the time to figure out what these dreams are trying to reveal. If we have too much to eat, or if we have been drinking alcohol, using recreational drugs, or taking

over-the-counter medications or prescription drugs, we may find ourselves having nightmares as well. Situations that frighten us during our waking hours can also trigger frightening dreams.

If you are interested in past life dreams, a good book to read is *16 Clues to Your Past Lives!*, by Barbara Lane.

If you want to learn more about dreams, there are countless books available to you, but *Dreamwork for the Soul,* by Rosemary Ellen Guiley; *The Inner Eye: a Guide to Self-Awareness through Your Dreams,* by Joan Windsor; and *Breakthrough Dreaming,* by Dr. Gayle Delaney are good books to get started with.

Now that you know how important your dreams are in your efforts to know and heal yourself, this medium will be used more and more by your angels, spirit guides, and higher consciousness to divinely guide you, so paying attention to your dreams is paramount.

LOVEWORK ASSIGNMENT

Make a conscious effort to remember your dreams for the next two weeks. For some of you this is going to be a very difficult assignment, particularly if you have trouble remembering your dreams, or if you have never paid much attention to them.

In order to remember your dreams, place a notebook and pen or a tape recorder beside your bed.

Before falling asleep, tell your subconscious mind to reveal whatever it is you need to know right now. Ask your spirit guides, angels, and anyone who has passed on if they have anything to tell you. Say over and over, "I will remember my dreams, for I know they hold the key to my psyche."

On the third and fourth nights, you're going to try practicing lucid dreaming. Before falling asleep, visualize a dream you'd like to have. Meditate on that thought before going to bed. If you dreamed that dream, or even just a part of it, record this information.

You can further practice lucid dreaming if you should wake up in the middle of a dream. Take a moment to suggest where you want the dream to go. See if this suggestion takes root in your dreams.

Notice if you've worked any external events into your dreams. For instance, when your clock radio went off in the morning, did you incorporate the song that was playing into your dreams for a while before actually waking up?

If you're to keep track of your dreams, you have to write down or record whatever you recollect as soon as you get up. Even if you can remember only bits and pieces of a dream, capture those.

Be sure to include all the people who showed up in your dreams. Write down any scenery or places you were dreaming about. Write down any objects that appeared in your dreams. Be sure to note any archetypal characters that showed up in your dreams, such as a "Wise Old Man," a "Beggar," or a "Vampire."

If you feel you've had a prophetic dream, write it down and wait to see if it predicted the future.

Be sure to write down the mood of the dream. Was it scary? Was it funny? Was it serene? Did any colors appear in your dream?

See if there are any messages from your angels, spirit guides, or a deceased loved one.

Are your dreams dealing with your relationships? What are they trying to tell you?

Pay attention to the parts of the dream that seem to be spitting back something you actually saw in your waking life. Do you think these everyday images have any significant meaning, or are they just something irrelevant that showed up?

After the two weeks are up, review each of your dreams. Is there a pattern of fear or unfulfilled desire? What insights have you gotten from your dreams?

If you continue to keep a dream journal, you'll come to understand the different purposes your dreams are serving.

What My Dreams Have Revealed to Me

I Vow to Begin Paying More Attention to the
Workings of My Subconscious Mind Through
Dream Analysis

Waking Dreams

Waking dreams are experiences and people that come into our lives at just the right moment to reveal what we need to know or to give us some kind of much needed confirmation.

For example: Two friends are in a restaurant talking. One of the friends is trying to explain what a divine coincidence is, but the other friend isn't buying into this "New Age" stuff, so they drop the topic. Next, the two of them mention a mutual friend and are wondering how her chemotherapy is going. All of a sudden, to their utter amazement, this mutual friend walks into the restaurant. This scenario represents a waking dream that was meant to show the skeptical friend that synchronous events do in fact take place.

A real life example of a waking dream was told to me by Susan, one of my Tarot card clients. Susan told me how her deceased mother used to love Monarch butterflies. On the anniversary of her mother's death, Susan went to the cemetery. Just as she was about to leave, she found herself hoping that her mother was resting in peace. A second later, Susan looked over at a tree filled with the most magnificent, large orange and black butterflies. This experience was a waking dream meant to comfort Susan and give her a sense of closure, confirming that her mother was not only resting in peace, but was still with her in spirit.

Waking dreams occur all the time. Just as we need to learn to pay more attention to the dreams that occur when we're asleep, we need to keep our eyes open to the revelatory experiences that occur throughout our waking life.

LOVING WITH THE BODY - SACRED SEXUALITY

When Soul Mates, who are deeply and passionately in love, engage in a blessed communion of hearts, souls, minds, and bodies, this holy union is known as Sacred Sexuality.

There's no denying that we live in a capitalistic culture in which sex sells. Day in and day out, we're bombarded by mass ad campaigns telling us that if only we had whiter teeth, bigger muscles or breasts, better toned bodies, fuller hair, sweeter breath, whatever, we'd be more desirable. Yes, sex sells. Sex is everywhere – on television, in the movies, on DVD, on the Internet, in magazines, in books, and if we're lucky, we might even be getting some in the bedroom. It seems we're having more vicarious sex than the real thing. This phenomenon epitomizes a pop culture mentality that fears not only commitment, but real intimacy as well. (Read more about the fear of commitment in STEP 17.) Consequently, we remain a culture fixated at a level of sexual development that is so junior high. This type of soulless sex, which is controlled by the shadow sides of individuals, is entirely different from Sacred Sexuality.

Sacred Sexuality naturally occurs between two people who are deeply connected via their hearts, minds, souls, and the bodies.

Sacred Sexuality

Sacred sexuality is the physical manifestation of love. Sacred Sexuality is part of our ancient human past, and it's destined to reappear and take hold again in this new millennium.

When we truly make love, we don't just engage in sexual activity; we join two holy quadrangles (two hearts, two minds, two souls, and two bodies) in the great cosmic dance of the universe.

This experience, unlike the fleeting, instant gratification of lust, is transcendent, loving, meditative, and prayerful.

The Jewish mystics have always recognized that the sacred union of two bodies and souls leads a couple to the ultimate union with God. The Jewish mystics further emphasized that the home is a sacred space and the bedroom is the holiest sanctuary of all.

It seems paradoxical in our dualistic western world to even put the word "sacred" together with "sexuality." In STEP 3, we discussed the Platonic ideal of love, in which a higher love was not a sexual one, but only spiritual and intellectual in nature. This erroneous thinking was later embraced by early Christianity, and for the most part, even in our modern world, sex and church don't mix. We've been brainwashed by the puritanical ideals of our forefathers into thinking that sexuality is an aspect of our lower, animalistic drives, and something that should be sublimated and/or repressed. This repression of sexuality, with its forbidden-fruit appeal, has led to a reaction formation in which all kinds of sexually obsessive and exploitive behaviors are acted out either behind closed doors or right out there for everyone to see. All the repression of our innate sexuality has ultimately served to reinforce the erroneous concept that sex is something dirty.

Sacred Sexuality allows us to transcend this dualistic, black-and-white thinking which labels every activity as good or evil, temporal or spiritual.

Tantra teaches us to honor the human body, for it is the holiest of temples.

Tantra

Tantra has become a buzz word thrown around a lot in "New Age" circles. Most of what is currently being espoused as Tantra is, at best, a watered-down version of the ancient, highly disciplined Tantric practices.

Let me assure you, much of what is being packaged and marketed by New Age entrepreneurs is not Tantra, but little more than glorified soft-porn. This kind of New Age Tantra is dangerous, since it still keeps us in bondage to our sexuality, while giving the illusion that we have mastered it.

True Tantra originated in India more than fifteen hundred years ago, and is linked to both Buddhism and Hinduism. Tantra is part of the yogic tradition, particularly Kundalini Yoga. Ultimately, Tantra is a spiritual discipline, philosophy, and path of life that leads to ever-expanding knowledge, eternal truth, and immutable wisdom.

Engaging in Sacred Sexuality awakens the sleeping giant known as our serpent power.

Kundalini Energy

In ancient times Kundalini energy, which is the Goddess energy as it manifests in the human body, was known as the serpent force. This energy is not only our libido, or sexual energy; it's also a great spiritual, psychological, and creative force. Think of it as your life force.

Our Kundalini energy remains dormant until activated through meditation, dance, Yoga, prayer, Sacred Sexuality, or a host of other activities. Once our Kundalini energy is ignited, it begins spiraling ever upward. This potent life force begins activating our entire Chakra System, from the lower energy centers (chakras) up to our higher energy centers (chakras). Know that Kundalini energy is a transformative energy that has the power to burn away all that is untrue in our being and in our very existence. Once Kundalini energy is released, it has the power to propel our souls quantum leaps forward – even into Enlightenment.

Unlike many other religious teachings, Tantra addresses the innate needs of the body as well as the heart, soul, and mind. It doesn't separate spirit from matter, but rather strives to unify the two. Tantric practices teach us to understand and master our sexual energy as a method of opening and expanding the portals to higher consciousness.

Tantric tradition professes that in practicing Sacred Sexuality, we will awaken our sleeping serpent power. This awakening of our dormant Kundalini energy begins activating our psychic powers as well. We then gain access into the higher realms of Cosmic Consciousness.

As we continue to engage in Sacred Sexuality, we experience a profound state of deep meditation in which we transcend self, time, and space. We're able to stop thinking about yesterday and tomorrow. We care nothing for our possessions and forget, momentarily, our fears, cares, concerns, and aspirations. For one breathtaking moment, we're content to be who we are, with whom we are, and where we are. We return to our true, natural, God-given state, in which we live peacefully in the moment, enveloped by a deep sense of bliss, love, and joy. We're at ease with our physical body and stop obsessing about our flaws. Everything is perfect. Sacred lovemaking is a deep, heartfelt fulfillment that touches our entire being.

Sacred Sexuality involves the perfect communion of two people. A melting, blending, joining, unifying, merging of two loving beings until all the world fades away. Only the two lovers exist. All is well in the world. It isn't an exploitation of each other, but rather an exploration. Sacred lovemaking becomes the vehicle that transports us to heaven on earth. We wholeheartedly engage in a divine act that unites our corporeal bodies and essential spirits in the ecstatic dance of the universe.

The practice of Sacred Sexuality becomes a vital and necessary part of our spiritual growth and self-actualization, for it allows us to become pure consciousness, thus gaining access to all the truth of the cosmos.

True Tantric practices liberate us from our illusions. Tantra is love: love of self, love of another, love of God, and love of the cosmos.

You don't need to work with a Tantrika (one skilled in the ancient ways of Tantra) to learn how to engage in Sacred Sexuality. You need only to follow the heart. The heart knows. The heart will initiate you into the sacred path of sexuality, and you'll come to know that when you're making love, you have entered the holiest of holy temples.

Sacred Sexuality as Our Life Force

Our sexuality is our life force. It's pure energy that flows through us and touches every fiber of our being. It recharges us, rejuvenates us, refreshes us, and relaxes us.

In the Western world, we're taught to concentrate on the ending of the sex act – the big "O." This concentration on the end result turns lovemaking into a sexual marathon at best, and never allows the experience to move to the higher spiritual level that Sacred Sexuality soars to.

In the Eastern tradition, you're taught to concentrate on the flame that is the beginning of lovemaking; the ending will take care of itself. As you engage in this sacred lovemaking, you and your beloved become two brilliant beacons of light and pure energy.

Remember, our immortal soul is housed in a temporal body. When we engage in a physical and spiritual union with another, we're uniting two planes – the earth plane and the heavenly realm. For this reason God made our sexual drive a strong one; one that isn't easily willed away, wished away, nor brainwashed away by religious dogma.

There are several very enlightening books on Sacred Sexuality that I would advise you to read, either alone or with your partner: *Tantra Spirituality & Sex* by Osho; *Tantra: the Path of Ecstasy,* by Georg Feuerstein; *Tantric Quest: An Encounter with Absolute Love,* by Daniel Odier; and *Sacred Sexuality,* by A. T. Mann and Jane Lyle.

Making love in a holy manner brings us back to the primal state of the universe when all was one, before the great division.

East versus West

The Christian tradition preaches that Jesus was born from a virgin mother. This religious teaching implants the subliminal message that sex is dirty and not to be discussed in church. Thus began the Madonna/putana (whore) duality of thought that is still prevalent in our modern-day world.

On the other hand, in the Hindu religious tradition, temples were decorated with phallic symbols and artwork depicting the sexual union in all its manifestations. This is a foreign concept to our westernized, puritanical way of thinking, in which religion and sex don't mix. These ancient temple sculptures reveal an adoration for the male and female genitalia since it was believed that these parts of our bodies have magical powers. They possess both black magic, with its evil and destructive powers that can lead us down the road to ruin, and white magic, with its good and creative powers that can take us on the path to Enlightenment.

Let these ancient Hindu temples serve as a concrete reminder that our sexual impulses and desires are a sacred part of our being and must be treated as such.

A compilation of this erotic temple artwork can be seen in the book *Khajuraho* by L.A. Narain, with photographs by D.N. Dube and Jean-Louis Nou.

The Kama Sutra

The ancient Hindu sacred text, the *Kama Sutra,* is a spiritual guide that leads couples to the understanding that lovemaking is a sacred form of joint meditation and prayer. This sacred manual strives to teach couples to transcend their physical bodies and become one united spirit.

Engaging in Sacred Sexuality makes it possible for two people to achieve Enlightenment as a direct result of the tremendous amount of Kundalini energy that is released. These Enlightened couples represent the living embodiment of the divine couple – Shiva and Shakti.

The Complete Kama Sutra, by Alain Danielou is a modern, unabridged version of this ancient Indian text. It's a book well worth owning, since it's an easy-to-read, uninhibited translation of the oldest sex manual.

Understanding Our Physical Body, Energy Body, and Astral Body

When we make love in a sacred way, we engage not only our physical body, but our subtle body as well.

We don't possess just a physical body – we have an energy body and an astral body as well.

The number and kinds of subtle bodies humans have are hotly debated subjects in mystical, occult, religious, philosophical, and New Age writings.

The Eastern traditions believe that we have only one subtle body, whereas the Adyar School of Theosophy believes in as many as seven bodies. I've come to believe the differences are not as contradictory as they appear to be on the surface, but are more a question of semantics. I personally don't have a clue as to how many energy bodies we have, and for our purposes here, it doesn't really matter. All you need to know is that we do have one or more energy bodies.

I do, however, believe in the existence of at least **three distinct densities of bodies,** as does Rudolph Steiner, the founder of the spiritual doctrine known as anthroposophy. **We're composed of the physical body, the energy body, and the astral body.**

The **physical body** is much denser than our **energy body.** Thus, we can see, feel, touch, smell, and taste it. It's our fetch-and-carry, aches-and-pains, changing-over-time self.

Our **energy body** either surrounds the **physical body** or exists within it. It houses the soul's memories of all of our lifetimes, including the present one, and all the teachings we've received while in spirit or on the earth plane. Our energy body gives and receives messages from the outside world and relays these messages to our physical body. It's our energy field that scopes out a new situation and relays to our brain whether this is a safe place or a safe person and we want to stay here; or this is a bad place or person, and we had better hightail it out of there.

The **energy body** is the body that remembers our *Soul Mates.* It's the **energy body** that remembers and signals to us that a person we're meeting houses a soul we recognize (*The Recognition Factor).* Our energy body is the seat of our gut feeling that instantly draws us to someone either positively or negatively.

The **energy body** stays with our soul after death and returns with us lifetime after lifetime. Our energy body is ever-changing since it records all that we do, experience, and witness in the here and now and in the hereafter, and it will continue to do so in our lifetimes to be.

The **astral body** is the true transport vehicle of the soul while we're on earth, and it stays with our **physical body** for a while after death. The **astral body** is free to travel (astral projection) anywhere in the universe and sometimes leaves us while we're asleep to travel all over the cosmos. Astral projection (sometimes referred to as out-of-body experience) takes place when the **astral body** of a person separates from the **physical body** and projects itself to another location; in other words, the spirit separates from the flesh. This can happen in a near-death situation, when someone is in great physical pain or danger, when someone wants desperately to communicate with another who is far away and for a host of other reasons as well. If *Twin Souls, Mirror Souls,* or other deeply connected *Soul Mates* are physically separated either by death, circumstances, or distance, their astral bodies may travel to each other to comfort, aid, commune, and even make love to each other.

Unlike the **energy body** and the **physical body,** which undergo great changes over time, the **astral body** remains pretty much the same throughout our lifetime. It's the original blueprint for the **physical body** we incarnate into, and it can be compared to the original blueprint of a house that remains the same, no matter how many changes happen after the house is constructed, burned down, gutted, added to, etc.

Suffice it to say that the **astral body**, the **physical body,** and the **energy body** are all vehicles for the soul.

There are many interesting books written on this topic, and I highly recommend the following: *The Projection of the Astral Body,* by Sylvan Muldoon and Hereward Carrington; the series of books by Arthur E. Powell, *The Etheric Body, The Astral Body, The Mental Body,* and *The Causal Body;* Rudolph Steiner's *Theosophy: An Introduction to the Supersensible Knowledge of the World and the Destination of Man;* and Barbara Brennan's *Hands of Light: A Guide to Healing Through the Human Energy Field.*

Understanding the Energy System of the Subtle Body

Just as our **physical body** is composed of different parts such as organs, bones, muscles, etc., our **energy body** or subtle body can be broken down into different components.

1. The **etheric body** corresponds to our **physical body** (Body).

2. The **mental energy body** corresponds to the mind (Mind).

3. The **emotional energy body** corresponds to our feelings and emotions (Heart).

4. The **spiritual energy body** corresponds to our soul (Soul).

Understanding the Etheric Body and the Chakra System

Remember, the **etheric body** corresponds to the **physical body.** Housed within this **etheric body** is the **Chakra System,** which is an energy system.

A chakra, which means "wheel" in Sanskrit, is any one of the energy centers. We have many chakras in and around our physical body, but for now, let's concentrate on the first seven.

Carl Jung called the chakras "the gateway of consciousness." These vital energy centers don't show up on any medical diagnostic tests such as a CAT scan or an X ray, although some clairvoyant people see the chakras as "auras" or colors, and in Kirlian photography these emanations appear as a glow that encircles the body.

Our different chakras are aligned vertically from the base of the spine to the crown of our head, and spin at varying speeds. Our first chakra spins the slowest, whereas our seventh spins the fastest.

The first three lower-chakras are concerned with our **physical body,** while the four higher-chakras are more concerned with our **spiritual well-being**.

When we're in an emotional, spiritual, sexual, psychological, and physical state of well-being, the energy flows freely throughout the Chakra System. Just the opposite occurs when we're distressed – the energy flow gets blocked, and we begin to feel off-balance. Since our energy body and physical body are hardwired to communicate with each other, we will experience these imbalances in the form of ill-ness, disease, and nervous energy.

The First Chakra

Our **first chakra,** often called the base or root chakra, is located at the base of our spine. The first chakra is concerned with survival and our ability to be grounded to the material world. This chakra operates at the level of consciousness that is concerned with putting food on the table, taking care of everyday, mundane tasks of life, and in gen-eral maintaining our physical body and its primary needs.

When we're fixated on day-to-day survival and material possessions, we begin to exhibit signs that our first chakra is out of balance. We become anxious and depressed. We have trouble making decisions, especially those concerning our careers and financ-es. We tend to feel mistrustful of others, sometimes even to the point of paranoia, as we find ourselves increasingly filled with worries and obsessions.

Because we begin to believe in the scarcity principle – the conviction that there's not enough in the world for everyone – we become selfish and greedy. (Remember that selfishness and greed are two of the Deadly Sins Committed in the Name of Conditional Love.) We come to believe the *Error in Thinking* that it's a dog-eat-dog world.

If our energy stays blocked here too long, we may turn to drugs, alcohol, or any other distracting addiction in order to numb our pain.

When the energy is flowing freely in our first chakra we begin to feel safe, and the world feels like an abundant place.

This chakra also houses our tribal energy or the feeling that we belong or don't belong to a particular family, culture, or society.

The Second Chakra

Our **second chakra** or sacral chakra is located between our belly button and genitals. This chakra is most closely related to our sexuality and to our deep-seated emotions. It's our pleasure center.

During Sacred Sexuality we learn to move the energy upward from this lower-chakra all the way to our crown chakra or **seventh chakra**, the seat of our higher consciousness.

If we keep the energy stagnant – in other words, keep it only at the level of the second chakra without moving it upward – we become fixated on, or stuck in, a kind of adolescent view of sexuality. We don't view sex as sacred; rather, we continue to view it as dirty or forbidden. Consequently, we'll either try to repress or suppress our desires, or seek destructive outlets for them in promiscuity, perversions, incest, and even rape.

If we're out of balance in this chakra, it will display itself as a fear of intimacy. We'll also have boundary issues. We'll inadvertently violate other people's boundaries and/or allow others to violate ours. We'll often find ourselves responding emotionally in inappropriate ways – we're either hysterical in our reactions, or we act like an automaton.

The second chakra is the energy center that deals with power, and how we use or misuse it. Additionally, it's the chakra that's concerned with human relationships, and how we manage our power within that context. This chakra also deals energetically with how we feel about and manage money.

When the second chakra is in balance we're capable of engaging in Sacred Sexuality, and we're free of any guilt or shame concerning our sexuality. In all our interpersonal relationships, we interact freely with others, while maintaining appropriate boundaries.

As far as money goes, when the second chakra is flowing freely, we begin to learn to respect money, but not be ruled by it.

The Third Chakra

Our **third chakra** is located in our solar plexus (the upper part of our abdomen where we feel "butterflies" when we're anxious). It's our intuitive center, where we experience that "gut feeling."

When this part of us is out of balance we tend to be hypersensitive, judgmental, and depressed because we feel powerless to alter, control, or change our life.

The third chakra causes a great deal of trouble for a lot of people, since it's activated during the turbulent teen years. Learning to manage this potent energy during our adolescence can be a particularly angst-filled experience. If we went through a great deal of emotional turmoil during this stage of our lives, we'll still have a lot of energy blockages at this chakra level even decades later. As a result, we become fixated at this juvenile psychological stage. This will manifest as an obsession with our physical appearance. If we don't balance this chakra as we begin to age, we'll have a massive midlife crisis, desperately fearing the loss of our looks and of the power and prestige we associate with our physical appearance.

Until this energy center opens up, our primal fear of rejection will be a crippling force in our lives. Consequently, we'll begin to feel more and more disempowered, so much so that depression and anxiety can become chronic conditions.

When this center is operating properly we demonstrate healthy self-esteem, instinctively knowing when and how to assert ourselves. We trust our gut instincts and become increasingly comfortable and confident about taking calculated risks.

The Fourth Chakra

Our fourth chakra is located by the heart and is the center of love. This chakra is a bridge between the first three lower-chakras and the fifth through the seventh chakras. This chakra is the seat of compassion and love. In reading this book, you're seeking to activate your fourth chakra.

The heart chakra is the energy center where we house and process our emotional experiences. When this center is off balance, we feel abandoned and alone, and our feelings of envy and jealousy run rampant. (Remember, envy and jealousy are two of the Sins Committed in the Name of Conditional Love.)

When our heart chakra is blocked or closed, we'll have a tremendous fear of abandonment as well as a fear of commitment, and these double-edged fears make having a lasting relationship impossible. (Read more about the fear of commitment in STEP 17.)

A closed heart chakra causes us to feel unceasing sorrow and despair.

Shyness and social phobia are also characteristic of a blockage in the heart chakra.

People with unhealed heart issues tend to draw into their lives other "wounded mates" who talk incessantly about their lousy childhoods, their bad mates, and any other victim consciousness that comes into their heads. They don't help each other heal, but rather feed on each other's hurts, continually ripping open old wounds and keeping new ones festering.

People who've shut down their heart chakra lose their sense of empathy and compassion, and they tend to follow what their minds dictate over what their hearts tell them. If and when they love, they love conditionally.

People who have closed heart chakras tend to become addicted to and/or highly dependent upon cigarettes and marijuana.

On the other hand, when the heart chakra is fully open and balanced, we radiate unconditional love to all and in everything we do. We regain that innate sense of joy, and people gravitate toward us to be bathed in the light of that love.

As we move our energy from our first, second, and third chakras up into the fourth chakra, we'll learn how to follow our hearts in matters of money and sexuality. When we engage our hearts in our choice of how we make, spend, or save our money, we've mastered the material world and are no longer enslaved to it. Remember, on our path toward Enlightenment we're asked to master two worlds – the spiritual plane and the earth plane.

As we move our sexual energy up from the second chakra to the heart chakra, we become capable of engaging in Sacred Sexuality.

An open heart, with its vortex of swirling energies, fills us and everyone who encounters us with hope and passion for life. We're in control of our emotions and operate from a place of emotional intelligence. This emotional intelligence has much more to do with our success and happiness in life than our mental intelligence. The main character in the movie *Forrest Gump* proves that with an open heart anything is possible.

To learn more about emotional intelligence read Daniel Goleman's groundbreaking book, *Emotional Intelligence.*

The Fifth Chakra

Our fifth chakra is located in the throat area and is our center of will. When this chakra is balanced we're able to communicate our thoughts, feelings, and creativity easily and effectively.

When we have a blocked throat chakra we're unable to honestly communicate how and what we feel. We tend to keep everything bottled up inside, feeling that no one really understands us. Our fears of judgment and rejection further serve to keep the gateway of this chakra closed.

An out of balance fifth chakra leaves us vulnerable to addictions, for we have lost the will power and strength to master them. Our addictions begin to make us feel out of control as we become more and more powerless to stop them.

Sometimes the imbalance in this chakra can manifest in a person having too much self will. He/she will try to will away everything and anything that appears to be threatening. If God brings love, and this type of person doesn't like the package it comes in (too old, too young, too this, or too that), he/she will try to override God's will by willing it away. There are many things you can will away, but love isn't one of them, and sometimes this attempt to will away love can manifest in drug addiction and alcoholism. A blocked fifth chakra won't allow us to "let go and let God."

When the throat chakra is open and balanced we come to the place of "Thy will be done." We turn our life over to the hands of God. We learn to use our own will to discipline ourselves, to help us endure, and to find the fortitude to do what we have been asked to do. We willingly honor the *Yang Factor* by answering our divine calling.

Our center of will is located between our heart energy and our mind energy, serving as a reminder that the heart has a will all its own, just as the mind does.

The Sixth Chakra

Our sixth chakra is called the "third eye" chakra or the brow chakra and is located behind the center of the forehead. This is the seat of our higher intuition. Through this chakra we're able to receive higher guidance. Ultimately, the divine guidance we receive from this energy center will enable us to overcome our fears of abandonment, rejection, and death.

When our "third eye" is blocked, we have trouble concentrating and thinking clearly. We feel we're all fogged out and can't trust our own judgment. We continually ask others what they think and lead our lives based on what they tell us. We can fall victim to cults, fads, dogmatic thinking, and herd mentality. Our primal fears of rejection, judgment, abandonment, and death run rampant and further cloud our thinking.

When this chakra is open, we can hone our psychic powers of telepathy, channeling, and clairvoyance. Our mind is open and functioning clearly. We can differentiate easily between dogma and eternal truth. In quantum leaps, knowledge and wisdom flow to us. We see our *Errors in Thinking* clearly, and we begin to trust our own judgment above that of "the tribe."

The Seventh Chakra

Our seventh chakra or crown chakra is called "the thousand-petaled lotus" and radiates halo-like over our heads. This chakra is the seat of Cosmic Consciousness and of Enlightenment.

When this chakra is closed, we become very attached to our physical body and the material world around us. We won't be in touch with true spirituality, although we might follow a particular religion in a highly dogmatic and fundamentalist way.

When this chakra is operating properly, we gain access to our subconscious mind and no longer fear the shadow. We receive much divine guidance, helping us to answer our divine calling (*Yang Factor*). Our mind becomes peaceful, as we return to the natural state of bliss in which God intended for us to live. Our spirituality becomes an integral and inseparable part of our being. We've learned to commune perfectly with our Maker, for we have become a mystic, truly free from the illusions of the world.

To understand more about the Chakra System a handy tool is *The Chakra Deck* created by Michelle Damelio. This deck is like having flashcards that you can refer to often.

Some good books to read to further your understanding of the Chakra System are: *Kundalini and the Chakras,* by Genevieve Lewis Paulson; *Anatomy* of the Spirit: The Seven Stages of Power and Healing, by Caroline Myss, Ph.D; and *Wheels of Life*, by Anodea Judith.

Understanding the Mental, Emotional, and Spiritual Subdivisions of Our Energy Body

Our energy body is further subdivided into three more parts. Besides the **etheric body,** which we just discussed, we have a **mental body,** which corresponds to our mind; a **desire body** or **emotional body,** which corresponds to our heart; and a **spiritual body,** which corresponds to our soul.

Each of these energetic bodies is further subdivided into two parts: one part which manages the lower energies of our personality and our egos (the Lower-Chakra System), and another part which manages the higher consciousness energies of our mind, heart, and soul (the Higher-Chakra System) and communes continually with the universal mind known as Cosmic Consciousness.

Just as one chakra interacts with and responds to all of the other chakras within the etheric body, all the subdivisions of our energy body – including the etheric body, the mental body, the emotional body, and the spiritual body – are responsive to each other and interact with each other, performing a delicate balancing act.

If our **emotional body** is suffering, the other subdivisions of our subtle bodies will be affected, and of course our denser – and, to many of us, "more real" – **physical body** suffers as well.

The subdivisions of our energy body are not always in agreement with each other, and this gives us the uneasy feeling that we're at war with our self. For instance, if our **spiritual body,** which houses the memory of our soul's calling (*Yang Factor),* wishes to perform a job or task that our **mental body** does not agree with, we'll feel splintered and paralyzed by these conflicting energies, and we'll continue to feel like we "just don't know what to do or which career path to take." When we feel this way, we must meditate and reflect long and hard. Eventually, we'll be able to ascertain that our **mental body** is responding to fear, usually economic in nature; while our **spiritual body** is acting from a place of faith, feeling that this is what God is willing us to do, and that God will not only provide, but will show us the way.

Making Love in a Sacred Manner

When we practice Sacred Sexuality, we engage not only our **physical body,** but all four of our **energy bodies** as well. Our spiritual body, our mental body, our emotional body, and our etheric body are all active participants in the Sacred Art of Making Love.

Our etheric body, via the Chakra System, will activate our dormant Kundalini energy. This potent energy is then released and spirals ever upward from our lower-chakras to our higher-chakras.

If a couple achieves Enlightenment by engaging in Sacred Sexuality, one or both of the parties involved have probably prepared themselves for this miraculous event through spiritual study, meditation, or practicing Kundalini Yoga. I'm sure there are instances where neither person had a conscious awareness that they'd actually achieve Enlightenment together, but their energy bodies carried this knowledge from another lifetime or from spiritual training one or both of them received while still in spirit.

Tantra is a highly ritualistic belief system that one is initiated into by a guru. Most of us are not going to receive this kind of intense guidance, but have faith that one doesn't have to engage in any rituals to practice Sacred Sexuality. Two willing hearts, minds, souls, and bodies are all the tools you need.

Any spiritual activities, especially those that engage both the physical body and the energy body, such as: Yoga, long distance running, or dancing, help invoke the assistance of gods and goddesses, spirit guides, and angels in activating our Chakra System. Caring for your body through proper fitness, health, and nutrition will further assist you in your goal of sacred lovemaking.

Prayer and meditation are useful tools. Ask God to assist you in your efforts to gain a better understanding of the true nature of sexuality.

If you're not with a partner at the current time, pray to acquire the knowledge you need to partake in this sacred form of lovemaking, so that you'll be prepared to do so by the time your beloved *Soul Mate* manifests.

If you're with a partner now, ask him/her to join you in praying for a sacred union. If your partner is reluctant, pray for guidance. Ask God to fill you with light and love and positive thoughts and feelings, and to help remove any negativity from your being as well as from your mate's.

Prepare your bedroom as a sacred space. It should be clean and orderly. Decorate it with paintings, statues, plants, or whatever objects make you feel in touch with God and nature. Read the recommended books on Sacred Sexuality both alone and with your partner. Keep them in a special place in your room. Vow to treat the sex act with reverence, knowing that when you are truly making love you have entered a holy temple. Honor this sacred union by allowing sufficient time for the experience to unfold. Make love often – it's a beautiful way to reconnect with your partner, and for both of you to recharge your physical and energy bodies.

Allow time for **cocooning. Cocooning is the art of deliberately locking the world away, so two lovers can timelessly and intimately embrace, energize, and enjoy each other.**

During Sacred Sexuality a vast amount of heat is activated between the two lovers' bodies as the Kundalini energy is released. Even just lying naked together produces this heat. It's advised that lovers learn to sleep naked beside each other, thus generating heat and warmth that envelops them throughout the night, keeping the flame of love burning.

Practice visualization. Visualize what Sacred Sexuality looks and feels like. Remember, in practicing Sacred Sexuality, we aren't concentrating on the end result. Rather, we're entering into this act without any expectations other than to love and be loved in return. Sacred Sexuality is unrushed. There is much tenderness exchanged via sweet words, passionate kisses, soft caresses, lingering touches, and gentle massages.

Meditate. Meditation can help us catch glimpses of this sense of "oneness." Slowly and effortlessly we learn to live in the moment, feeling one and at peace with everything. *CELLpH LOVE Meditation CD,* by Marcy Neumann is wonderful to listen to alone or with your *Soul Mate*.

Perhaps the most important thing you need to do, if you want to have a sacred and intimate relationship with another, is to heal your own personal issues. Throughout this book, I'm continually asking you to do just that. You have to remove the inner blocks, clear the energy in your chakras, so that your life force can flow freely throughout your entire being. You have to deal with your shadow self and free yourself of any shame or guilt associated with sex. You need to work on your self-esteem and self-love issues so that you won't feel inadequate or self-conscious when you're naked and exposed.

You must come to know in the deepest part of your being that Sacred Sexuality is a great gift from God. God doesn't wish or ask for you to deny your body. God wants you to know bliss. When you know bliss in one area, you'll bring that same kind of pure joy to other aspects of your life.

A blissful world is a peaceful world.

LOVEWORK ASSIGNMENT

Take some time to reflect upon Sacred Sexuality. Can you honestly say that you've ever engaged in such an activity? If you have been so blessed to have had this experience, write about it. If you haven't, write down some of the issues you might have to work on before you can practice the art of Sacred Sexuality.

My Reflections on Sacred Sexuality

I Vow to Use My Sexuality as a Tool for Awakening my Spirituality

Where We Go from Here

This long, involved STEP showed why and how you must *love* your *Soul Mate* with your entire heart, soul, mind, and body.

The following STEP, Understanding The Fifth Golden Rule of Love – Surrendering to the Power of Love, is a short STEP sandwiched between this long one and another rather lengthy one – STEP 17.

STEP 17 will teach you why and how you have to *commit* to loving someone with your entire heart, soul, mind, and body to ensure a long-term positive outcome for your *Soul Mate* reunion.

In STEP 16, we'll cut right to the chase to learn why you have no real choice but to *surrender* to love.

Learning to love with your entire being is one of the most important STEPS you've taken thus far, on your cosmic journey toward a higher love.

STEP 16 – UNDERSTANDING THE FIFTH GOLDEN RULE OF LOVE

Surrendering to the Power of Love

"Lay down your arms, and come without defense into the quiet place where Heaven's peace holds all things still at last."
(*A Course in Miracles*, Lesson 190)

<u>The Fifth Golden Rule of Love</u> – **True love calls for us to surrender our entire heart, soul, mind, and body to its power. We must take down the barbed wire, let the guard dogs go, and drop the weapons of mass destruction that surround our being.**

Sweet Surrender

When we surrender to love we stop trying to play God. Once we stop trying to control everything with all our *Errors in Thinking*, defense mechanisms, manipulations, and half-truths, we can begin the real process of healing.

How to Surrender to the Healing Power of Love

- ◆ You're here on earth to love.
- ◆ You must want love above all else, and then surrendering comes naturally.

♦ You must not only have the will to love, but consciously choose to love. (True love is not a choice initially, since it comes from the will of God, bypasses logic, and crash lands so hard and so fast into our lives that we don't know what hit us. After the initial jolt of high voltage love, though, due to fear and unhealed issues, some people flee from this earth-shaking event by trying to will or wish it away. It's at this terrifying crossroads of love and fear that we have to consciously choose love and fight for it with every ounce of courage and fortitude we can muster.)

♦ Once you consciously choose love, the universe will assist you along the path to sweet surrender.

♦ Next, you must learn to value love more than any worldly goods or earthly endeavors, so that if the love you're given demands that you forfeit these things in order to abandon yourself to the experience, you willingly do so, knowing that only love is real.

♦ Surrendering to love means we don't question the package love comes in. **This may prove difficult at first, particularly if your newfound love interest isn't really your type, or doesn't match your idealized vision of what your *Soul Mate* should look like or be like; or if this person doesn't fit the usual criteria that your family, friends, or society approves of.**

♦ In surrendering to love, you stop trying to will or wish it away.

♦ In surrendering to love, you're giving allegiance to your heart and to your immortal soul above all else.

- ◆ In surrendering to the love God offers, you're saying, "Thy will be done." Hallelujah!
- ◆ Surrendering to love is a choice – the only karmically correct one.

When you surrender to love, you honor your Soul Mate Celestial Contract.

LOVEWORK ASSIGNMENT

Before proceeding with this STEP, go back to STEP 5 and reread the sections titled "Understanding Our *Celestial Contracts*," "Honoring Our *Celestial Contracts* with our *Soul Mates*," and "*A Sacred Betrayal*," to refresh your memory about these all-important concepts.

Understanding our Romantic Celestial Contracts

- o Between lifetimes, we spend a period of time in spirit. How much time we spend in spirit being guided by our angels, spirit guides, saints, Ascended Masters, and God is determined by many factors, such as: how much guidance we need before we incarnate again, or how quickly the earth world needs our particular frequency of light or our particular skills. Thus, we could die and be reborn almost instantly, or we might stay in spirit for hundreds or even thousands of years.

o   Those beings that have learned all their karmic lessons become Ascended Masters who might never return to earth; however, in times of dire world crisis such as world wars or epidemics, these totally Enlightened beings might choose to come down in droves to help humanity.

o   When we're in spirit we go through what's called a **life review.** During this life review, the karmic lessons we've learned during our lifetimes, and the ones we still need to learn, will be discussed. If we're older souls, we might help decide which *Cellmates, Razor's Edge Mates,* and *Soul Mates* we'll meet in the next lifetime. If we're younger souls, we usually won't get to choose which romantic mates we'll meet, since we don't really have a good enough understanding of what lessons we need to learn or the best way for the universe to teach them to us. We will, however, usually get to see a brief preview of the *Cellmates, Razor's Edge Mates,* and *Soul Mates* who have been chosen for us, so that our energy body will recognize them more readily when they are brought to us (*The Recognition Factor*).

o   After our romantic mates are chosen, we make *Celestial Contracts* with them, which basically state: **When we meet one another, we'll try our best to heal our issues, and to learn and/or teach each other the lessons we've incarnated together to experience. If either of us becomes a hindrance to the other, we vow to move on so that our other *Cellmates, Razor's***

Edge Mates, and *Soul Mates* can step in to help further both of our souls' evolution.

○ In this new millennium, more people, through the vehicles of meeting with their earth guides, meditation, dreams, mystical experiences, psychic readings, spiritual studies, and near-death experiences, will be having life reviews without having to cross over first. These life reviews in the here and now allow people to see where they're honoring their ***Celestial Contracts*** and where they're falling short of this goal. This type of life review will allow us to correct our *Errors in Thinking*, provide insight into the karmic lessons we've learned, and point out what we still need to learn in our journey toward Enlightenment. Armed with this knowledge, we'll take quantum leaps in our spiritual growth, evolving several lifetimes in a matter of days, months, or years.

○ **Remember the Karmic Five-Year Cycle that governs relationships, which we discussed in detail in STEP 8?** (If you feel a little rusty about this topic go back and reread the sections "Karmic Relationship Cycles" and "An Example of the Karmic Five-Year Cycle.") At this point in your study of love, you've already learned that the sooner you learn your karmic lessons with a *Cellmate,* the better. Whether you learn your lessons in a day, or you take a full five years or longer to learn, doesn't really matter. God asks only that we learn and either move the relationship up *The Ladder of*

Love or move on. Of course, when ending our relationships, we must always try to end them in a karmically correct manner. (If you've forgotten what it means to leave a relationship in a karmically correct manner, go back to STEP 8 and reread the section "Leaving a Relationship in a Karmically Correct Manner.")

○ If we receive a *Soul Mate* relationship, God hopes we'll be able to surrender to this love, so that we'll heal our issues and honor the great love that we've been given. If we don't resolve our issues in a reasonable amount of time while in a *Soul Mate* relationship, then we're under karmic obligation to end that relationship and move on. Ending a *Soul Mate* relationship that is not a healing one is part of our *Celestial Contract.* Ending that relationship in a karmically correct manner gives us an opportunity to move on and learn what each of us needs to learn, either by spending a period of time alone, or within the framework of another relationship. Depending upon personal karma, this other relationship might be a slide down *The Ladder of Love* to a *Razor's Edge Mate* or even a *Cellmate* one, or perhaps you'll be given another *Soul Mate, Twin Soul,* or *Mirror Soul,* if that's what God thinks your soul needs to evolve further.

God will give you whatever level of love you need to heal. It's then up to you to surrender to it.

To learn more about life reviews read *The Tenth Insight: Holding the Vision: An Experiential Guide,* by James Redfield and Carol Adrienne. To learn more about our pre-birth contracts read *Sacred Contracts,* by Caroline Myss, Ph.D.

When God blesses us with a Soul Mate, if we surrender to that love, we're being given a chance to learn our karmic lessons through love, peace, and joy.

What Keeps Us from Surrendering to the Power of Love?

We resist surrendering to love because we innately know that when we're in that deep place of love, all of our unhealed issues will surface. (Read more about this issue in STEP 18, Understanding The Seventh Golden Rule of Love – Heal Thyself.) This is God's compassionate way of allowing us to be in a safe place, before we're asked to confront our greatest fears, our deepest wounds, and our biggest regrets.

Love reveals all. Anything that's hidden will be brought forth. Remember – what we keep hidden, locked away in our shadow bags, will destroy us, and what we bring forth into the light of love will heal us.

This revelatory period becomes the emotionally rocky junction in a relationship when many people jump ship or run away in fear. These people tell themselves the biggest lie of all: *Before love came into my life everything was okay, but now that this person is here all this anxiety, fear, and panic has set in.* But the truth is – that all the angst was always there. Love just brought forth what was buried deep inside. Hidden fears and unhealed issues are like a deadly cancer that eats away at your insides whether you're aware of it or not. Love simply reveals what was hidden beneath the surface all along.

Until we're healed beings – a great love will always bring forth a great fear.

Meeting at the Treacherous Crossroads of Love and Fear

When you meet a *Soul Mate* you're at a crossroads. You can choose to continue keeping all of your unhealed issues tightly locked away in your shadow bags and go on walking the known path – the path of fear, which eventually becomes your own road to ruin; or you could choose to take a giant leap of faith and plunge headfirst into the dark, uncharted waters of your psyche, and start walking down the path of love, which is the way to salvation. This can become the hero's moment for you, when you decide to be the master of your destiny and take your life where you want it to go; or this could be another coward's moment for you, when you decide to turn your back on love and flee in fear.

Becoming the Master of Your Destiny

You become the master of your destiny when you find the courage to follow your heart, which is telling you to forge forward, even though every bone in your body screams at you to flee.

You can start being the author of your life by being yourself and telling the truth. If you're not sure what you're feeling, or why you feel like you're jumping out of your skin, talk honestly to your *Soul Mate* about the chaos you're feeling within. Don't pretend everything is okay, when you know that it's not. Don't shut this person out. Trust in the love you've been given. Have faith that love is perfect even when we're not. Surrender to your feelings. Surrender to love. Remember: *only love matters.* Have faith that the two of you – together – can weather any storm.

Ask your angels, spirit guides, and deceased loved ones to shed light on the situation. Know that prayers for guidance are always answered. Pay attention to the people you encounter, to the songs that move you, or to a movie, television show, book, or magazine article that hits home. This is how divine guidance shows us the way.

Pray for the strength and endurance to face what you must face. Take a few minutes a day to meditate and ask for clarity and healing.

Continue to act in a loving and kind way to your *Soul Mate*, even though you feel like running away. If you find yourself engaging in petty fights, stop yourself. All that bickering is your subconscious mind trying to drive your lover away, so you can go back to hiding your head in the sand.

Love instantly changes everything, and this scares us to the bones.

Remember that most human beings don't like change. They usually prefer the known path, even if it's the wrong one. If you're one such person, then your karmic lesson is to learn that change is an inevitable part of life. You need to learn that change can be a good thing, in fact, a very good thing, if that change came about due to the power of love.

If you've always been a control freak and God gives you a high *Soul Mate,* the kind of irresistible love that takes you by storm and grips your heart, soul, and body, completely bypassing your mind, know that you'll feel terror of the greatest magnitude when the dust settles over your relationship. God wants you to learn to let go and let love.

If you have trouble embracing change, read *The Zing,* by Ronald P.Villano, M.S., ASAC. *The Zing* teaches a level of living in which change is always good.

LOVEWORK ASSIGNMENT

Reflect upon all of your romantic relationships. Have you ever surrendered to love? If so, write about how it felt to let go and let love. If not, why not? Write about it.

Did I Ever Surrender to Love?

To Truly Love Someone We Must Find the Courage to Surrender

After Sweet Surrender, the Next Step is Commitment

In the next STEP, we'll explore one of the main obstacles that stands in the way of our ability to surrender to love – the fear of commitment.

When I first began writing this book, it was channeled to me that I would need to devote an entire STEP to the fear of commitment. I thought, *How absurd is that?* I felt a page or two would surely do the trick. From that moment on, my angels and spirit guides began working frantically to reveal to me the magnitude of this fear, and just how wrong my initial response had been.

I look back at that period of divine guidance with utter amazement. Even now it's hard to fathom the sheer number of devastated people who landed on my doorstep for Tarot card readings, attempting to make some sense out of the heartbreaking consequences of either their inability or their partners' inability to commit to their relationship.

After a while, I began noticing that for most of these people, this wasn't the first time the fear of commitment had wreaked havoc on their relationships, and I began to see a pattern emerging. I realized that some people wore their fear of commitment on their sleeves for everyone to see, and I referred to these people as **Classic Commitment Dodgers.** Still others managed to keep their fear of commitment hidden (often even to themselves), and I called these people **Closet Commitment Dodgers.**

Nothing short of serendipity led me to a book that I've since come to call the Bible of Commitment Issues, *He's Scared, She's Scared: Understanding the Hidden Fears that Sabotage Your Relationships,* by Steven

Carter and Julia Sokol. I discovered this treasure buried among the books for sale at my local library and purchased it, thinking that I'd take a quick look at it, if and when I ever got around to it. (I got to it sooner rather than later because my spirit guides kept screaming at me to read it!) It didn't take long for me to realize how the universe had conspired to guide me to this illuminating book, proving that what we need to know, learn, or teach will be brought to us one way or another.

After finishing the following STEP, if you should suspect that you have a fear of commitment, either a "Closet" case or a "Classic" one, I strongly suggest that you read, *He's Scared, She's Scared* – cover to cover. Since this is an entire book devoted to this topic, it goes into much greater detail about the fear of commitment, its causes and consequences, than I can ever do in just one short STEP.

I can just hear many of you thinking right now, *Oh, I can skip the next STEP, since I know for a fact that I don't have a fear of commitment.*

Don't bet the house on it!

Learning to let go and let love is the key to recognizing and cherishing a higher love.

Pray for the strength to surrender.

STEP 17 – UNDERSTANDING THE SIXTH GOLDEN RULE OF LOVE

Committing to Love

"I seek a future different from the past."
(*A Course in Miracles,* Lesson 313)

<u>The Sixth Golden Rule of Love</u> – **True love asks that we commit to our *Soul Mate* with our entire heart, soul, mind, and body.**

The Fear of Commitment

The fear of commitment has become a New Age collective unconscious fear; however, its strangulating roots run deep into our primal collective unconscious fears.

Since the latter half of the twentieth century, the fear of commitment has spread like wildfire throughout the modern world as a direct result of the many lifestyle choices that have opened up to us. For instance, we can choose to marry, not marry, or marry many times over. We could also choose to never have a monogamous relationship and to stay a player indefinitely or remain relationship-free for the duration or remain celibate for a time, without bearing the stigma that in the past such alternative lifestyles might have incurred. With so many options available to us, how can we be sure which one is best? For this reason, there are gazillions of people out there who can't make up their minds one way or another as to what relationship style suits them best, and so they continually take steps toward and away from intimacy.

The fear of commitment, at the simplest level, is really the fear of making the wrong decision or the wrong choice. We can overcome our fear of commitment if we accept our humanness with all its imperfection, misperceptions, and flaws. We've incarnated on earth school to learn, grow, and evolve. God loves us unconditionally and says, "Make mistakes. Make many mistakes. Just don't keep making the same ones over and over. Choose again." Correcting your mistakes and *Errors in Thinking* helps you learn to listen to your heart, soul, and higher consciousness, so that you'll be able to choose the lifestyle that will best serve your higher good.

Learning to Make Intelligent Choices

In the not-so-distant past, marriage didn't represent a restriction of our freedom; rather, it was viewed as an initiation into the adult world. The marriage license granted us permission to engage freely in sexual activity and allowed us to take charge of our own life without having to answer to our parents.

With the advent of the birth control pill in the 1960s, the sexual revolution was born. In the decades that have followed, sexual activity outside of the context of traditional marriage has become more and more socially acceptable. This phenomenon opened up our current lifestyle options.

Getting and staying married is no longer an absolute must. The decision to have children or not to have them is up to us. Even how and when to have them is our choice: We can choose to have children in the framework of a traditional marriage, or we can opt for single parenthood. We can be part of either a straight couple or a gay couple raising children. Even the way we have children has also opened up – we can conceive them naturally or artificially, or allow a surrogate to carry them for us. We can adopt them from anywhere in the world without regard to race, creed, or color. Brady Bunch-type families are commonplace now, with people blending together the children they had with other partners to form a new family unit, and then sometimes adding to this motley tribe by having some more children together, making the terms "stepsister," "stepbrother," "half brother," and "half sister" household words.

In a relatively short period of time, the rules of the game of life changed, wreaking havoc on the human mind.

This present-day, paralyzing fear of commitment stems from the realization that if we choose one option, then we may be shutting out others. Factoring in all this, is it any wonder that modern people are a splintered lot with one foot in one location and the other foot out the door?

The only way to know what kind of lifestyle best suits you is to know yourself inside and out. When you know who you truly are, you'll instinctively know the kind of life you wish to live, and you'll find yourself, ready, willing, and able to fully commit to it.

The fear of commitment is a powerfully destructive force that can and does wreak havoc on our most intimate relationships. Taming and mastering this Goliath calls for us to face head-on our greatest personal and transpersonal fears.

All the Things We Really Fear when We Fear Commitment

1. **THE UNKNOWN** – True love is uncharted territory for most of us. If I commit to you, will I **survive** this love?
2. **BETRAYAL** – If I love you, and you betray me, will I **survive**?
3. **ABANDONMENT** – If I commit to you with my entire heart, soul, mind, and body, and you leave me, will I be capable of **surviving** without you?
4. **REJECTION** – If I commit to you with my entire being, and you reject me, can I **survive** without you?
5. **NOT ANSWERING OUR CALLING** (*Yang Factor*) – If I commit to you, will I still be able to answer my calling, and if not, will I **survive**? We fear not answering our calling because we think that God may punish us for not doing so by striking us dead, or by taking away our or our loved ones' health, or by wreaking havoc on our material world and goods via some natural or unnatural disaster. Additionally, we fear if we don't answer our calling, we'll be severely punished in the afterlife.

6. **LOSING CONTROL** – When we truly love someone, we're not in control of our heart, mind, soul, or body, leaving us to wonder whether we will be able to **survive** without this person.

7. **JUDGMENT** – If I commit to you, what will others say and think? What will God think or do? Our **fear of judgment** brings up our **fear of losing face,** which translates into the **fear of rejection,** which boils down to our **fear of abandonment,** which translates into **fear of not being able to survive,** which is really our **fear of death, which ultimately boils down to our greatest collective unconscious fear of all – our fear of God.**

8. **DEATH** – What if I commit to you and you pass away? Will I be able to **survive** without you?

This New Age version of the fear of commitment packs a tremendous punch because it encapsulates within it so many of our everyday fears as well as our massive primal, collective unconscious fears. As you can see from the above list, these terrifying fears wear numerous masks and take many different forms.

By reading this book, you are joining me in the work of rewriting the human collective unconscious, which is overridden with fear, and inscribing within it a Cosmic Consciousness rooted in love.

All the alternative lifestyle choices in this new millennium – and the fear of commitment that these choices bring with them – are God's brilliant way of guiding us to rapidly overcome our personal fears, as well as our deep-seated collective unconscious fears, so that we can become beacons of light and love.

What Does Committing to Someone Have to Do with Love?

Love without commitment is a mere shadow of an intense feeling that is destined to go nowhere. In the past, it was mainly men who had commitment issues, but now with the economic and social liberation of women, they too are facing the commitment demon.

Committing to someone doesn't necessarily mean you have to get legally married to him/her. Traditional marriages (the old archetype of marriage) have often been little more than a legal partnership and/or a business association between two people who may or may not be totally committed to each other in heart, soul, mind, and body. The new archetype of marriage recognizes that two *Soul Mates* form a sacred union by loving, surrendering, and committing to each other with their entire beings.

Commitment in the New Age of Aquarius is concerned with loving, surrendering, and honoring your *Soul Mate* with your entire heart, soul, mind, and body. To God, that and that alone constitutes *Holy Matrimony*.

Remember – the very fact that we're free to choose from a host of lifestyle options in the twenty-first century has contributed vastly to the fear of commitment. In order to overcome this fear we have to readdress the entire issue of what it means to truly commit to another person.

What Are Some of the Reasons that People Might Fear Committing to One Another?

1. **We've already discussed the transpersonal fears that can lead us to fear commitment, such as fears of abandonment and rejection.** If you never really commit to someone, then you never have to fear that that person will abandon or reject you.

2. **Then there are the common, everyday fears that can get in the way.** For example: "Can I afford this commitment financially?" "Will I be able to remain faithful to this person?" or "Will my partner be able to remain faithful to me?"

3. **Oftentimes we fear commitment because we view commitment in the prison-like sense, since this is what we saw all around us when we were growing up.** We have to learn to stop viewing a long-term relationship as the traditional "old ball and chain" thing. We have to reprogram ourselves to realize that our marriage or long-term relationship can be as open as we choose. For example, just because

you're married doesn't mean you have to do everything as a couple. If you like to ski, but your mate hates it, then by all means plan a ski trip with your friends and let your mate plan a different trip. (Of course, we have to tame the jealousy demon first in order to do this.) Understand that life as you currently know it doesn't have to come to an end just because you have a ring around your finger. Work out the logistics together, as a couple, and do what works best for the two of you. If you're involved in a relationship right now, but are fearful of committing to it, sit down and talk honestly with your mate about your fears. Tell your mate about the kind of committed relationship you would like to be in, and the kind of committed relationship that makes you want to bolt out the door. See if your mate's idea of commitment suits yours. **Remember, love is not a compromise as far as the big issues go. If you and your mate have sizable differences on what commitment means, then you have to face the fact that your relationship isn't going to work over the long haul.**

4. **In this day and age, people have come to fear commitment because they don't want to go through all the angst, not to mention the financial bloodbath that traditionally accompanies a divorce.** We have to come to understand that ending a committed relationship doesn't denote failure, nor does it mean that we have to come to hate our mates and drag them through the mud. Ending relationships in a way that is karmically correct is paramount

in this new millennium. (In STEP 19, we'll be paying homage to the ending of relationships.)

5. **If our own parents' marriage was a train wreck, we can fear duplicating this catastrophic scenario.** In reading this book and doing your *LOVEWORK ASSIGNMENT,* know that you're going a long way in healing your own childhood issues so that you won't be doomed to continually repeat the past.

6. **Sometimes we fear committing to another person because of our own self-esteem issues.** We fear that if someone ever really got to see and know us on an everyday basis, he/she would come to see all our flaws and shortcomings and leave us. Once again, these kinds of feelings reveal that we still need to work on our self-love issues.

7. **The fear of commitment can manifest after a relationship we really cared about ended, either through death or other causes.** For example, if we lost a beloved parent, particularly when we were young, our fear of abandonment can become so overwhelming that we never allow ourselves to love someone that much again. Subconsciously, we vow never to commit to another person, because we never want to feel that kind of heart-wrenching pain ever again.

8. **Sometimes we fear commitment because we know that even if people tell us they'll love us forever and will never leave us, they could unwittingly abandon us by going and dying on us.** This fear of abandonment due to an un-

timely death of someone we love can result in our inability to commit our entire being to another person.

9. **Our energy body contains the emotional memories of other lifetimes in which we were involved in disastrous marriages that we couldn't get out of.** Up until the latter part of the twentieth century, if you married, for the most part you stayed married no matter what. Our energy body remembers this emotional imprisonment, and this haunting memory warns us to beware of getting ourselves into something we can't get out of. For the most part, this is an irrational fear now, because terminating a marriage has become easier and more socially acceptable at this point in time.

10. **Most of the time our fear of commitment is rooted in one or more of the above stated reasons.**

Committing to a person is a choice.

LOVEWORK ASSIGNMENT

Reflect upon your own relationship(s). Has the fear of commitment (either yours or someone else's) ever played a factor? How did this affect you? Where do you think this fear emanated from? For instance, did you or your mate have parents who had a bad marriage? What issues do you still have to come to terms with?

After you finish the rest of this STEP, I want you to revisit this assignment to see if your answer has changed. Perhaps you thought that you weren't afraid of commitment, but have come to see that you really are a Closet Commitment Dodger.

If you've never had a romantic relationship, do you think your own fear of commitment could be the reason why? After finishing this STEP, try revisiting this assignment to see if your answer has changed.

My Experience with Commitment Issues

True Love is a Commitment to Love Another with our Entire Heart, Soul, Mind, and Body

A great love (Rungs Six through Nine on The Ladder of Love) will momentarily override the fear of commitment. Two Soul Mates willingly rush into this relationship, but soon the fear of commitment rears its ugly head, leaving a trail of broken hearts, dreams, and promises in its path.

Telltale Signs that You're Dealing with Someone Who's Afraid of Commitment

The main warning sign to watch for is your own gut feeling telling you that every time you appear to be getting closer to this person, he/she suddenly becomes unavailable and/or begins acting evasively and emotionally distant for no apparent reason. Another sure giveaway that you're dealing with commitment issues is the way that your mate seems to be giving you a lot of mixed messages, which run the gamut from hot, hot, hot and passionate to frigid cold and emotionless. For instance, one minute this person tells you that he/she loves you, and next minute he/she is running in the opposite direction.

There are two kinds of Commitment Dodgers: the overt ones, or Classic Commitment Dodg-

ers, who wear their fears on their sleeves for every-
one to see; and the covert ones, or Closet Commit-
ment Dodgers, whose fears are often well-hidden.

Classic Commitment Dodgers
(How to Recognize One)

1. Phone calls, text messages, and emails from their mates go unanswered or unreturned for no apparent reason.

2. Plans with their mates are canceled or excuses are made at the last minute to renege on some prior commitment.

3. Classic Commitment Dodgers are the masters of mixed messages. Their words say one thing, their actions another. For instance, they tell their mates they love them, and then break up with them.

4. Classic Commitment Dodgers are known for "pulling a geographic," in which they decide almost overnight to move far away, or take a job on the other side of the country, or enlist for military service without consulting their mates.

5. The way they make love changes in that the intimacy that was once there is gone. They no longer make love in a tender, caring way and

reduce the whole experience to just having sex. Or suddenly they say, "I just want to be friends," and stop having sex all together in an attempt to cool off the relationship. Sometimes they only allow you to have "phone sex" with them in lieu of the real thing.

6. "I love you" is said by them one moment, and then in a blink of an eye Classic Commitment Dodgers become either emotionally or physically absent.

7. The usual gestures of love are missing. For example, if and when given, the birthday cards or Valentine's cards Classic Commitment Dodgers choose are perfunctory in the words used, and gifts are impersonal at best. Sometimes they choose to forget or ignore important dates like birthdays and anniversaries altogether.

8. Classic Commitment Dodgers make their mates continually feel as if they're never sure if or when they'll see each other again. If these bewildered mates should be so bold as to inquire when the two of them will get together again, the question is answered defensively, evasively, or totally ignored.

9. More and more boundaries are set up to limit getting closer. For example, a rigid dating schedule is enforced in an effort to put the brakes on the relationship and control everything. Classic Commitment Dodgers erect

these walls because they don't want their mates to get to know them too well. They also put off meeting their mates' close friends and family and won't permit their mates to meet theirs.

10. Suddenly Classic Commitment Dodgers claim to want to start seeing other people or profess that they've fallen in love with someone else almost overnight.

11. Classic Commitment Dodgers are famous for cheating on their mates just when everything seems to be going great, and they make sure that they get caught. Subconsciously, they hope that their mates will be so hurt by the discovery of the affair that they walk away – thereby, letting them off the hook.

12. Out of the blue they appear cold or unresponsive. When confronted with the sudden change of heart, they become hostile and belligerent. Classic Commitment Dodgers, who may otherwise be kind and compassionate human beings, can show extreme insensitivity and downright cruelty if they begin to feel "trapped." A dead giveaway that we're dealing with someone with an over-the-top fear of commitment is this unexplainable cruel behavior from an otherwise kind human being.

13. Classic Commitment Dodgers act like cornered animals when their mates ask questions or expect an answer.

14. When their frustrated, angry, and hurt partners finally get fed up and move on, Classic
Commitment Dodgers resurface, wining and
dining their partners in an all-out effort to win
them back. They stay only long enough to play
out a condensed version of the whole relationship in record time. Basically, this boils down
to this scenario: You leave/I'm back/I win you
back, and then – I'm out of here!

15. Classic Commitment Dodgers keep their
mates in a constant state of confusion, in which
they never seem to know what will happen
next.

16. Classic Commitment Dodgers appear to be
able to end meaningful relationships on a
dime, often walking out when the relationship is really heating up, leaving the remaining partner in a state of emotional devastation,
wondering what in the world went wrong.

17. Some Classic Commitment Dodgers can never
say, "I love you." Others only say it right before
they bolt out the door. Still others say, "I love
you" and then list all the reasons why the relationship can't work, won't work, or shouldn't
work.

18. Classic Commitment Dodgers often can't
even commit to spending a special occasion
with their mates.

19. Some Classic Commitment Dodgers leave
when the relationship is still in its infancy,

wanting to nip the whole damn thing right in the bud. For instance, after a great first date, they'll never contact that person again.

20. Sometimes Classic Commitment Dodgers stick around for a while, but still leave before the relationship affects too much of their heart, soul, and life. In other words, they run away before they get in too deep.

21. Sometimes Classic Commitment Dodgers go to extremes of behavior, hoping their mates will get fed up and leave. For instance, they arrive three hours late for a date or forget about it altogether, or they start nagging their partners continually.

22. Alcoholics, workaholics, and any kind of "-aholics" often have Classic Commitment issues. They use their addictions as weapons to keep their partners at bay.

Because Classic Commitment Dodgers leave and never look back, they don't see the emotional devastation they have wrought upon their mates. There appears to be no closure; many questions remain unanswered, and many important things remain unsaid. **This is such a tragically painful parting that the heartbreak can last forever. After such a heart-wrenching love experience, the jilted partner can, and often does, become a Closet Commitment Dodger.**

If you continually find yourself being drawn to people who just can't commit to you, examine your own heart. What part are you playing in this dead-end scenario? Could you be afraid of commitment? Do you choose people who are afraid to commit to you, because in reality you're afraid of commitment? If so, then you're a Closet Commitment Dodger.

Closet Commitment Dodgers (How to Recognize One)

1. Closet Commitment Dodgers continually "fall for" people who just can't seem to commit, or who are already involved in a committed relationship. This is a mind game they're playing with themselves. They make themselves appear to be victims of Classic Commitment Dodgers, rather than face the fact that they have their own commitment issues. By continually falling for unavailable partners, they don't have to confront their own commitment issues.

2. Closet Commitment Dodgers spend all their time obsessing about why their partners are doing what they're doing, rather than concentrating on why they would choose to stay in such a nerve-wracking relationship in the first place. (Once again, they're distracting from and avoiding their own commitment issues.)

3. Since Closet Commitment Dodgers continually get involved with people who make it clear from the beginning that they don't want a committed relationship (Classic Commitment Dodgers), they spend all their time complaining and whining to everyone about the situation. This way, they can feel as if they're in a relationship, but it doesn't force them to confront their own commitment issues because they know full well the relationship is never going anyplace anyway. If, however, their Classic Commitment Dodging mates should have a change of heart and want to commit to them, these Closet Commitment Dodgers suddenly lose all interest in the relationship.

4. Closet Commitment Dodgers always seem to be involved in relationships in which they care more about their partners than their partners care about them, or they pick partners who care much more about them than they could ever care about their partners.

5. When Closet Commitment Dodgers meet someone who is ready to be involved in a committed relationship, they find a million reasons why that person is not right for them. Or when they do find someone they care about, they start playing the game of "Blemish." They begin to see everything that's wrong with the other person, and rationalize why this relationship won't work.

6. After a relationship ends, Closet Commitment Dodgers avoid getting involved with anyone else for an unreasonably long time because they're still pining for the one who got away.

7. After a disastrous marriage or long-term relationship ends, or after the death of a beloved partner, some people become Closet Commitment Dodgers because they fear ever putting themselves in a position where they could get their hearts broken again. As a result, they're subconsciously drawn to Classic Commitment Dodgers, knowing that these people will never want to bring the relationship to the next level.

8. After a really good first date, Closet Commitment Dodgers make up a million reasons why they should never see that person again.

9. Closet Commitment Dodgers stay in a no-win relationship because it keeps them from going out and finding another partner who would be willing to commit to them. This way they don't have to face their own hidden fear of commitment.

10. Closet Commitment Dodgers are continually drawn to "bad boy" or "bad girl" types such as drug addicts, gamblers, and alcoholics who care more about their addictions than about anyone or anything else. These relationships move around the

dysfunctional Transactional Analysis triangle from victim to rescuer to persecutor, so that no real intimacy ever really has to take place.

11. When Closet Commitment Dodgers are in good relationships, they do things to sabotage their relationships. For instance, very jealous Closet Commitment Dodgers might drive their mates away by constantly checking up on them, by constantly accusing them of things, and by acting out countless other insane behaviors. Although on the surface it would appear that these jealous mates desperately want the relationship, the giveaway is that nothing is done to try and control all their crazy jealous behaviors – no matter how many times their mates warn them that they will leave if it continues.

In other words, Closet Commitment Dodgers do the same thing Classic Commitment Dodgers do – they engage in over-the-top behaviors in an unconscious effort to drive their mates away.

Is it Possible to Be in a Committed Relationship and Still Fear Commitment?

Absolutely! A person can commit to coming home every day to you on a physical basis, yet remain unavailable to you on the emotional, psychological, and spiritual levels.

A person can be in a long-term, committed relationship, particularly one on the lower end of *The Ladder of Love,* in order to **avoid intimacy.** The boundaries these *Cellmates* construct might be invisible, but they're impenetrable all the same.

These "Committed Commitment Dodgers" choose mates who'll allow them to hold all the cards. Committed Commitment Dodgers control everything, reveal only what they wish, and never truly let anyone in.

Committed Commitment Dodgers may never leave a bad relationship, but they sure as hell will run away from a good one. Or they'll play it safe by carrying on a long-term affair with someone they truly love, knowing they'll never have to commit to that illicit relationship as long as they stay safely nestled in their lousy marriage. When pressed about the issue, they'll give all kinds of reasons why they can't get a divorce. The bottom line is this: to leave the bad marriage and embrace the good relationship would mean facing head-on the frightening fear of commitment.

People who are in long-term relationships, but still have commitment issues, will reveal themselves in other aspects of their lives. For example, they never seem to hold on to a job, and oftentimes they can't even commit to a career. One week they're a bartender, the next week they're going back to school to be a teacher. When they finally get their teaching degree they never teach, but go back to school to become a dental assistant, and so on and so forth. They may also have a hard time making decisions, buying things, choosing where to live or where to go on a vacation, or even what to eat for dinner.

Commitment issues are boundary issues. If we've been raised by people who have raped our boundaries, which are our private spaces, we come to fear that intimacy means an invasion of self.

By now you're coming to understand that commitment issues can be overt, right out there for everyone to see; or covert, hidden, and not so easy to detect.

Signs that You're Dealing with Your Own Set of Commitment Fears

1. Your relationships never last long, no matter how much love is involved.
2. You constantly play the "Blemish" game, and no one can meet your ego's ideal of the so-called perfect mate.
3. You've chosen a profession that calls for frequent travel or moves. Since you never really stay rooted in one place for long, you never have to commit to anything or anyone on a permanent basis.
4. You had your heart broken once, and now you're paralyzed by fear at the mere thought of ever loving that much again. So, you avoid becoming involved with anyone you're really drawn to.
5. You never go to places where you could actually meet a potential mate.
6. When asked why you're not looking for a relationship, you list a million things you've got

to do first, such as: lose weight, get a better job, or fix up your place before you can have anybody over. All this would be well and good, except that you never get around to doing any of those things, either.

7. You ignore or refuse to see the kind and loving signals a potential partner is throwing your way.

8. You make yourself unattractive (voluntary ugliness) so that no one will be attracted to you. (Nonstop weight gain, dressing in a slovenly way, etc.)

A fear of commitment is really a fear of true intimacy. When we're truly intimate with a person we must let down our guard. We must allow our true self to be revealed, and this makes us quake with fear.

Where Do We Go from Here?

In STEP 18, we'll explore The Seventh Golden Rule of Love – Heal Thyself.

This STEP will help you understand that we all possess the inner knowing that when we're given a higher love, all our unhealed issues will surface. For this reason, people can be reluctant to surrender and commit to love.

If you want to be granted a higher love, then you have to be willing to love yourself, know yourself, and heal yourself, so that you'll be able to surrender and commit to the great gift of love when it's given to you.

A higher love asks us to confront and conquer our greatest fears. The next STEP will show you how to do this, as we examine why love brings forth all that is hidden within us.

Furthermore, we'll summarize the entire book to show you step-by-step the process of healing that you can do on your own, in preparation for a higher love, be it a new love or a current one that you wish to bring up *The Ladder of Love*. The more inner reflection and homework you do on your own, the easier it will be to confront the other issues that surface when you're in a place of love.

By completing this STEP, you have told the universe that you are ready to commit to a Soul Mate relationship with your entire, heart, soul, mind and body.

STEP 18 – UNDERSTANDING THE SEVENTH GOLDEN RULE OF LOVE

Heal Thyself

"You do not see how limited and weak is your allegiance, and how frequently you have demanded that love go away, and leave you quietly alone in 'peace.'"
(*A Course in Miracles,* Chapter 29)

The Seventh Golden Rule of Love – Know that when we're in a place of love, all our unhealed issues will surface.

When we're in a place of love, the floodgates of our unhealed issues burst open because we finally feel safe and protected enough to look deep into our hearts, minds, and souls to see what's buried deep within.

Bringing Forth That Which Is Hidden

Unfortunately, this aspect of love – the revealing, and thus healing, element – causes many people to run away from love because they're too afraid to face what they must face.

People delude themselves into thinking, *If this person weren't in my life, then I wouldn't be feeling all this angst.* True, you might not consciously feel all the angst, but subconsciously all the hidden truths would be eating away at your heart, soul, mind, and body all the same. At this crucial junction in the relationship, you might choose to run away from love and go back to living the half-life you've always lived. Eventually, in this lifetime or in another, you'll meet at this crossroads of love and fear again and again, until you finally muster the courage to walk forward through the cleansing fire.

If you want to be granted a higher love, then you must consciously choose to heal. Tell God that you want to get the issues out in the open so that you can get over them and get on with living the real life you were meant to have. Then vow to face what you must face.

Our shadow self – the good, the bad, and the ugly – wishes to be known.

Ultimately, we're here on earth to learn and to evolve. God truly wants us to choose to learn our karmic lessons through love. God waits compassionately for us to begin the painful process of self-healing until there are comforting arms to hold us and catch us should we fall. If, however, you run from love because you fear the lessons to be learned, know that God has no choice but to allow you to learn these same lessons the hard way – through suffering. Choose to learn through love, even though you may be filled with fear at the mere prospect of what's going to be revealed to you.

At this point you're expected to muster up courage. Courage gives you the strength to forge forward despite your fears. So what will you choose? Will you choose to flee from your lover when the Pandora's Box of your fears flies open? Will you wait until you're forced to learn your lessons through deep suffering, or will you choose to stay put and sort through each issue, one by one, in the shelter of your lover's embrace? The choice is yours.

Love brings us to wholeness. Eventually the shadow and the persona fall away, making way for individuation, self-actualization, and the emergence of our authentic self. In running from love we run from the chance to heal, grow, and become all we're meant to be.

If we stand firm, love will show us the way.
Love is the answer. Only love matters. Love is God.

True love changes everything in an instant, and this scares us to the bones.

True love calls for us to bring forth and heal our personal issues as well as to confront and conquer our primal, collective unconscious fears.

LOVEWORK ASSIGNMENT

Examine your love relationships closely and see whether you've ever run away from love because you were afraid of all the complex feelings this relationship was stirring up inside of you.

What were the consequences of this action? Did you suffer? Do you still feel regret and remorse? What was it that you needed to learn or heal, but were unable to do so at the time? Armed with the knowledge this book has provided, if you were given a chance to do it all again, would you choose to do things differently?

Have I Ever Run Away from Love Because I Was Afraid to Heal?

I Vow to Work on My Healing Issues Every Day of My Life

A Summary of the Things You Can Do Right Now to Pave the Way for a Higher Love and to Minimize the Amount and Magnitude of Unhealed Issues that Will Surface when this Great Love Manifests

The first thing you need to do is begin to monitor your thoughts, words, and deeds continually, to see whether they reflect your desire to walk the path of love or keep you chained to your fears.

For instance, did you find yourself gossiping about someone today? Did you judge someone's actions or words? Were you critical of others? Did you act in a mean or vengeful way? Were you petty, envious, or jealous today? What made you feel this way? Did you feel like a victim today or whine about how someone was taking advantage of you? Did you lack the courage to speak the truth or assert your rights? Did you act like a Pig Parent today, berating others and dictating what they should or shouldn't do? Were you violent or did you scream at someone today? Did you find yourself acting in a controlling or manipulative way? Did you abuse drugs or alcohol?

Learn to become more and more aware of the kinds of behavior that represent fear-based emotions. Each day, make a conscious effort to act from a place of love. This way, when your *Soul Mate* comes into your life, you'll already know how to act in a karmically correct manner, and that will make the road to healing that much easier.

When you find yourself being kind, forgiving, generous, humorous, joyful, thankful, honest, trustworthy, passionate, patient, hopeful, compassionate, and empathetic, know that you're acting as the living embodiment of love and demonstrating to yourself and to the world that you're a healed being.

The more you act on a day-to-day basis from a place of love, the easier it will be for you to continue acting that way when a *Soul Mate* is brought to you. Consequently, your desire to run from love will be greatly diminished, and your desire to stay put and figure out what issues are being revealed to you by this great love will increase exponentially.

You'll also need to become consciously aware of all of the false beliefs and *Errors in Thinking* that are still dancing around in your head. You'll need to read this book continually to keep your *Errors in Thinking* in check and to help you recognize and remember what love is and what fear is. It's easy to fall back into our old patterns of thinking and reacting, so you'll have to make a conscientious effort to watch your words and actions from now on. For example, when someone asks you for advice about a love relationship that's just ended, stop talking from an unhealed place that accepts jealousy, vengeance, and conditional love as truth. Guide this person using the knowledge this book has given you. By now, you're well aware of the fact that not all romantic relationships are meant to last forever. Share this knowledge with that person. Ask this person what lessons he/she was supposed to learn while in this relationship, and what lessons he/she can still learn from the ending of it. In other words, the advice you would have given this person prior to reading this book should be dramatically different from the kind of advice you can give now. By teaching others what you have learned, you're not only educating them, but you're reinforcing in yourself the truth of what you've discovered. In doing this, you'll help put an end to all the romantic *Errors in Thinking* that still exist in the world, as you replace them with eternal truths. Your karmically correct words will help the evolution of all human beings, one person at a time.

Start seeing the significant others in your life as part of your Group Soul. As you advance your soul, you begin to lift the souls of your entire group. In teaching others how to behave in a loving and karmically correct manner, you're practicing and demonstrating *Agape* love, the unconditional love for humanity and all God's creations.

Now that you know the difference between a *Cellmate*, a *Razor's Edge Mate*, and a *Soul Mate*, you'll begin to see every relationship with new eyes. When you watch a movie or a television show, pay close attention to the love relationships portrayed there. Try placing these relationships on *The Ladder of Love.*

Practice the art of giving and receiving love within the framework of the relationships that currently exist in your life. Spontaneously offer a hug! Learn to give and receive compliments. If you try to see the good in people, praising them will then come easily and naturally to you. On the other hand, when someone pays you a heartfelt compliment, learn to accept it graciously. For example, if someone tells you that you look great today, accept the compliment by saying, "Thank you," and not, "Oh, no, I don't," and then going on and on with your usual modus operandi – a longwinded litany as to why you really look like hell.

You can also practice Random Acts of Kindness and graciously accept the Random Acts of Kindness that will begin flowing your way. If you learn to see love as a two-way street that entails the giving and receiving of love, when your *Soul Mate* comes into your life this sense of loving and being loved in return will seem second nature to you.

Begin taking steps to have a more intimate relationship with God and with your angels and spirit guides. Pay attention to the divine guidance given to you. This way, when a higher love is brought to you, you'll truly trust the advice you're being given about how to make this love true and everlasting.

Talk to God – often! Tell God of your efforts to know, love, and heal yourself. Tell God of your great desire to have a higher love in your life, and humbly acknowledge the concept of "Thy will be done."

While you're waiting for a higher love, use this precious alone time to get to know yourself inside and out. If you're a shame-based person, go to therapy or talk with a trusted friend about the things in your life that make you feel worthless and ashamed. Start opening up your shadow bags and explore the contents within. If you've been keeping a lot of good things about yourself hidden, start revealing them. If you have a deep desire to pursue something, or a talent you'd like to work on, do it now. If you have an addiction to conquer, join a twelve-step program, sign yourself into a rehab center, or seek therapy.

Work on loving yourself. Try practicing the mindset of "I'm OK, you're OK" with everyone you meet.

If you're the master of the game called "Blemish," consciously tell yourself to seek the good in others and stop magnifying the bad. By the same token, if you have a history of being hurt by people because you refused to acknowledge the evil that lurked within their shadows, then you need to stop practicing the defense mechanism of denial and see things the way they truly are. This doesn't call for you to judge these people, but it does ask that you learn how to protect yourself from being hurt by them time and time again.

If you're guilty of practicing the Five Deadly Sins Committed in the Name of Conditional Love, work on healing those issues. If you're a selfish person, try putting others ahead of yourself sometimes. If you're a person who's afraid of being selfish, and so you've learned to always put others first, then you need to learn to put yourself first once in a while. If you're always obsessed about the way you look, put a little less effort into the superficial side of yourself, and put more effort into cultivating your spirituality. If you find yourself envying others, work on being in gratitude for the things you have. If you envy someone because they've achieved some goal you'd like to achieve, use this envy as a catalyst for your own work toward obtaining that goal. If you're a greedy person, try being more generous and see what generosity feels like. If you've always been a jealous person in all of your relationships, then you need to study STEP 13 often to see what unhealed aspects of yourself the jealousy demon is revealing.

Learn to honor and believe in the Sacred Law of Synchronicity. If you desperately want a higher love, please don't get discouraged if it doesn't come at the exact moment you want it to. To bring two *Soul Mates* in alignment with each other requires a divine conspiracy between heaven and earth. Know that this higher love will be brought to you at the exact right time and place. Just go on doing all you can to be the living embodiment of love, and wait patiently, knowing full well that it's just a matter of time (divine timing) before the miracle of love enters your life.

In the meantime, work at opening your heart. Learn to give generously of yourself without worrying, *What's in it for me?* Practice being kind, compassionate, and tolerant with everyone you encounter. Laugh a lot. Have fun and keep the Natural Child alive inside of you.

Practice the art of blending the energy of your soul with others by engaging in meaningful, heartfelt conversations. Nurture your soul on a daily basis by surrounding yourself with the beauty of nature and art. Good music helps our souls to soar, so surround yourself with the gift of song. Expose yourself to new kinds of music and watch your soul expand. Continue to read spiritual books and surround yourself with like-minded people.

Keep exploring your subconscious mind by paying attention to your words and actions to see what unhealed issues are continually being revealed to you. Remember to pay attention to your dreams. What are they trying to tell you?

Stop using all your defense mechanisms to keep real intimacy at bay. Learn to be yourself and tell the truth. Work on cultivating the Adult, Nurturing Parent, and Natural Child states within yourself. Recognize when you're acting like a Wounded or Spoiled Child or an irrational Pig Parent, and consciously try at those times to hook the Adult within and stop these crazy behaviors.

Stay away from movies and television shows that seem to pander to the lowest denominator of human behavior, glorifying promiscuity and senseless violence. Remember, violence begets violence and vengeance inspires vengeance. If you surround yourself with pornography and movies that exploit the sex act, the art of Sacred Sexuality will be all the more difficult for you to practice when the time comes.

Pay attention to your energy body. Try to learn all you can about the Chakra System and the mind/body connection. What is your energy body revealing to you? Our unhealed issues will oftentimes manifest first in our energy body and then in our physical body. For instance, a closed heart chakra or one that has been ripped too wide open from some emotional devastation can manifest itself in heart disease. What is your heart disease trying to tell you? Sometimes, it's telling us to start treating our body like a holy temple and not like a refuge site for all the junk food we can pour into it. At other times, it may be trying to tell us that we haven't dealt with the pain of losing someone we love, or we haven't dealt with the traumatic events from our childhood.

If reading STEP 16 and STEP 17 brought to your consciousness the idea that you have trouble surrendering and committing to love, then your job is to look deep within yourself to discover why these aspects of love terrify you so. The more you deal with your own fear of commitment now, the easier it will be to surrender to love and commit to your *Soul Mate* when he/she manifests.

Healing your own issues and acting on a day-to-day basis from a place of love are vital to obtaining and keeping a higher love.

Lifetime *LOVEWORK ASSIGNMENT*

Each night before falling asleep, take a few minutes to reflect upon your day. When were you proud of your words and deeds? What did you say or do that you wish you hadn't? Where did your actions fall short of your intentions? Examine the incongruities in your words and deeds to see what aspects of your inner self still need healing.

Embarking on the Final STEP

The final STEP in this book is probably the most painful one that any of us will ever have to master – Practicing the Art of Blessing Our Relationships Before Letting Them Go.

Goodbyes are never easy, but STEP 19 can help ease the pain by teaching you how to pay homage to endings.

According to the ancient science of numerology, 19 is a karmic number (representing accrued good karma) that signifies the completion of the second part of a journey.

When you finish the all-important 19th STEP, be prepared to reap the positive reward for completing this journey – a God-given higher love!

The STEPS you've completed need to be practiced on a day-to-day basis.

Reread this book often to keep yourself walking the path of love.

STEP 19 – UNDERSTANDING THE EIGHTH GOLDEN RULE OF LOVE

Practicing the Art of Blessing Our Relationships Before Letting Them Go

"Miracles are both beginnings and endings..."
(*A Course in Miracles*, Chapter 1)

<u>The Eighth Golden Rule Of Love</u> – If two people meet and then separate, know there were powerful lessons to be learned in their communion, and still more powerful ones to be learned in their separation.

We must come to trust the destiny that brought two people together and the fate that drove them apart.

Paying Homage to Endings

Know that an act of kismet and the Laws of Karma conspire to blow a relationship our way. Understand that the selfsame divine workings of kismet and karma might beckon it away, caring little for what we mere mortals profess to want, will, or wish.

Now that we've reached the final STEP, it should be increasingly clear to you that all of us possess many *Errors in Thinking* regarding relationships. If you remember, in STEP 2 – Debunking the Wives' Tales Surrounding Romantic Love, you learned that not all relationships are meant to last forever.

Many friendships, romantic relationships, and even family members are meant to be in our lives for only a limited amount of time, and when that unique moment in time passes, we must bless these relationships and let them go.

If we refuse to accept the inevitable comings and goings that life hands us, we'll find the ending of all things, not just relationships, to be extremely painful.

If I were to pick one word that best characterizes the experience of life, I would pick the word "change," for life is ever-changing. If you can learn to meet the inevitable winds of change with a sense of hope and courage, rather than panic and fear, you'll be able to see all the possibilities that the universe is opening up for you, and you won't get caught up in prolonged mourning for what has passed. Learn to embrace the philosophy that when one door closes another opens. Think positively and trust there is something better waiting for you on the other side of that newly opened door.

If we play the "Blame Game," blaming our mates for leaving us and placing all the responsibility for the ending of the relationship on them, we'll continue to dwell in the stagnating realm of victim consciousness. In playing the "Blame Game," we don't have to face our part in contributing to the ending of the relationship. This kind of futile game playing is extremely harmful, for it allows us to remain in denial about the inevitably changing nature of life it-self and about our own issues that need addressing.

If you learn to look at your relationship ob-jectively, you'll come to understand your ex-mate's point of view as well as your own, and this will help dispel some of the rage, disappointment, and sorrow you might be feeling. Looking at the relationship honestly and objectively allows you to face the truth and see that the relationship might have been more dead than alive for a long time. You might come to admit that you stuck around in the hopes that some-thing would change for the better; and yet, if you were to be perfectly honest with yourself, you know in your heart of hearts that you never actually did anything to remedy the situation. You could also come to recognize just how many core issues you or your partner were compromising on in order to stay in the relationship.

Perhaps the relationship came to an untimely ending because you or your mate couldn't surrender or commit to it, or maybe one or both of you ran away from love rather than face the issues that needed to be faced. Learn to accept responsibility for your ac-tions, and try to see the other person's point of view, so that you can come to that inner place of peace and acceptance.

If the relationship ended as a result of some-one's death, we often find ourselves filled with anger and rage toward life in general and God in particu-lar. It might take us a long time to see the karmic lessons inherent in this painful ending – and, sadly, these lessons will be learned the hard way – through great suffering.

All Meaningful Events or Relationships that Come to an End Will:

- o Bring up all the other losses we've ever suffered.
- o Put an end to life as we know it.
- o Bring to an end many of the plans for the future we may have counted on.
- o Stir up a host of our most terrifying primal fears.
- o Leave us badly wounded, emotionally paralyzed, and psychologically scarred, sometimes beyond recognition.

As we progress through our life's journey, by the Grace of God and through our own will to live, we can move beyond this place of total devastation to a place of healing, if we allow ourselves to learn the many karmic lessons this painful experience has wrought.

You're under karmic obligation to search your heart, explore your soul, and sift through your thoughts to uncover the lessons you were supposed to learn from the ending of any relationship.

There Are Countless Lessons You're Asked to Learn from the Ending of a Relationship

Listed Below Are Some of Them:

1. **You might be asked to learn that love goes on, even in the physical absence of that person.** If this is the lesson God is asking you to learn, you'll be divinely guided as to how you can commune telepathically with that person. You can do this regardless of whether the person is still walking the earth plane or has crossed over and dwells in the spirit realms. Telepathic communications are carried on the strong current of love. Anytime you find yourself missing someone you love, try communing with this person telepathically. To do so, first find a quiet place. Next, close your eyes and send this person love – pure, unconditional love from your heart chakra. Then concentrate on your brow chakra or "third eye" chakra, located behind the center of the forehead. Remember, this is the seat of your higher intuition, and as you concentrate on this chakra you can tell the soul of your missing beloved that you need a message or a sign from him/her. Pay attention as the days unfold, so that you won't miss the messages that are being sent. A message can come in the form of a song you hear on the radio that answers your question, something someone else reveals to you, or something you stumble across that seems to answer the question perfectly. Sometimes the answer comes in the form of a thought. This crystal-clear thought appears to come out of nowhere, but it leaves us with a feeling

of peace and contentment, knowing that our question was heard and answered.

2. **Perhaps God is asking you to learn how to love unconditionally.** God might want you to go on loving this person even though you're separated. If this person ended the relationship, this can be an extremely difficult thing to do, but if you learn to see his/her point of view, you can come to a place of acceptance, knowing this person needed to leave you for compelling reasons of his/her own. God might wish for you to learn that it's possible for you to still love this person unconditionally without any personal agenda in it for yourself.

3. **You might need to learn that only love matters.** The two of you might have let every obstacle, both real and imaginary, separate you. If this were the case, then as time goes by, you'll come to learn that only love was important – that everything else should have fallen by the wayside, but the love was meant to last. This lesson is a very hard one to bear at first, for it can fill you with deep feelings of remorse and regret, but if you truly absorb this sorrowful lesson into every fiber of your being, you can take comfort in knowing that you'll never let love slip away again.

4. **You might need to learn how to listen to your heart and not to other people.** If you ended a relationship because of the way your friends or family felt about this person or because you feared their reaction, the heart-wrenching suffering you'll be forced to endure will make you realize that what others say or

think is not as important as what your heart tells you.

5. **You might need to learn how and when to speak your mind and assert yourself.** Perhaps you let too much slide, or nagged about all the wrong things and never really spoke up about the real issues. Perhaps you wanted peace at any price and allowed your mate to get away with violating your basic human rights, until the relationship got so far off course there was no turning back. In this case, your karmic lessons would involve working on your self-worth, self-love, and self expression issues.

6. **Perhaps you need to learn not to push people too far.** If you were the one who took advantage of your mate's kindness, unselfishness, or innate goodness, then by honestly examining your heart, you'll be able to fully comprehend why your mate finally got fed up and left. In this case, you needed to learn the importance of never taking people for granted, or expecting them to do for you what you are perfectly capable of doing for yourself.

7. **Perhaps you need to learn how to deal with your dependency issues.** God is asking you to grow up, take responsibility for your own actions, and stand on your own two feet. Don't expect your lover to be your babysitter. We're under karmic obligation to grow up, be responsible, and take care of our own needs to the very best of our ability.

8. **Maybe you need to learn that love is not about control.** Are you a control freak? Do you have to tell everyone when and how to do

everything? Then you're asked to learn to live and let live, and let go and let God. Have you ever had to leave a relationship because your mate was too controlling? Then you were asked to learn to be the master of your own destiny, to trust your own ability to run your life, and stop putting your fate in the hands of another.

9. **Maybe you need to learn how to set and honor healthy boundaries.**

10. **Perhaps you need to learn who you really are.** Did you find yourself doing things or acting in a way that pleased your mate, but betrayed your core values? While in this relationship, did you pretend to be something or someone other than yourself?

11. **Maybe you need to learn that everything you need to survive is within yourself, and that you don't need a knight in shining armor or a fairy princess to rescue you.**

12. **Perhaps you need to learn endurance, courage, compassion, tolerance, or patience.**

13. **Maybe you need to learn to accept the things you can't change and to change the things that you can.** Did you need to learn the difference?

14. **Perhaps you need to learn that love isn't about money or possessions.**

15. **Maybe you needed to learn that some relationships are only meant to last for a while.**

16. **Perhaps you need to learn how to end relationships in a manner consistent with the Laws of Karma.** We're under karmic obligation to be kind and fair in our parting. If we vowed "till death do us part," but our marriage ended in

divorce, it's still possible to honor this vow by remaining lifelong friends. This is particularly important when people have children together. Remember, it's possible for two divorced people to become *Soul Mate* friends later on. If you're divorced, put into practice the lessons you've learned in this book, and watch your relationship with your ex-spouse change for the better.

17. **God might be asking you to come to terms with the concept of revenge.** The need for vengeance is still a strong part of our collective unconscious. Since ancient times, the idea that vengeance is right and just has been hammered into our heads from the historical and mythological viewpoint. This concept is still continually reinforced in our own culture via television shows and movies, as we cheer on the protagonist seeking vengeance in all sorts of highly vindictive ways. Learn to stop thinking that you have to even the score. God is asking us to move from victim consciousness toward an understanding that there are positive karmic lessons to learn in whatever experiences life might hand us. Leave karmic reckoning up to God. God knows best how to dole out the experiences that will teach others what they need to learn.

18. **Maybe you need to learn that endings are an inevitable part of life, and that every ending is a new beginning.** Do you need to face your fear of the unknown and embrace the ongoing adventure of life?

19. **Perhaps you need to learn the big life lesson of forgiveness.** We learn to forgive by trying to

walk a mile in the other person's shoes. This allows us to see why this person might have acted in the way that he/she did. We further learn to forgive by praying and asking God for help. To forgive is divine, and all humans need divine intercession when the forgiveness issue is a big one. After we pray, we then begin to say, "I forgive you." Even if you don't believe that the words you're saying are true or ever will prove true, keep on saying them. God, hearing your sincere efforts to forgive someone, will take away the pain and bring forgiveness to your heart, when you have learned all or most of the lessons inherent in that life experience. If you're still having trouble with forgiveness, then you need to realize that we forgive someone because in doing so it sets us free, since we're no longer a victim of this person or his/her actions. We can then move on with our life without this person or that situation draining our energies. If the crimes against us have been horrific, we don't have to forgive the **things** this person has done to us, but we forgive the person all the same. Sometimes it is ourselves that we need to forgive, and this can be one of the hardest karmic lessons of all.

20. **Perhaps the biggest lesson we learn is to face head-on our collective unconscious fears of abandonment, betrayal, rejection, judgment, and death.** You've been working hard in reading this book and doing your *LOVEWORK ASSIGNMENTS* to recognize these fears so that you can conquer them, either in this lifetime or in another.

21. **Maybe you needed to do some inner healing, and the ending of a relationship left your heart ripped open and so vulnerable that you sought the help you needed in order to face what you had to face and heal what needed healing.**

22. **Perhaps you need to learn how to bury the relationship, mourn it, and let it go.** See a relationship that has ended as something that has died. Don't try to bypass the mourning process. Allow yourself to feel the sorrow, the rage, the despair. Feel what you feel, learn what you must learn, and then bless the relationship and let it go.

23. **Maybe you need to learn that relationships don't end the moment the actual physical connection stops.** Long after two people have parted ways, their souls might go on communing with each other in an effort to take care of some unfinished business. This is why you might find yourself thinking about this person, or dreaming about your ex-mate for quite some time after the relationship appears, on the surface, to have ended. Pay attention to these thoughts and dreams. What unfinished business still needs closure? At some level every relationship we've ever had is an eternal one, for it was a soulful experience that altered us, affected us, and forever influenced and changed some aspects of our being and our life. The ending of a relationship doesn't erase its existence from the face of the earth. Accept the fact that a complete soulful and heartfelt severance may never take place, because this is the soul's way of honoring,

respecting, and memorializing what was good in the relationship.

24. **Perhaps you need to learn that love is not a compromise.**

25. **Maybe you need to learn how to love someone with your entire heart, soul, mind, and body.** If two people don't love each other with their entire being, whatever need is not being met will guide one or both of them out of that relationship and into another one.

26. **God certainly didn't mean for you to learn that all men/women can't be trusted, or that love stinks.** God never wants us to come to think in those kinds of negative and harmful generalized ways.

27. **Maybe you need to learn how the human soul works.** The human soul has an innate need to grow and ascend. If someone has left you and you're wallowing in self-pity, perhaps you need to understand that the person who left you might be answering the call of his/her soul. Know that sometimes we're the person answering the call from our soul to move on; at other times, we're the soul who's been abandoned and needs to learn the lessons inherent in this heartbreaking experience. If you're the one who's doing the leaving in a relationship, try to send compassion to the person you left behind. Try sending this person unconditional love so that he/she won't feel rejected or abandoned. Ask this person's soul to try and understand what your soul needs to do, so this person will be able to make some sense of the ending and move on with his/her life. If you're the one who is feeling betrayed and

abandoned, try to see why this person needed to move on, and with that understanding wish your ex-mate a heartfelt Godspeed in his/her journey through life, and then get on with yours.

Sending Love on the Soul Plane

There's no denying, that a **Sacred Betrayal** can leave us devastated. (If you don't remember what a **Sacred Betrayal** is, go back to STEP 5 and refresh your memory.) We can find ourselves yearning for our beloved *Soul Mate* day and night. During these heartbreaking times, continue to send your *Soul Mate* love on the soul plane, and then pray for the inevitable reunion of your souls in this lifetime or in any other time or space. Sometimes, our out-of-body dreams can bring us much comfort, as we find our beloved in the dreamscape or in the astral world. If your *Soul Mate* has passed away, know that you can continue to send love on the soul plane, commune with him/her telepathically, and visit with each other in the world of dreams.

The Last LOVEWORK ASSIGNMENT

Reflect upon your romantic relationships, concentrating on how they ended. If you've never had a romantic relationship that ended, then substitute any relationships with friends or family members that have come to an end. Try to think about each of these relationships in chronological order. From the ending of each of these relationships, what lessons do you think you were supposed to learn? Did you learn them, or do you keep encountering the same lessons over and over again?

Write down your observations and vow to put into practice these all-important lessons. Ask God to help you forgive those who must be forgiven – including yourself, if this is the case.

Lessons I've Learned from the Endings of My Relationships

This Last *LOVEWORK ASSIGNMENT* Marks the Beginning of Your New Life

Congratulations!

EPILOGUE

By now you've come to realize that *Soul Mate* relationships are first and foremost spiritual partnerships in which two people agree to help each other grow and evolve as human beings.

Soul Mates are under karmic obligation to willingly allow room for personal growth and change within themselves and within the relationship. Therefore, learn to encourage and embrace your beloved's personal growth, knowing that as your *Soul Mate* evolves, so do you.

Soul Mates who see each other as two separate beings embarking on a spiritual journey together instinctively know that they're still expected to follow their individual hearts and spirits throughout their conjoined lives. Take comfort in knowing that what's right and truthful for your *Soul Mate* is ultimately right and truthful for you as well.

Some Characteristics of Spiritual Partnerships

- ◆ These blessed *Soul Mates* have a strong belief in their love.

- ◆ They have a deep sense of trust and faith in each other and in their relationship.

- ◆ They're kind and compassionate to each other and to the world at large.

♦ They know that kindness matters.

♦ They're not envious of their *Soul Mates'* accomplishments and honestly do all they can to help each other answer their divine callings and honor their *Yang Factors.*

♦ They maintain a heartfelt devotion to God, honor the sacredness of all God's creatures, and demonstrate reverence for the entire universe. They are living embodiments of *Agape* love and Cosmic Consciousness.

♦ They live in a constant state of gratitude; deeply appreciating the sustaining love they've been given.

Never Underestimate the Importance of Your *Soul Mate* Relationship

In this new millennium, as God reunites more *Soul Mates, Twin Souls, and Mirror Souls,* the world will take a giant leap toward peace, love, and joy. Never underestimate the importance of human love affairs. Children born to *Soul Mate* couples will know the peace inherent in true love. As grown-ups, they won't be interested in waging war, for they have borne witness to two people who solve their differences in loving, generous, compassionate, and kind ways.

Know that the universe urges you to master what you have been seeking to learn by reading this book. The very survival of the human race depends upon it. Remember, as your soul evolves, you lift the souls of all humans, particularly those souls that you come into contact with at work, at home, at play, and wherever your life may lead you.

When you first picked up this book and began setting off on your path toward a higher love, you probably did this because you felt a personal need to love and be loved in return. Valid as this may be, the universe also guided you on this path because the world so desperately needs for you and your *Soul Mate* to become beacons of light and love. Every time you give love, conquer a fear, forgive someone, perform an act of kindness, or act in a tolerant, nonjudgmental way, you're helping to advance the evolution of all human beings.

Remember to refer to this book often, as you progress through life. Share this book with your friends and lovers, so they can better understand where your newfound thoughts and feelings are coming from. When talking about relationships and love with others, try to use the words and terms you've learned in this book. Willingly share the knowledge you've acquired with others. When you find yourself falling into your old patterns, see this as a message for you to pick up this book and read it again.

If you want world peace, then make peace within your own heart, in your own home, and within all of your relationships.

Vow to settle for nothing less than a million-watt love.

EXODUS

As our journey together closes, I leave you to reflect upon the Ten Commandments of *Soul Mate* Love and The Six Pillars of *Soul Mate* Unions.

Learn them, live them, and joyously shout them from the mountaintops, for they are the means and the way to honor and cherish the greatest miracle of all – true, everlasting love.

May God grant each and every one of us a higher love.

Godspeed!

The Ten Commandments of *Soul Mate* Love

I. **You shall turn your love life over to God.** If you're going through a rocky patch in your relationship, ask God to guide the two of you and watch miracles happen.

II. **You shall tell your beloved over and over, time and time again, "I love you with my entire heart, soul, mind, and body."** To truly love someone, you must love this person with your entire being, and you must be willing to say so.

III. **You shall stand on your own two feet and not expect your beloved to carry your cross.** In other words, don't expect your *Soul Mate* to be your surrogate mommy or daddy.

IV.   **Honor your *Soul Mate* and help, encourage, and support your beloved to become all he/she was meant to be.** We're on this earth plane to learn, grow, and evolve. Encourage your *Soul Mate* to pay homage to the *Yang Factor* by answering his/her divine calling.

V.   **You shall practice the art of Sacred Sexuality.** Strive to learn the difference between having sex and making love.

VI.   **You shall love your *Soul Mate* unconditionally.**

VII.   **You shall not take advantage of your beloved's unconditional love.** You're fully expected to heal your issues in the midst of such a divine showering of love. To do otherwise is sacrilege.

VIII.   **You shall be your true self.** This one's easier said than done.

IX.   **You shall tell the truth.** Remember to temper your honesty with kindness.

X.   **You shall not take your beloved for granted.** We hold this truth to be self-evident.

The Six Pillars of *Soul Mate* Unions

I.   **Vow to cultivate an attitude of gratitude –** Ceaselessly honor and cherish your relationship, for it's truly a miracle. Live in a state of continuous appreciation for the great gift God has bestowed upon the two of you.

II. **Vow to love each other unconditionally –** Monitor your behavior continually. Acknowledge openly when you're coming from a place of fear. Put into practice the lessons learned from studying the 19 STEPS to bring yourself and your relationship back to the heart of love.

III. **Vow to surrender and commit to your relationship with your entire heart, soul, mind, and body.** Work arduously to resolve the issues that keep you from opening up to your *Soul Mate*, and encourage your *Soul Mate* to do the same.

IV. **Vow to help each other answer your sacred callings by continually paying homage to your *Yang Factors*.** You and your *Soul Mate* will have some joint undertakings to perform. However, you may need to complete other tasks, and even your main life calling, essentially on your own. The encouragement and support you and your *Soul Mate* provide for each other will greatly contribute to the success of all of your endeavors.

V.   **Vow to honor the sacredness of your *Soul Mate* relationship above all others.** At first this pillar might sound selfish, but in truth, it's anything but. The universe needs *Soul Mates* to stay together for these relationships prove to the world the power of unconditional love. Even if two *Soul Mates* raise children together, the primary relationship remains the romantic one. Remember – children are a byproduct of that higher love, and are blessed to be raised by *Soul Mate* parents who truly love and honor their relationship. Never forget that our children are ours only for a short while, and then they must go out into the world to find their own lives; but our *Soul Mate* relationship can and will last way beyond those years, if we learn to honor and cherish it above all else.

VI. **Vow to allow your love to be a beacon of light for all to see.** The gift of a higher love is meant to be shared with the world. If you and your *Soul Mate* keep each other locked away from the world, you're not allowing other people to bear witness to the peace, love, and joy that are inherent in a *Soul Mate* union.

Remember,
This is not the end…
This is the beginning.
God is love.
Love is God.

Made in the USA
Charleston, SC
25 June 2010